LITTLE WHITE LIES,
DEEP DARK SECRETS

LITTLE WHITE LIES,
DEEP DARK SECRETS

The Truth About
Why Women Lie

SUSAN SHAPIRO BARASH

ST. MARTIN'S GRIFFIN
NEW YORK

LITTLE WHITE LIES, DEEP DARK SECRETS. Copyright © 2008 by Susan Shapiro Barash. All rights reserved. Printed in the United States of America. For information, address St. Martin's Press, 175 Fifth Avenue, New York, N.Y. 10010.

www.stmartins.com

Design by Susan Walsh

The Library of Congress has catalogued the hardcover edition as follows:

Barash, Susan Shapiro, 1954–
    Little white lies, deep dark secrets : the truth about why women lie / Susan Shapiro Barash.—1st ed.
      p. cm.
    Includes bibliographic references and index.
    ISBN-13: 978-0-312-36445-8
    ISBN-10: 0-312-36445-8
    1. Women—conduct of life. 2. Truthfulness and falsehood. I. Title.
BJ1610 .B365 2008
177'.3082—dc22

2007047087

ISBN-13: 978-0-312-36446-5 (pbk.)
ISBN-10: 0-312-36446-6 (pbk.)

First St. Martin's Griffin Edition: January 2009

10   9   8   7   6   5   4   3   2   1

In memory of my grandmothers,
from whom I learned the truth

This book is based on extensive personal interviews with women and experts in the field of psychology and counseling. Names have been changed and recognizable characteristics disguised for all people in this book, except the contributing experts. Some characters are composites.

CONTENTS

For a moment the lie becomes the truth.
—FEDOR MIKHAILOVICH DOSTOEVSKI,
The Brothers Karamazov

Enduring Tales: Enabling Choices

Ever since we were little girls, we have been encouraged to keep secrets.

I was raised a good girl, like most women in America, where instinctively we knew that a secret was sacred, I was taught never to betray a trust. The fact that a mishandled secret could endanger someone was shown to me by my mother, my aunts, my grandmothers, so I knew to believe this. I remember feeling special when someone shared a secret, and choosing carefully with whom I shared my secrets. By high school, secrets between girlfriends were a big part of the picture; who had a crush on whom, how far someone had gone with her boyfriend, who had been out all night while her mother thought she was sleeping at a friend's house.

When I was a young wife, and friendly with other young married women, secrets had taken on another hue. We whispered about shopping excursions, avoiding our mothers-in-law, how we could put off pregnancy or accelerate getting pregnant, about how much money we made at work, how much our husbands made. By the time we had children the circumstances had shifted, and our secrets changed; now we had secrets about our children. We now lied to the kindergarten teacher about our children's science project or to our boss about why we were late for work, careful not to disclose that it had to do with our child.

Throughout it all, I had the sense that these were lies of necessity, but not highly immoral. I believed that women lied to get through socially and as mothers, daughters, wives. These weren't essential secrets and lies.

Or were they?

The first definition of a lie told by either gender, according to *Webster's Collegiate Dictionary,* is "to make an untrue statement with intent to deceive." *Webster's* definition of the truth is "sincerity in action, character and utterance." If we take these definitions literally, would it mean that women are liars? Or is the value of the truth for women found in a version of a female lie?

In fact, every woman lies and sometimes it works, sometimes it doesn't.

Women use secrets to facilitate their lives in a culture that encourages us to be deceptive. Out of the five hundred women interviewed for this project, from diverse backgrounds, ages, and areas of the country, the same comments were made over and over again. "Of course I have secrets, women *always* have secrets," my interviewees said. "Sure, I lie, women *have* to lie, don't they?" these women asked.

Despite the great strides of the women's movement and the ever-increasing options for women in the work world, in politics, in choices to marry or not, to mother or not, there is a sense of missing out, a lack of satisfaction in the lives of many women. That's when the lie becomes part of the process; whether a woman benefits from her covert activities or brings harm not only to herself but to those close to her, the secret and lie are irresistible. A woman's lies to friends, children, husband, lover, adult siblings, and coworkers are societally induced—it's a tool used when we're missing out, when the life we dreamed of eludes us, when the going gets tough. It's interesting how women recognize a lie coming from another woman (men often miss the lie, as do children, especially sons) and often endorse the behavior. Unless a woman's lie deliberately hurts another woman, it's as if we all belong to the same club, where the expedience of our lies proliferate and rule the day.

WOMEN TELL ALL SORTS OF LIES

There are infidelity lies, financial lies, lies about children and their achievements, plastic surgery lies, and smaller, white lies about time and commitments that border on excuses. There are bigger secrets, the ones that require real work to maintain. Some are dark and haunting and demand a selective brand of secret telling, such as lies about domestic abuse, a drinking problem, or having a husband or child with an addiction. If women's lies and secrets are used as a survival technique, it is also a means by which women get what they want. Where a man will lie for a secret as a quick fix and be sloppy in his lie, a woman will carefully guard her secret— this secret is a part of her existence, it can make her feel powerful.

For every book I've written, and for every study I've conducted, women have confessed their secrets. In my books on second wives; unfaithful wives; mothers-in-law and daughters-in-law; sisters, stepmothers, and mothers, I have listened to women reveal credit card debts, sisters admit to seducing their sibling's boyfriend or husband, married women having secret trysts, and a lifelong pathology of family secrets.

What could be more riveting than a secret, defined by *Webster's* as "working with hidden aims or methods"? In the classic film *Belle de Jour*, Catherine Deneuve's character works at a brothel, which her husband knows nothing about, all the while feigning she is a pristine wife. And isn't Daisy the one driving her husband's car when she inadvertently runs down her husband's lover in F. Scott Fitzgerald's novel *The Great Gatsby*? Candace Bushnell's novel *Lipstick Jungle* offers female characters who lie to get ahead and to manage their lives. These dramas resonate with real life. Not only does it seem to be part of our nature to lie, but we've been taught by our grandmothers, mothers, and other female role models that a shade of gray is the standard, rather than white against black.

While I neither condemn nor condone the lies women tell, I recognize how central they are to a woman's existence. For the majority of women, the hard work of the lie is the payoff—as long as we pretend to be good girls, cleverly covering our tracks.

FEMALE LIES ARE EASY TO SPIN

Women justify how they profit from a lie, using it as their armor and shield. This falls into the "greater good" theory, a safeguarding of family or ourselves, and therefore has an ethical explanation. There are many instances where women feel comfortable not only with their secrets but with the lies begotten for these secrets. In a patriarchal culture, our secrets and lies can strengthen us, get us through ordeals.

Even though we are raised to be "good girls," women are quite invested in having secrets. When it comes to mothering, rivalry, and status, we're willing to lie, to distort the facts, to twist the truth. Women choose this path when it aids them in their ambitions. Oftentimes our own mothers have taught us to operate this way.

Women are adept at having secrets and choose to have secrets. A woman lies with intentional deception because she is convinced of the exigency of her lie. A woman instinctively perfects her lie, which offers the advantage of not being detected or criticized. A female lie appears much more satisfying than a male lie.

REVEALING FEMALE LIES

We are surrounded by women with secrets, from the intrigue we see on television and in film, to the barrage of weekly magazines, saturating us with the personal activities of Hollywood stars, to everyday women. In all of these cases it's about public persona versus the private self. What is so striking is how my interviewees described themselves in a myriad of situations—facile at having the secret and committed to the importance of the lie. For example, Irene, a thirty-seven-year-old mother of two daughters, views her kleptomania not only as thrilling but as an experience she owns.

I walked into the store with my two children, one in the grocery cart, and began with the children's clothing aisle. The place was crowded, on a Saturday, around lunchtime. I saw so many things that my husband would say we didn't really need and that somehow gets me into this game. No one knows that I shoplift, and I have it down to a science. I dress well so that no one is suspicious of me. I'll take makeup, lotion, even clothes and it's getting to be a bigger part of my life. I'd say I do it every time I go out now, every time I shop. I put stuff in the cart and walk out. My plan is that if I ever get caught, I'd act sorry and surprised. I'd be totally shocked and get away with it. I doubt my husband would stand for this if I got caught. He's so particular, such a good citizen.

What I love about this secret is how it makes me feel. Even if sometimes I'm worried, usually I'm exhilarated that I got away with something, that I'm not what I seem. I feel like in this life you have to take things as you can, that's how I see it. But this secret is so safe that I don't have to lie about it, I just keep it my secret. I don't believe anyone can find out, so I don't have to cover my trail. I feel like I'm beating the system and I get a kick out of this. This secret is on my time, not my boss's schedule, not my husband's, and not my girls'. It's all mine.

Little White Lies, Deep Dark Secrets was a natural segue after writing *Tripping the Prom Queen: The Truth About Women and Rivalry.* I felt it was time to research the ways in which women use societal lies and clandestine acts as a means to an end. Since our society remains complex for women, still doling out the mixed messages—the myth of having it all, that motherhood is the ultimate female experience, that we marry for true love—I wanted to know how a woman's omission or distortion of the truth has a loss/gain ratio.

With technology so much a part of our lives, we can have secret e-mail accounts, block our cell phone calls, deceive others of our whereabouts, and create a private world, all the while posturing as a good mother/good wife/good employee. The fluid travel and increased opportunities for women only make it easier for them to integrate their secrets, even exotic and daring ones, into their everyday lives. In *Psychology of Women,* Juanita H. Williams points out that "A central issue in the development of ideas about female personality has always been . . . the degree to which they are biologically or environmentally determined."

In order to appreciate the ways in which women lie, we have to look at how lies and secrets have sufficed both positively and negatively in our lives. Certainly, we've been raised to believe in honesty as inscribed in the Bible—"The truth shall make you free" (John 8:32). Yet for convention-bound women who shared their secrets, there was also an ability to dispel the truth. As David Livingstone Smith writes in his book *Why We Lie,* "Deception is a crucial dimension of all human associations . . . ," but it's a woman's *style* of duplicity and the areas in which she lies that is outstanding and unique from men.

HOW CAN WOMEN NOT LIE?

I decided that for this project, I would place ads on craigslist as well as network through my interviewee pool, and I devised a questionnaire. I was stunned not only by the number of women who replied, but by the range of secrets and lies they confided in me. What was also unexpected was the gratitude these women expressed in being able to tell their stories, anonymity guaranteed. These secrets concerned children, family, work, sex, status, abuse, money, rape, friendships, and relationships. While some women's lies were of tremendous magnitude, others were more ordinary in scale, but always at the heart of the matter. This created a duality in the women's lives; one in which appearances were deceiving and desires ran deep. Repeatedly I heard phrases such as "I'm not hurting anyone, and this works for me," "What no one knows won't hurt them," "I lie well if I have to," and "I have plenty of secrets."

Although in some situations the results were less than optimal, oftentimes these women were triumphant, the lie improved their lives. Throughout I remained glued to my subjects' tales of greed, deception, gain, and vindication. I was uplifted by the determination these women had, which was manifested in the lies they told so cautiously and bravely. In prying open a woman's secrets, we come face-to-face with the struggles and yearnings of women in the twenty-first century and the provisions they cull to prevail.

- More than 80 percent of women of various backgrounds believe in beneficial lying.
- 80 percent of interviewees believe that women lie more cleverly and successfully than do men.
- 75 percent of women say they have to lie in the workplace to sustain their positions.
- 50 percent of women have mixed emotions about mothering.
- More than 75 percent of women feel justified in having a secret to protect.
- 70 percent of women attribute "living a lie" to how they've been positioned in marriages, the workplace, financially, or as mothers.
- 75 percent of women say they lie about money to boyfriends, husbands, and family members.
- 60 percent of interviewees admit to an addiction secret.
- More than 50 percent of women caught in their secrets and lies were prepared to defend themselves.
- More than 60 percent felt they could wiggle out of their lies once discovered, and not suffer the consequences.

INTRINSIC LIES: THE SIX STYLES OF DECEPTION

What is the criteria for a successful female lie?

In collecting personal stories, I realized that women choose very specific kinds of lies, lies that might not even occur to men. *Compassionate lies,* uniquely female in nature, are the most innocuous type of lies, manifesting as "I'd rather lie than hurt your feelings." This is a familiar form of lying, something we've known our entire lives, and it softens up the hard truth. We tell our best friend she looks good in a dress when it's unbecoming, we apologize to a boyfriend/husband/mother not because we mean it but to get on with our day, we don't speak of the gory details of a grandparent's illness or the prognosis with our children.

This choice may seem a no-brainer, but it also sets a template that women frequently use. Lying to protect, to avoid pain, can also be misleading, even if it seems like the right idea. It can actually create distance between the woman who chooses to lie and the person for whom or about whom she lies. And if this person discovers the truth it can backfire, yet women lie this way to avoid conflict.

But if lying is used to avoid serious conversations, it can also be isolating and counterproductive. *Why don't we trust our children, friends, and partners to hear the truth?*

Another female lie used to assuage the status quo is the *betterment lie:* "I lie to improve the situation." This particular lie certainly has its pluses, and most women say it's the bread and butter of female lies. A betterment lie enables us to ameliorate the situation, a trick women have finessed over centuries, mainly as compensation in a male-dominated society. We do it for ourselves, our children, our partners. As Dr. Donald Cohen, a psychologist who treats families, sees it, "Women are maternal, more centered on their children and husbands—they do what they must for those they love."

In the work world, women already feel, in enough cases, that they aren't getting their fair share of the pie. The competition is steep, as I discuss in my last book, *Tripping the Prom Queen: The Truth About Women and Rivalry.* Ninety percent of women in that study reported that they compete only against other women in a variety of work environments. So, when it comes to a bonus, a raise, or promotion, a betterment lie could expedite matters, it could make all the difference that women tell these lies in order to be recognized.

This brings us to our next category of female lies, *survival lies*, which translates into "I lie to preserve; without my lie, I'd be nothing." Survival lies are the most dire of the six types of lies, and can get us into trouble. It isn't that I found any criminals in my study, but women are willing to go out on a limb for a survival secret and its accompanying survival lie. Janet Fitch's novel *White Oleander* comes to mind. A single mother purports to protect her daughter, but in truth, in a narcissistic rage, she kills her former lover by poisoning him, is found guilty, and taken from her daughter to prison. While the mother weaves the lie of her innocence and male suppression from her jail cell, her daughter is bounced about in foster care, acquiring her own survival lies to literally withstand the system. Women are invested in survival lies, as they cope with personal and work situations on an ongoing basis.

For instance, Sarah, a thirty-nine-year-old waitress and mother of three, guards a profound secret.

> I have never told my husband the truth about our third child. It's a secret I'll take to the grave. He isn't the father of our youngest son. In fact, he was in the army when I became pregnant. I'd had a fling with a man who I knew from work, someone I had liked for a very long time. Then my husband was on leave a few weeks later, so I was very lucky. When our son was born he only weighed in at six pounds. I told my husband our son was born early. I have to think about what I did and why I did it all the time. I never change my mind about my secret, though. Telling the truth would be a big problem; it would ruin everything. But every day I look at my son's face and I think about it.

At this point, we ask ourselves, what's the harm in *designated lies*? The message here is "I have too much to lose if I unveil my secret, my lie overpowers my moral code." So we lie about a specific situation, our past, our education, our family life. The secret helps, it buffers the bad stuff in a woman's life. As Benedict Carey pointed out in his article in *The New York Times* on January 11, 2005, "The Secret Lives of Just About Everybody," "Psychologists have long considered the ability to keep secrets as central to healthy development." Since women are excellent at deception, a designated lie can be easily integrated into our existence.

Pop culture has underscored women's designated lies in film and television over the past several decades. In *Breakfast at Tiffany's*, Audrey Hepburn, playing Holly Golightly, is posturing in her New York City life, while in reality she has run away from life with her farmer husband. Two popular sixties shows, *I Dream of Jeannie* and *Bewitched*, succeeded on the premise that one woman was a genie and the other a witch. In the nineties came darker tales, such as Angelica Huston's and Annette Bening's characters in *The Grifters*, where both women are con artists swindling innocent people. Yet this film is tame compared to Angelina Jolie's character in *Mr. & Mrs. Smith* (2005), where Jolie's character lies to her husband, played by Brad Pitt, about her real job, that of assassin.

This brings us to the next part of the equation, the *acceptable lie*. Whenever a woman is lying for her child, her marriage, her job, it's fairly convincing. A woman's rationale is, "I can get away with this, this lie will be accepted if I'm held accountable." Remember how Julia Roberts was forgiven for being a "runaway bride" in the film of the same name? Rather than think badly of her, we view her not as a liar, although she broke her promise to marry each of these men, but as a skittish woman whom we excuse. In the novel *The Bridges of Madison County*, we are sympathetic to Francesca, an Italian war bride married with two teenage children. Women embrace her secret tryst (a secret she takes to the grave) with Robert Kincaid, a photographer who knocks on her door one day. In moral terms, there are those who would say her tryst with Kincaid betrayed a trust. Yet in the book and in the movie (starring Meryl Streep and Clint Eastwood), we side with Francesca and her longing for her lover.

Finally, there is the *beneficial lie,* justified by women for its conviction. A woman's explanation of this kind of lie is "it's more important than the truth." My friend Mary, who owns her own bookstore, illustrates this position. "How could I have built this business if I hadn't buried my secret? If anyone had known my past debt, what happened to my husband in his business, I would never have gotten approval on the lease for the building. Maybe a man would have had an easier time with my credit history, but fifteen years ago, as a widow with two small boys, I knew what to hide to get ahead. I told my lie for the rewards."

The parameters of acceptable lies in the twenty-first century expand as the world opens up to women. The trick becomes self-evident: earmark your secrets carefully, file your lies thoughtfully. There is a protocol for female deception that ranges from the superficial to the profound.

THE CAT OUT OF THE BAG

What is profitable in all these secrets and lies?

In the first two sections of this book, "The Myth of the Truth" and "Through Glass Darkly," I explore the ways in which women lie and how it has affected their lives as mothers, daughters, sisters, wives, friends, and working women. The last third of the book, "Living the Lie," investigates how our culture feeds into our need for secrets and lies. I'll look at the outcome of secrets as negative and positive elements, when a lie is harmful, or strategic, or advantageous. Progress for women can be found in the ability to discern acceptable lies versus the lie that is debilitating. The key to comprehending ourselves is in knowing how and why we tell female lies.

PART I

THE MYTH OF THE TRUTH

ONE

Spinning Yarns: Our Mothers' Lessons

HOW WE LEARNED TO LIE

Our mothers are our role models, our springboard to the world, and their influence upon us, in all areas of our lives, is heartfelt. In certain instances our mothers have shown us what to do, as we'll see in this book, but also what not to do. Whether our mothers kept secrets and lied for the cause or disdained such a path, or openly criticized lies on moral grounds all the while lying themselves, it has impacted us as daughters. Whatever decision our mothers made concerning female deception, the explicit message that came both from our parents and from society at large is that a lie is bad and the truth is good. Yet according to my interviewees, their mothers' lies, or lack thereof, became evident over time. As the daughters themselves approached womanhood, the ramifications of their mothers' actions had an effect.

It may seem a contradiction that a mother, sexless creature that she is supposed to be, a martyr to her children, would have a need for secrets, would yearn for an inner life, for dreams beyond her prescribed reality. It's a hefty load to carry, no wonder so many women confided in me that the genesis of their lies comes from their mothers. These women lie as mothers, about their mothers, to their mothers, and beyond—spilling into the other parts of their lives. Some women describe the advantage they have in lying because their mothers did it, big and small lies that make it familiar, easier to do. What an admission this is—that our own mothers have shown us how to lie.

The Lies Our Mothers Tell Us

As Jollie, twenty-two, a substitute teacher from Washington state, recalls her childhood, it was continually about her mother's problems. Jollie has taken her mother's example as a deterrent.

> The biggest secret I've had in my life is my mother's drug addiction. She told everyone she had a serious illness and we believed her. Really she was addicted to painkillers. I had to watch my younger brother and sisters since she couldn't. I don't want to end up like my mother.... I'm still ashamed and upset by her. I pity her. My father was in on her secret and fibbed to us, which made it even harder for me. I was older and I ended up being the one who took care of her. We thought she was dying, and we were so afraid. It was sad for her children . . . and I don't understand why she didn't think of that, why she didn't care. Finally, when I was around twelve, I figured it out. Still, my mom lied—she was lying all the time. Now I have my own children and I keep my distance from my mom. My friends have mothers who come to babysit, to help out, but I can't have my mother come. So I say she's far away . . . she works . . . I won't do to my own children what she's done to us.

In Jollie's case, the shame of her mother's lie—part survival lie, part designated lie—haunts her. Having a family of her own is a chance to right the wrongs that she suffered at the hands of her mother. Jollie's determination is to mother her children in the way she wanted to be mothered. Yet she hasn't disclosed her entire past to her husband or friends.

> I got married young and had babies young, and it makes me feel like I have a shot at a healthy life. I don't say much to my husband about my mother, maybe because I'm so trained to tell her lie, about some grave illness. I still hide her secret, it's what I know how to do. I used to think I did it for her, but I do it for her and for me. We both needed to lie about her life.

The Lifetime television movie *Homeless to Harvard*, the story of Liz Murray, played by Thora Birch, is about a family torn apart by the mother's drug addiction. Murray's mother, an AIDS-infected drug addict, needed not only to be mothered by her young daughters, but for the daughters' attempts at normalcy—going to school, having friends—to be cushioned in a lie. Sadly, Murray's mother dies. Afterward, Murray ends up graduating from high school and winning a scholarship to Harvard, but she's been robbed of a healthy childhood and is spooked by her mother's trajectory.

For daughters so burdened by their mothers, there is both the attachment to the mother and the pulling away, as we have seen in Jollie's case. These survival lies, for the sake of the mother and the sake of the daughters, are shrouded in fear. When Liz Murray roams the streets and subways, homeless at fifteen, there is a terrifying melancholy surrounding her that she is desperate to rise above.

There are our mothers' lies that aren't as dark and ominous, but have tremendous influence over how we live our lives as adult women. As Tyne, forty-six, living in Georgia, recalls her divorce, she couldn't have managed it without her mother's choice set before her. Like Jollie, Tyne's decision is in reaction to her mother; she has purposely chosen another kind of life for herself.

If my mother hadn't stayed married to my father all these years, still today, I wouldn't have had the guts to leave my own lousy marriage five years ago. I saw her tough it out, her cross to bear, with six children to raise. Her secret was her hope that he'd die or he'd be the one to leave her or her life would miraculously change. I knew her secret because we were so close. She said nothing, but I saw it and felt it, and one day I picked up and left my marriage, blowing wide open my mother's pretense. I was brave enough to say to the world, my marriage isn't okay, that's the truth. Her lie wasn't my lie, but it sure was my example. She was floored when I did it—not that she said, oh you bad person. I felt absolved, for both of us.

Tyne's action is proof that her mother's example, of living a betterment lie, wasn't enough for her. So what we start as small girls lasts a lifetime; we are entwined in our mothers' opinions, decisions, and secrets; it becomes a jumping-off point. Although the trajectory of a mother/daughter relationship can have peaks and valleys, 80 to 90 percent of women in midlife, according to Dr. Karen S. Fingerman in her book *Aging Mothers and Their Adult Daughters: A Study in Mixed Emotions,* claim to have a good relationship with their mothers. According to Dr. Fingerman, adult daughters still seek their mothers' approval and dislike their disapproval.

In the 1998 film *Dangerous Beauty,* starring Jacqueline Bisset and Catherine McCormack as mother and daughter in sixteenth-century Venice, Bisset's character convinces her daughter that she'll have independence only if she becomes a courtesan. She herself was a famous courtesan, and to this end, Bisset's character teaches McCormack's character her secrets. In return, her daughter exceeds her mother's dreams, becoming a kind of feminist as well as the best of the courtesans. This example shows a mother's secrets and wiles as a positive force in her daughter's life.

OUR MOTHER'S VOICE

Modern-day women describe how much their mothers' secrets and trumped-up tales become theirs. Lisa, thirty-nine, lives in the Midwest and works part-time for a large retailer. She believes that she's taken on her mother's habits when it comes to being deceptive.

> My mother is a shopper, and from the time I was in kindergarten I've watched her hide her purchases from my father, the cleaning lady, everyone. I do the same thing. And I bet my girls will do it, too, since they watch me unload the trunk of the car, and sneak in through the back door, scurrying with my bags into the bedroom. I quickly hang all the new stuff up, just like my mom did. My mom also encouraged me to make my own money and stash it away, do conservative investments, make sure my money isn't available to anyone but me. I do it and I tell my girls they'll have to have their own money, any way they can get it, in this world. My mom was always secretive about who she'd meet for lunch in town, and it somehow gives me license to do the same. Who knows who she was with—and who knows who I see at lunch? I know she'd approve.

Who understands our secrets better than our mothers?

As adult women and, for many of us, as mothers ourselves, we continue to look to our mothers for their input. Oftentimes our mothers become our trusted confidantes when we engage in a secret and lie. More than 80 percent of the women in my interviewee pool felt that their mothers were their greatest advocates when it came to their ability to lie. Angela, thirty-four, mother of two, remarks:

> My mother supports me no matter what. I've been having an affair and trying to figure out if I should leave my husband. My mother even covers for me, babysits the kids, so I can see this guy. She just wants me to make a clean break, or stay in my marriage. Whatever I decide, my secret is safe with her.

Perhaps mothers and daughters are in cahoots not only because mothers and daughters align historically and culturally, but for daughters with their own children, motherhood itself can trigger a few lies. An underlying problem seems to be our society, which doesn't really support mothers, yet has many preconceived notions of how they are supposed to be. Ann Crittenden, author of *The Price of Motherhood,* observed that women are diminished as mothers with a "mommy tax," meaning women lose economic security to some extent once they have children. The children suffer as well from this lack of respect for women. And when a third of divorced women, according to her study, go on welfare as primary caregivers for their children, it's no wonder women will lie and cheat to get what they need, what they deserve.

Daniella, twenty-five, grew up in a family of six; her mother held down two jobs to support the children, and her father saw them several times a year.

> My mother was respected in our neighborhood because she could make ends meet. The people who lived around us had more problems than we did, but that's only because our mother worked hard to avoid them. No one helped her and no one cared; she did it herself. But she used to tell me to get a college degree even if I had to beg and steal for it. And get

a job with some respect. I did that, I worked as an intern in a media center and I went to school at night at the local college. No one did this, and my mom didn't boast about it, she kept it a secret. Today, she still doesn't say much, she's afraid people will be jealous. She taught me to lie on my résumé, and she taught me to do it so I wouldn't clean toilets like she does. I think it was right what she told me to do. I have a job with health insurance now, and I am a manager.

Daniella's story raises the question if it's okay to lie because our mothers instructed us this way, to ameliorate the situation, as a betterment lie. It's as if Daniella's mother's voice is ringing in her ears as she forges ahead. According to Wray Herbert, in his article in *Newsweek* on August 21, 2006, a new study by Anita Kelly, a psychologist at the University of Notre Dame, found that people with secrets (about families, sex, romance, health) have fewer psychosomatic symptoms than do people with clear consciences. Based on my research for *Little White Lies, Deep Dark Secrets,* I recognize the agility with which women lie; if men feel okay about their secrets, women feel convinced of theirs. Our mothers' secrets have seeped into our subconscious, providing unspoken consent for our own deceit.

There are our mothers' lies and our own lies.

Whatever style of truth or lie our mothers have, we have our own individual genetic makeup and tendencies. For mothers with more than one daughter, the example they set can be influenced by birth order, the mother's frame of mind combined with the psyche of each daughter. Was the mother rigid with her firstborn daughter and progressively less so with the daughters who followed— offering more leniency? And how did this affect each daughter's style of secret telling? Christine, sixty, from a southern city, believes that her two grown daughters were influenced by her moods and the environment of their childhoods.

> I didn't have to teach my daughters not to lie or to lie, it's in them. My first daughter would lie when the truth would serve her better and my second daughter never lies. I was such a different mother with my first child—I was so concerned about doing the right thing. With my second daughter, I was single and poorer, and I allowed more mistakes, and so she doesn't tell lies. I cut her a break. Later I had sons and they aren't the same when it comes to lies. I didn't care so much about not being wrong with the boys but I had to be right with my girls
>
> I told the girls that lies have short legs but to keep a secret. I taught them that women should always keep something to themselves, don't tell all. Something has to be sacred. You aren't obligated to answer questions, you have to learn to be a best friend to yourself. I don't like the word "lie" and I hope my girls know this, it's what I've said, many times.

For Jasmine, thirty, who lives in New Jersey and is a part-time nurse's aide with three children, her mother's lie was similar in nature to her own.

> I lie to protect my children when it comes to the real story about their father. He abandoned them and I got a court order. He can see them, but it's court-mandated. The same thing happened to my mom with my father, and she kept what he'd done a secret from us, and told me when I was twenty. It's my own life but I see her influence. I do some things like she did and some things I do my way because I prefer it. But I'm thinking of her, of what she's been through and what I have ahead, with my children.

Unlike Jasmine, Tiana says her mother's secret has become hers and her sisters' secret, too. A forty-year-old photographer living in southern California, Tiana can't recall a time when the family wasn't enmeshed in her mother's lie.

Our family is probably too close, it's just my sisters, our mother, and me. Our mother knows everything about us and we know so much about her. It's agreed by all of us that we don't tell anyone the truth about our father, who has nine children and has had several wives. Instead we act mysterious, our mother tells us to, like he's missing or dead, when people ask. We never mention him or what he's done to us. Our mother wants it this way. I respect her, but her life has made me not want to be a wife and mother.

Glory, twenty-eight, lives in the Northeast. She views her mother's secret and accompanying lie as a necessity, yet was encouraged not to lie by her mother.

My mother lied about our religion because we lived in an intolerant area. She wanted us to fit in and thought this was the best way. Then she used to tell me that if you lie about who you are, you're nothing. She was this really honest woman who never told lies, except this one big lie. It was confusing, but I understood her decision. She was right, there was such bigotry. I moved away after high school—she encouraged us to leave as soon as we could—and have been truthful about myself, who I am, what religion and background I'm from, ever since. I think my mother decided this path and stuck with it, but she wasn't very happy about it.

The lies told by our mothers and the lies we, ourselves, tell, are a way to get through the labyrinth of life as adult women.

While Christine in highly invested in veracity and has gone to great lengths to teach her daughters this, Tiana and Jasmine use deliberate, beneficial lies, and if victory or opportunity is the result, it's a relief. This applies to Glory's mother's lie, too, although the desperate edge to her mother's choice categorizes the secret as a survival lie, and her mother's overall honesty is noteworthy.

THE EVOLUTION OF THE FEMALE LIE

Our Mothers Set the Stage

It can be reassuring that our mothers have shown us the ways in which women lie and what they lie about. What could be more comforting than to know, when one is lying, that it's ritualistic, an acquired talent, endorsed by our mothers, and media-driven? After all, our mothers have lied in countless ways—to their coworkers, friends, sisters, husbands, and children—for the options the lies provide, the "seeing is believing" quality it adds to their lives, the wishful thinking it presents, the choices it creates.

There is a close identity with other women's lies and secrets, whether a woman tells the tale or is affected by another woman's story. In this way, women's secrets have passed from generation to generation. Consider Jesse, thirty-four, the mother of three young children, who has been married for nine years.

> My mother had an affair and left our father for this man. For years this was fine for my mom, but somewhere along the line she started an affair with her high school sweetheart. She still sees him whenever she can. I knew all of her secrets, but my brothers knew nothing. This secret life is the thing that helped her unhappiness. So now I find myself wanting to be with someone other than my husband and I know I can do it, just

like my mom did, twice. I wonder which was better, her divorce or the affair in her second marriage? And what about all the gossip—people talk, no question. I know she thinks it's a secret, but people say things, I can tell.

Even if my mom didn't care if she was caught in a lie, she tried to keep it a secret. I work for a bank, something my mother didn't deal with, and I worry about getting found out, about nasty text messages and mean e-mails about me floating around. I feel like I'm becoming my mom without the guts she had, that I need to stand by my lie better.

It isn't just our media-driven culture but our sophisticated technology with Internet access, news flashes, and instant messaging that create vehicles for gossip and secrets. This kind of easy access not only fuels gossip but underwrites the lies. Gossip is perceived by some as detrimental, by others as a healthy part of social intercourse, and surely we have observed our mothers knee-deep in the game. For females, gossip is a part of the social canvas of our lives, from grade school through old age. Kate Fox writes in her essay "Evolution, Alienation and Gossip" that regardless of negative connotations, gossip has beneficial social and psychological functions.

"You only have to worry when they stop talking about you," my friend Lara, forty-nine, was taught by her mother. Lara regards gossip in a positive light and seems not to care if her female friends are spreading rumors about her. There can be the right results from a lie that's looped into gossip. This is the case for Nina, thirty-nine, who, unlike Jesse, acted on her emotions and had an affair. She explains how a spilled secret and subsequent gossip created her happiness. The fact that her mother supported her secret was the gravy.

We're all from this little town where my cousin Sheryl decided to divorce her husband. She called me first and said she was miserable but didn't want anyone to know. I'd always been crazy about her husband and had a few lunches and quiet meetings in the park with him. We were about to have an affair when Sheryl decided she wanted a divorce. But it wasn't really a secret by then and women were talking about it. I knew I had to do something. My mom told me to go for it—I think she had her own reasons, and that gave me courage.

I divorced my husband, and got to be with this man. It's true I used Sheryl's secret to get what I wanted. It's true I lied to her as long as possible. Our boys played together while I was listening to her complain about Carlo and at the same time planning my life with him. It worked out for everyone that it happened that way.

Not every mother's secret and her daughter's mirroring of it revolves around illicit love affairs. Still, these are common for both mothers and daughters because women continue to be disappointed in their long-standing, monogamous relationships. Thus, the mother's actions have a direct influence upon their daughters if the younger women find themselves in a similar predicament. The mothers' beneficial lies are fodder for the daughters' own lies.

The Good Girl + Power = Female Lies

When we overheard our mothers speaking in code when we were younger, confiding in other women, we emulated their style. It was a way for us, as young girls, to bond—over a shared secret, a form of communicating. Our mothers' example proved that secrets render us potent in a world were women have fewer auspices than do men. Using a lie to get what you cannot otherwise have is a keenly female trait. A secret that begets a lie is shown to us by our mothers, our mentors, and our female peers as worth pursuing.

So if good girls wouldn't venture to fool anyone outright, a lie that seems to have no consequence is a throwaway. If a secret makes the day easier, it can't be all bad. But can't these "light lies" enable women to lie more easily about serious matters since there is now a precedent? For instance, Louisa, forty, has been taught by her mother to deny any of her cosmetic procedures to her husband and friends.

My mother taught me that looks are your greatest weapon in this world. She was so panicked over losing her looks when I was in grade school that I always knew that aging was a huge problem. By the time I was in junior high, my mother was on her second procedure, a face-lift, after an eye lift and lots of special facials, whatever they had in those days. She told none of her friends—she even went to California to have the face-lift. Instead of looking at my mom and thinking she shouldn't be lying when her friends asked her what she'd done, I decided I'd be just the same. I got Botox and collagen treatments ahead of anyone I knew.

My mother acted like we'd murdered someone when we went to the doctor's office together for my first Botox injections. She kept looking around as if the enemy would show up in the person of one of my friends or worse, one of hers. When I had my eyes done a few years ago, I told my husband that I needed it for my sinuses and he believed me. I told my friends another story, that I was only doing my lower lids for a tearing problem. Some of them seemed skeptical but I insisted it was the truth. My mom thought I'd gotten away with something. She said that my father always fell for her excuses when it came to her beauty secrets, and her friends were out to rat on her.

The trickery involved in Louisa's beauty lie to her friends is an example of how women lie to each other in a separate style from how they lie to a husband, boyfriend, or child. For her friends,

Louisa needed to have more details, a more convincing explanation. Louisa is well schooled in lying about this matter, her mother
has been a skilled coach.

Similarly, Darren, thirty-three, well schooled by her mother,
whose age remains a mystery, is already lying about her age.

> On my twentieth birthday I was panicked. I told friends I was
> eighteen and had skipped a grade to be a sophomore in col-
> lege. My mom warned me always to be the youngest, and if it
> wasn't the truth, just say I was the youngest. She did. I doubt
> my father, or any of her children, ever knew her real age. She
> was obsessed with it, with what would happen to her if she
> was old. It's weird and sad that she died young, and my aunt
> says she was lying about her age to the very end. No one
> could find her birth certificate, but my aunt says she got five
> years on her tombstone.
>   So I lie about my age, I say I'm twenty-nine, and before
> that, when I was younger, I lied younger. I think my mom
> would like this, she saw no problem in never telling your
> age—she saw a problem in telling the truth.

On another topic, as equally affecting as Darren's mother's influence, is Nora's experience with her mother. At thirty-six, Nora
remarks on her mother's keen consciousness about her husband's
(Nora's father's) status in the neighborhood.

> We were poor growing up but my mother came from a fancy
> family. She was always pretending that things were okay when
> they weren't. Our father couldn't keep a job and that was a se-
> cret. My mother kept saying he was at a job that he'd lost
> three years earlier, and either everyone believed her or every-
> one knew she was lying. I know people whispered things and
> she wanted to defend my father. But mostly it was so she still

looked like she had this life, the way she'd been raised. And how it was when our father had money, early on.

As disparate in theme as Louisa's lies (and her mother's) about cosmetic procedures, Darren's mother's lies about her age, and Nora's mother's lies about financial status, the impact upon the daughter is the common thread. In these instances, the lies are central to each of the women's identities and manifest as acceptable lies. The cover-ups for each kind of lie *feel* necessary; these women instinctively avoid the truth.

Our Mothers' Secrets Trump Any Other Persuasion

Just as I was finishing up my interviews for this chapter, women began to tell me that their mother's impact in terms of secrets and lies was the only factor in their decision to do the same. For this group of women, the media and cultural influences were of little importance; since they'd been young girls, an implicit approval for female lies was a direct message from their mothers. The benefit of the lie versus the drawback of the truth was the example set before them. That their mothers' experience, in the fifties or early sixties, rendered them without a voice only made the daughters more strident in their secrets and lies.

Anya, a fifty-one-year-old mother of two daughters, lives in a suburb in Maryland, where she teaches. Anya believes that her mother taught her all that she knows about lying and circumvention, and was atypical of her time and place.

> The way that I am is because my mother had no regard for the truth. She saw the truth as an impediment. Even though she led a traditional life, she was cunning and shrewd and a total rule breaker. She was a navy wife and it was all about conformity, towing the line. Her whole existence was about how

to cross that line and I followed her example. It was a training issue for me, I was bonded to her and I admired her.

But when I was in college, I chose a husband whose whole creed of life was about honor, someone who didn't know how to scheme or cheat. My mother was surprised, she couldn't understand my choice—she was someone who couldn't constitutionally tell the truth. Here I was with a husband who believed in the truth, and I tried to be like that, but I'd been led by my mother. I had watched her go to great lengths to be devious, she was very scrappy. In the end I chose my mother's way and I've had secrets all along—my days are not pure as the driven snow. Secrets at work, secrets about money, about other men. My mother would approve of all this.

Likewise, Marie, fifty-one, living in southern Florida, views her mother's influence as tantamount to her own take on secrets and lies.

Anything my mother did was deliberate and suspicious and at the same time she'd achieved a lot in her life. She'd gotten her college degree during the depression so she cared about how accomplished someone was—she measured them for that. Her view was that it didn't matter what it took to get there, as long as you got there. She also wanted me to have a better life than she had. She wanted me to marry someone who had a secure income since my father never had that. She liked men to be smart and told me to marry a man with a profession, so I did. And then I lied to him like she lied to my father. And it was okay since my mother had done it. She believed in lying your way into anything that could help you—socially, money-wise, job-wise. She was clever and she taught me how to do the same. I even keep all these secrets from my sister, who never understood what our mother was about, she wasn't into it. My sister is honest, and not very useful. I'm my mother's protégée, I'm the one with the moves.

For Ellie, forty-four, who has a twenty-one-year-old daughter, there is disappointment in how little her daughter has been able to glean from both Ellie and her mother when it comes to being disingenuous.

Years ago, when I first read about Machievelli and the idea of people being Machievellian, I didn't know what the big deal was. I remember thinking, so what's wrong with what he does? I know for sure that my mother would agree with my viewpoint. My motto is that I lie to get what I want as long as I don't hurt anyone. This is exactly what my mother told me to do, what she did herself. But my daughter couldn't survive this kind of life, she can't cheat or lie or have a secret about anything. She isn't capable, it isn't in her and yet my mom and I raised her and she respects us.

My daughter is in a long-term relationship and I watch her be so honest with her boyfriend. My mother and I flinch, neither of us would have done it that way. Since she got to college, my daughter has purposely not been like my mother and me. She'll ask me how to navigate this relationship or what to tell her boss if she's going to be late, and then she'll absolutely reject my advice. In all fairness, she has something I don't have in my marriage, a loving, reciprocal relationship, but she won't even cut corners with her studying, it's not just the boyfriend. She doesn't see things like my mother and I do, she won't listen, won't sneak around.

Blanche, twenty-five, working in a southwestern city in marketing, uses lies less than her mother, and is trying to break free of her mother's pattern.

If my mother hadn't longed for a good life, and if she hadn't been so ambitious for me, I'd be stuck where I grew up. I watched my mother and my grandmother lie to my father and my grandfather, to anyone in our hometown. They were so miserable and I was their hope. My mom even wanted me to lie on my college application and my first job applications. So I exaggerated how I'd done at a job and made a two-week internship seem like it stretched out all summer. It helped. There's no question that my mom's tactics work. But I'm not good at it.

There's something to be said for telling the truth and I try to do it. When it gets messed up I think maybe my mother is right. Why tell my new boyfriend that I still see my old boyfriend sometimes? Why tell my boss why I'm really late? But I don't want to be like my mom, able to lie about things even if her secrets are good for her.

Vicki, thirty, whose mother told all sorts of lies, is like Blanche and considers the truth an option.

As much as I know my mom is smart and has gotten through some pretty awful ordeals, I don't want to live a life of lies like she has. I watched how she had to lie to my stepfather and to my father about money, about our schools, about our schedules. I watched her lie about work. I know she had to do it, but I want a different kind of relationship with people, even with my boss, definitely with my husband. I want to say it like it is. This doesn't mean I won't lie, since I know how to do it really well from my mother. It means I'll try to be honest, to do it that way first.

These interviews illustrate how impressive mothers are and how the modeling of a mother can obliterate any other authority.

While Anya's lies are beneficial in nature, Marie and Ellie employ the betterment lie. Blanche's has a compassionate component, as she enters the gray area that has ruled her mother's life, and Vicki recognizes her mother's survival lies as she breaks with the tradition. If a mother sanctions deception, it becomes familiar to the daughter, who then makes her own decisions. It's the lives that women lead versus the faces they wear that is the trick, the sleight-of-hand.

A DAY IN THE LIFE OF AN AVERAGE FEMALE LIAR

Credit Card Hell—Costco to Bloomingdale's

Your mother always shopped to assuage her disappointment, she always lied about her purchases to your father, her friends, sometimes herself. In the past few years, you've imitated your mother's pattern, walking into stores every time stress increases in your life.

Now you haven't been shopping in almost a month and you feel extremely virtuous, but you're also itching to get back to it. Any store that sells women's clothing, makeup, hair and face care products, and bargain purchases, from computers to cashmere sweaters, will do. Not that you are alone, your girlfriends are your cohorts on these shopping excursions. But they seem to handle their purchases better than you have, especially in the past year or so. It's been a long haul; your husband was laid off, the insurance company is refusing your daughter's asthma medication, and the raise that you expected at Christmas was a bonus instead. The tension of your husband being at home, day in, day out, is enormous and he can't be convinced to pitch in around the house.

During these shopping excursions, your problems are forgotten, albeit temporarily, and you feel lighter, there's a spring to your step at the mall. When your husband insists you curtail spending, you

promise to comply. And for two weeks afterward, you don't enter a
store. Then life became hellish, your children's needs, usually man-
ageable, became unbearable.

The first time you broke the rule, you felt denied, having returned
home with one lousy eyeliner and a new lipstick. After that, you sim-
ply lied about your shopping excursions. You kept your secret well,
having been approved for another MasterCard, in your maiden
name. As the debt escalated from $2,000 to $10,000, you felt a pang
of remorse. You promised yourself that you'd scrimp and save to pay
the debt, and better yet, give up the stores.

Deep in your heart you consider this a benign secret compared to
your cousin who is having an extramarital affair and your coworker
who is slowly siphoning money from her and her husband's joint
bank account. Isn't this what your mother instilled in you?

Demands of Mothering

Your day begins on the wrong side of the bed, and you have slept
through two alarms. The children are now late for school and your
eight-year-old son is asking about his lunch bag. You give him lunch
money and tell him he's to buy food in the cafeteria on Thursdays
from now on. When he seems perplexed, you assure him it's a new
rule.

Your thirteen-year-old daughter cries that she was supposed to be
up forty-five minutes earlier to study for her math test. When she be-
comes hysterical that she'll fail, you proceed to write an excuse from
math due to a long-standing dentist appointment, requesting your
daughter make up the math test the next day.

You toss your youngest child into the car in her pajamas, telling
her that preschool is canceled and she can stay home with her
nanny. The older children give you an odd look and a wave of ex-
haustion sweeps over you. You know your mother would never have

allowed this, she would have been organized and honest with her children. But then, she didn't have your career and three children, did she?

Once the older children are dropped off at school (they missed their bus), you call your office on your cell and announce that your little one is "under the weather" and you'll be in as soon as your nanny arrives. Just then your husband calls from Toronto, where he had a business meeting, and you tell him everything is fine. And it is, isn't it? It's just that so much is expected of you, the endless responsibilities, big and small. An hour later you drive to work realizing it's unlikely that the truth would have proven any better. You wonder if the falsehoods you've told all morning can be categorized as merely fibs. You push any thoughts of your mother out of your mind.

Behind Closed Doors

For a year you've buried a secret, a secret few would believe. To the outside world, you have an attractive, successful husband, two terrific sons, and a great job in fashion that you enjoy. As a family you take interesting vacations, having traveled to Asia and Europe in the past year. Your life appears close to perfection.

But the reality is that your husband has a serious alcohol problem and is abusive when he drinks. Nonetheless, it is the quiet times, when he is "behaving," that get you through the difficult times when his behavior is out of control and you feel demoralized and hopeless. This isn't alien territory, your own father was an alcoholic, and the worst part is, your mother lived a similar lie to yours.

Three months ago your husband was arrested two states over for drunk driving and disorderly conduct while returning from a sport outing. Not only did you pay a lawyer to make it go away, but you told no one, not even your mother or sister, both of whom had such

*high hopes for you to escape your past. Now you drive your husband
to work and pick him up, since his license has been revoked. Your relationship with your husband gnaws at you, in light of this most recent event. You ask yourself how long can you tolerate this and for
whose sake do you pretend? For the sake of the boys, for your reputation in your town, for your own need to have order in your life? You
promise yourself one more incident and you'll blow the lid on this
false life. Then you feel your mother's shadow, she never squealed on
your father, she lived the lie.*

A LEGACY OF LIES AND WHISPERS

The recent film *Because I Said So,* starring Diane Keaton as a
single mother who raised three daughters and Mandy Moore
as her unmarried daughter, addresses how far-reaching the
mother/daughter connection is. With the best intentions, Keaton's
character decides to advertise online for a lifelong partner for
Moore's character. Not only is Keaton not honest about her med-
dling, but when two men both fall for Moore, Keaton steers her
daughter toward her favorite of the two, without any disclosure as
to how it all came about. Since Moore prefers the other man, she
ends up a two-timer, lying to both men in order to please her
mother. This is a film where the secret unravels in order to clean
up the mess, but the underlying theme is that of a mother's strong
influence over her daughter.

In speaking to the women who answered my ad on craigslist,
I heard of more secrets that were kept than were revealed. The
majority of women claimed their mothers were responsible for
their ability to have hidden agendas. What we have learned from
our mothers covers the gamut from lying to our husbands, children, and friends to hiding a drug addiction, to embellishing our
children's achievements, to squandering money, to buying lottery

tickets. Women confided that they'd been sexually and emotionally abused, others had lied to save their reputations, some had lied to survive, still others to protect their families.

In justifying their secrets and lies, more than 80 percent of the interviewees reported their mothers' effect, and some adult daughters were not very troubled by their own actions. For example, Charlotte, a thirty-five-year-old woman who found herself tearing up credit card receipts from restaurants and hiding her purchases, felt the genesis of her acceptable lie was her mother's blessing.

> There's nothing in my life that is so huge I can't get away from it. I can escape any of my lies, but I choose to lie instead; I go shopping and don't tell my live-in boyfriend how much I spend, I go to a bar with girlfriends and tell him I'm at the movies. It's just easier. I don't want to be judged, but I want to do what I want to do. I sometimes wonder if I had another kind of boyfriend if this would be any different, but I doubt it. I've always lied to whatever guy I'm with. No one seems to get me. I figure a lie is easier than the hard work of trying to explain. The only person who knows what I do is my mom. Sometimes she thinks I could get a better boyfriend, but she also understands that I do this to make life easier.

BURDENED WOMEN: HOW SOCIETY ORCHESTRATES FEMALE LIES

Our mothers have endorsed our secrets, even coached us in deception; the culture fosters a climate where women choose to lie.

Let's face it, lying is instinctive, a part of the hard wiring in both genders. Yet female lies go deeper, reflecting societal expectations and used as a method to defy the construct. When a woman is adept at dishonesty as a way to keep afloat, she feels in control in the midst of her complicated life. It's ironic that as options have expanded for women, the need to lie becomes more central and more prevalent.

There are a few ways in which female lying not only aces male lying, but can be viewed as necessary *and* distinctive.

Female Lies Can Be Trite or Significant

If women lie to their male partners about the price of clothing, face creams, and shoes, it's easy—it affords them material goods without anyone in their lives passing judgment. But what of the more serious lies, the ones that have greater reverberations? Regardless of the scale of the secret, I found women such as Janine standing up for the decision to lie.

For Janine, a thirty-two-year-old administrator, an extramarital affair meant she had to lie to her husband and two sons about her whereabouts for more than a year. As with other interviewees, Janine confided in her mother, who encouraged her daughter to use the affair to shed light on her present situation. Janine's secret tryst was an eye-opener; she used a compassionate lie to put this into effect.

How much can I hate myself for lying when it made me rethink my life? I was raised to be a good wife and mother. I was also raised to be financially independent. And I was told by my mother to take care of myself. I know now that my husband never liked that about me, he resented that I had a good job, that I wasn't with him for his salary, that I wouldn't tolerate any bull. When I met a man who really respected me at work, I couldn't tell my husband how I felt and obviously I couldn't say what I was doing. And he never learned about it. He was better off with my lies about working late—he was even better off with my lies about why I was asking for a divorce. . . . I told him I was stifled, miserable, I didn't say I'd fallen for another man. When I doubted myself I would call my mother. She always advised me to keep it all quiet, to keep it a secret and make the best choice for myself.

If Janine used her secret as a means for serious changes in her life—such as getting a divorce—she never lay bare that she'd had this double life. There are women who echo Janine's choice in how to implement a lie. It's not by merely omitting the truth (*Webster's* defines the truth as "fidelity, constancy"), which she did, but also by using the experience to create a new beginning. It's at this point that a betterment lie kicks in and alters the status quo.

We're Taught to Be Unimpressed with Male Lies

Few women reported that their fathers had any say in how they came to keep secrets, nor did they mention male mentors or father figures as influential. Yet many of us have discovered a husband's or boyfriend's lie, and noted how easy is it to get to the bottom of their secret. It isn't that men don't need to have secrets, but their skills at keeping the secret and their choice of secrets seem rudimentary compared to a woman's style and requirements. Women go much deeper with their secrets and lies than do men, often describing them as "having a life of their own."

Narine, forty-three, aligned with her mother when her parents divorced thirty years ago, and was struck by how hollow her father's lies were.

My father would promise to visit my sisters and me on a Saturday and never show up. My mom lied for him and sometimes we believed her. But we never believed him. He just wanted to be with his girlfriend, not us. He didn't even know how to lie, and the odd thing is, my mother did. When she said that our father was at the office or on a business trip, it seemed credible, even though we suspected she was covering for him, just to save our feelings. His lies were a joke, he was never credible. This showed me that men are crummy liars, and women have a reason to lie.

How cleverly women lie is a balance of nature versus nurture, but socially created situations do cause women to lie. Since women can be more tentative and more willing to please than men, they use the compassionate lie, as does Narine's mother on behalf of her ex-husband.

When it comes to romance, children, marriage, careers, and friendships, there is less satisfaction and more complexity than many of us bargained for.

From the start of this project, I learned that even the most moral of women (mothers) can be deceptive. There are female lies that are scheming and those of a more innocent nature—we tell a friend she looks well when she doesn't, we say we are late due to traffic, we embellish our child's score on a standardized test. In any case, women accommodate the cultural expectations; their types of lies facilitate the process. When push comes to shove, although a woman's life should be virtuous, the ethics of female lying are about *not* getting caught.

Seth Shulman, a social worker whose practice includes women's issues, remarks, "For women, a resentment builds in relationships and in other parts of her life. A woman will seek what she needs, and lie to get what she wants, if she has to. Entitlement is a payback for what's gone on."

"It's a woman's nature to keep secrets," Dr. Donald Cohen, a marriage and family therapist, explains. "Even if it seems that they are sharing with their female friends, they're absolutely capable of internalizing and being inward."

Each week on *Desperate Housewives*, various characters, as mothers, lie and cover their tracks. What makes it so fascinating is how high the stakes are raised in the case of Bree, Marcia Cross's character, who in the second season banishes her son, Andrew, leaving him on a country road after his repeated mistreatment of her. This is after Bree has hidden her son's hit-and-run accident that resulted in the death of an elderly woman. Bree's neighbor, Betty, played by Alfre Woodard, has a secret equally dark when she hides the son who murdered a young woman, only to discover that she's hiding the wrong son. How deeply a mother guards her secrets is a recurrent theme on the show, one that fascinates us but doesn't surprise us.

WEBS OF DECEPTION

Our mothers have shown us how resourceful women's secrets and lies can be, and also draw the line on certain tall tales. In my study I discovered three societal directives that keep women invested in their secrets and lies, to varying degrees.

The Shame Factor

Disclosing a lie can make us look bad, and as "good girls," our mothers raised us to shun such behavior. Actually, many women would prefer to delude themselves when it comes to the ramifications of having a secret rather than face their shame. These shameful feelings tend to surface only when a lie spirals out of control and a woman's place in the world is jeopardized. Women are keenly conscious that they can be disgraced by a discovered secret and they take great care to cover their tracks.

In Misty's interview, we see the repercussions of an early secret, perpetuated by her mother's designated lie. Although the constant weight of this caused Misty, fifty, to be ashamed, today the healing process has begun for her.

> I've had a serious health problem since I was small and it gave me shaky hands and a nervousness that I can't control. So I always tried to be normal but I always felt something was wrong with me. I was afraid I'd fall apart and my mother gave me two different messages, one was that nothing was wrong with me and the other was that she'd do everything for me. I walked around feeling like I'd die, like I'd fall apart, and I had to go to the hospital for treatments. It was like my body had left me, deserted me compared to other people, and I worked hard at no one ever knowing what was really wrong. Even though people commented on the way I was, only my family knew the nature of it. We never explained anything, we kept it a secret. This was my mother's doing.

The Guilt Game

Guilt is another emotion women avoid when it comes to their secrets. Guilt is linked to shame but a woman who feels ashamed believes that she *didn't measure up;* a woman who feels guilty believes that she *did the wrong thing* (such as not taking action, not telling the truth, hoarding a secret that affects others). When we feel guilty we want to shed the guilt, to return to our mothers' image of the "good girl." The person who feels shame struggles with feeling undeserving and unsuccessful, by action or inaction. Like shame, many women are able to avoid guilt by justifying their ability to lie—and once again, our mothers have shown us the ropes.

Dealing with the guilt becomes a process for women and expedites the secret telling. For all sorts of female lies, women find a way to legitimize their tales and perpetuate them. Madeleine, twenty-five, living in a small town in South Carolina where she is in graduate school, dispels her guilt over her tryst with a married professor. Throughout, Madeleine has been aware of her mother's lack of enthusiasm for her situation and disapproval for her daughter's secret.

I was raised not to be involved with someone who is married with kids. I was taught to marry the right guy and bring up a nice family and at first I felt guilty about what I was doing. I felt even guiltier when I told my mother since I know she wants me to have no part of this. I sometimes tell myself this isn't a full-blown affair but something that's in my life. It's been going on for a year and we both have to pretend that nothing is happening. I don't think his wife knows and this makes me feel better about it.

Running around in secret is wearing me down, telling my mother I have a date on a Saturday night [when I don't] is tiring. At first it was that I'm doing something wrong that upset me the most, but now it's the frustration with the stolen hours. After a year of this, I know it's been worth it to be with him, and if it's wrong, it isn't as big a deal as not knowing what's ahead. I just want it to all work out.

Finally, Madeleine looks to her chances with her lover rather than the culpability of her relationship. While at first she felt guilty about her secret, especially concerning her mother's judgment, her shift is now to the possibility of a future with this man. Yet she is well aware of what it would take for her lover to be truly available to her, which brings us to how denial affects women's secrets.

The Denial Quotient

This is how women dismiss guilt and shame. Our mothers' lies are living proof a secret and accompanying lie can validate a woman. And it's easier *not* to dig deep enough to acknowledge the need for the lie, to deny the dark side of lying. This applies to serious secrets that women preserve. As we have just witnessed with Madeleine, it isn't out of strength that she denies her part in the deceit, but out of necessity. She chooses not to acknowledge her part in her married lover's duplicity as she waits for it to be resolved somehow. That would require that major steps be taken by her lover in order for the two of them to be united.

Another woman who denies any part of the secrets she keeps is Kerry, who, at thirty-four, has managed to refute her lies since high school.

> I learned how to lie early, from my mom, and to act like you aren't into your own lie. My mom did it with my dad and she did it with her office and it worked. I do it when I go out for drinks with friends and order vodka, which doesn't smell. That way I can keep it from my boyfriend that I've been drinking, since my drinking really bothers him. I call in sick to work when I want a day off, and I don't see anything wrong with any of this. It's the only way to get what I want done. I'm not causing anyone any grief, really—if there was another way, I'd do it.

This slippery slope that Kerry describes, of denying the result of a lie, intensifies over time. Yet the fact that her mother did it gives an imprimatur to beneficial lying for Kerry. Nonetheless, when we deny the weight of our actions, we can't possibly benefit from the lies that spill forth, and minimizing those secrets only complicates matters.

PLAYING YOUR HAND

Lies choreograph life as we hoped it to be.

If our mothers felt cheated and the expectations placed upon them seemed impossible to fulfill, the truth was beside the point. If a woman's craftiness seems counterintuitive, it's that the lies provided a tool with which women could manage their lives. This way of thinking has definitely been passed down to us as daughters in a world where the pressure has increased for women to excel in every component of their lives. Guarding a secret can be an act of responsibility to oneself.

The National Scruples and Lies Survey 2004, conducted in the United Kingdom, revealed that women lie frequently. As reported by Edward Black in *The Scotsman,* nineteen out of twenty women lie to their partners or husbands and 83 percent confessed to "big, life-changing lies." This is seductive enough that for some women, the guilt, denial, and shame are discarded in favor of personal satisfaction. Apparently, for women, lying is not only about the *kinds* of lies but about the *success rate* of the lies. The beneficial lie is often dependent on how well one keeps a duality going.

If more than 80 percent of my interviewees reported that their mothers have been the impetus for their deceptions, 50 percent were offended when they were lied to by their children, husbands, boyfriends, coworkers, and friends. I was surprised to learn that the other 50 percent simply didn't care, viewing it as a reality of life or that they were too preoccupied with their own secrets. The message from a mother is often that it may be wiser to be cryptic than tell all, but beware the lie that takes over your life and keeps you from facing your actuality and finding clarification. What is intriguing is the balance between the lie and the truth, how we've been educated to contain our secrets and revise our lives.

As Ben Best notes in his essay "Some Philosophizing About Lying," each of us needs to have credibility in our lives to ensure trust. Yet this credibility "is also required if one is to be believed when lying." If Best's theory is put to use, women are ahead of the game in a society that assumes women are credible. Therefore women are capable of what he calls "the perfect lie." He defines this as one "that produces a benefit and which will never be discovered."

Men can't possibly compare in imagination and finesse to how women manage their covert behavior. As Carolee, thirty-two, whose mother is "the best liar of all," comments:

> My boyfriend couldn't wrap his mind around what I do during the day. He imagines I'm sitting at my desk for long hours, that I don't even take a lunch break. He thinks I put my paycheck in the bank and that I dream of what to cook for dinner. How I really live my life would blow him away. The one person who would never be surprised is my mom, she's been at this forever.

TWO

Sex, Love, and Buried Secrets

WHEN IT COMES TO ROMANCE, WOMEN LIE EASILY

In a culture where the notion of romantic love is subsuming and sex the ultimate declaration of such a commitment, women keep secrets. I remember reading Edith Wharton's *The House of Mirth* and marveling at Lily Bart's decision to hold out for romantic love in turn-of-the-century New York society, where women had little choice but to marry for money and status. Although Lily Bart secretly loves Lawrence Seldon, she can't possibly marry him since he isn't up to snuff socially. In the end, she loses out by not making her secret known to him and by never meeting a man who is socially suitable and for whom she has romantic feelings.

Is it so different today, one hundred years later, when we avidly read of the love lives of the rich and famous? Are we not titillated by love affairs gone awry—such as Britney Spears's demand for a divorce from Kevin Federline—and the reasons behind these breakups? Each week, *People* magazine and *US Weekly* inform us of new unions and failed relationships, encouraging our preoccupation with secret trysts and betrayals. This information, fed to us by the media, tells us that romantic experiences are worth lying for, if need be.

In the feature film *Sweet Home Alabama*, we learn that not only was Reese Witherspoon's character already married once, but she's not even divorced yet. Her secret is discovered as she's about to marry a sophisticated New Yorker who knows nothing of her past. How she managed to keep this from her fiancé is impressive, but once revealed it makes her life and her final decision unpredictable. In *Closer*, the 2004 film starring Julia Roberts and Natalie Portman, the women two-time their two-timing partners and manage to confess on a need-to-know basis. There's so much lying going on that when Natalie Portman tells the truth, she's punished for it. An uneasy marriage between Hope Davis's character and Campbell Scott's character in *The Secret Lives of Dentists* is all about trust. Scott suffers for his wife's secretiveness, convinced she's having an extramarital affair. The audience never knows the truth, but is intrigued with the possibilities of her secret.

Women explain their romantic secrets as a way of keeping their options open, and female guile is inevitably part of the package. "There is great importance placed on relationships for women," psychologist Claire Owen notes. "Women need to be in these relationships to feel successful, so they'll pick a male who they think will fulfill their needs. Sometimes they maneuver the situation when another man comes along, or as things progress."

This is familiar to Alexa, thirty-three, a recently married account executive living in the Northeast. Her shamelessness about her past manifests in a compassionate lie—she hides the truth in order to placate her husband.

When I met my husband and we were first dating, I had to rewrite my past. He couldn't stand that I'd been with other men, that I'd been so wild, and I thought he was crazy. But I decreased how many guys I'd been with, as if I was somehow becoming a virgin for him. After awhile, it seemed the right way to be. So now my past sex life is a secret. I even deny it, because I don't want this marriage to fail, I don't want to feel dirty . . . I lie for that feeling to go away. I want to be married . . . it works for me.

My marriage is not the great romance I thought it would be and my attitude is, what guy could have done that for me? I wanted to be married to him; I wanted to be his wife. The reason I keep secrets from him is because there's no advantage to wearing my heart on my sleeve. I act like the sex is amazing when I really wish it would last longer. I act like any dinner we go to is a thrill, any night out a big deal. . . . It is what it is. If my husband knew how many guys I'd really known, he'd be upset, he'd be jealous. Who needs it? I think men are interchangeable and the problem is you don't know it till you've been at it for a while. So I stay buttoned up and fantasize the rest.

Since a double standard for women remains embedded in our culture when it comes to one's sexual history, women minimize their true desires. Positioned to feign how they feel and what they want in long-standing or monogamous relationships with men, women seem to have little choice but to lie.

SECRET YEARNINGS

Our puritanical precepts have divided women into good and bad, sexless and sexual, the proverbial lady and the tramp. At the same time, the emphasis for all women to look young, beautiful, and sexy has increased in the past fifteen years. Now the typecasting of women is overshadowed by the pressure to be all this, and more. The assumption that wives and mothers are lustless creatures has existed for centuries, yet a recent demand that women be glamorous and alluring in these roles is now juxtaposed with this traditional view. No wonder it was so provocative to watch Diane Lane's character in the film *Unfaithful*. After all, she had a great life, married to a nice husband, played by Richard Gere, with one malleable young son and a pleasant home in suburbia. Did she even know her own inner longings existed when she began an affair with a stranger? Her secret was the affair, obviously, but a deeper secret was how much she hungered for her lover, something few women feel for their husbands.

In my book on female infidelity, *A Passion for More: Wives Reveal the Affairs That Make or Break Their Marriages*, I came across some jolting and provocative statistics. Of the women with whom I spoke for this study, 65 percent of the interviewees reported that sex was better with the lover than in the marriage, and 90 percent felt no guilt but a sense of entitlement in conducting the affair. Likewise, Shere Hite reports in her research for *Women and Love: A Cultural Revolution in Progress* that 60 percent of her interviewees felt an affair was "a way of enjoying myself . . . having one person appreciate you in a way that another doesn't." Hite also reports that 13 percent of the women in her study are "in love" with their husbands, while 82 percent love their husbands, which is defined as "caring and/or companionship." My research over the years concurs with Hite's results, since 65 percent of my interviewees have confided that once there are children in a marriage, the romance disappears, and 70 percent are dissatisfied with the sex.

These findings explain a need for lies when it comes to women and their sex lives, let alone romantic longings. While it is standard fare to complain about a husband up to a point, an affair is off-limits. Sure, women will confide in a sister, a best friend, someone who will cover her tracks; these secrets are worth protecting. Women go about their business as wives and mothers with a lover on the side. For those women willing to risk having a lover

(60 percent of married women conduct extramarital affairs, according to my research), lies of all sorts unfold. In *Little Children*, the 2006 feature film starring Kate Winslet and Patrick Wilson, Winslet's character's affair is successful because she works it around her duties as a suburban mother to a young girl. How can she and her lover be faulted for having sex in the laundry room while their children are together, napping upstairs?

Women excel at romantic and sexual deceit.

Yearning for someone else while in a monogamous relationship can be an arresting and possibly rewarding secret for some women. Nadia, forty-three, a teacher in South Carolina, is married with two children and has had a lover for thirteen years.

> What is the point of my husband knowing or not knowing? I think it would infuriate him that I have a boyfriend, so I keep it to myself. I'm good at this secret and I love having it. I don't want to give up the affair to be able to tell the truth. . . . I bend the truth. I keep parts of it to myself. . . . I don't consider myself a liar, I consider myself someone who doesn't deliberately hurt other people.
>
> My marriage works and my mothering is better because of my secret life. It isn't that I go around promoting affairs, but this is something that has enriched my life. I only feel badly when I see how open my husband is about every morsel of his life. He will call me from his walk to the gym, at the end of his workout, when he gets to the office, if he's going to be an hour late at night. So I'm very careful to tell him my whereabouts, as best I can. I don't say I'm going off with my lover—that I lie about. But it's better to be vague all week so on my days with my lover I don't feel I'm acting any other way.

Nadia's decision to keep her affair going is singular; she is willing to lie to her husband in order to have the affair and disinclined to give it up. Her ability to keep a secret is well-honed and contributes to her lack of remorse. It's her confidence in her decision that colors this compassionate lie. Yet unlike Nadia's beneficial lie, some women have an affair and are deathly afraid of being found out. Lollie, who at forty-three is in a second marriage and has four children from her first marriage, was petrified of getting caught while she was having an affair.

> Just because I cheated on my first husband toward the end doesn't mean it was easy. I did it because I was so happy to be with this man. I had kept my bad marriage to myself and didn't have the courage to do much about it before the affair. I kept this secret really well because I was so afraid of losing my children if my husband knew. He never found out. That's how good I was at it. I saw this man for three months, and he helped me, he was someone who cared and listened to me. I stopped because it was too hazardous, it was wrong for me to put myself in that position. But still it gave me the strength to leave, to go for a better life. I see this affair as a kind of stepping-stone, I lied to do it and I ended up better off.

While the betterment lie Lollie told ended up being the catalyst to enhance her life, Jossie, thirty-four, describes her secret affair as a "sexual encounter" that made her feel ashamed. Living in Washington state, where she is the editor of a magazine, Jossie met a very young man through work.

> I'm still wondering why this happened, I suppose it's because I was feeling lonely and I met someone who made me feel good about myself. He's of legal age but very young. What made it so wrong is that he's the nephew of my employer.

Unfortunately, it had to do with lots of lying, and I'm not a good liar. I had to retrace my steps and make sure that no one ever knew. I was always in fear that he'd say something. He's promised not to, but he's so erratic. . . . I ended up quitting my job over this relationship . . . his aunt is my boss. We were involved sexually, and he said he was in love with me. I had to be so careful; I had to make up a reason why I was leaving my job because I couldn't go there anymore once this had happened. . . .

I'm sorry that I ever had him in my house, that we ever had sex. Once it was over, I had to change my e-mail address and my home phone number. He so guilted me—he attempted suicide after I broke it off and then called me. I felt trapped at that point, and whatever had been exciting about a secret relationship was finished. I had so many second thoughts about our age difference, about the attraction we shared. I feel so troubled by all that happened, I still worry about him, I care but I can't be in touch. This is a secret I'll take to the grave.

Old love is haunting and demands secrecy.

Another way in which women lie about their love lives involves old boyfriends and ex-husbands and the finality of those relationships. As Angie, thirty, a freelance journalist, explains her behavior, the new boyfriend is not working out as well as she had expected.

I always keep in touch with my old boyfriends. I call them if I need them and sometimes take up with them again. I lie to the new boyfriend and the old boyfriend when this happens. But I keep it going, it's worth doing.

Ruth, forty-four, from the Midwest, has been advised by her closest girlfriends to utilize a designated lie when she meets potential mates.

I can't get over my husband, who just asked for a divorce, but I want a boyfriend. I really miss my husband but I know it's not going to work out. So when I meet men and they say it's too soon to date you, you're in the beginning of a divorce, I lie, I keep my feelings about my husband to myself. I say that I want to be divorced and am open to a new love. Really I'm just trying to get through, but my heart belongs to my husband, who packed up one day and was out of here. How else do I stand a chance? Not by saying how I really feel.

A lie about sex and love often manifests as a shortcut in long-standing relationships (I have a headache; Sure, I still love you), but are also about past disappointments combined with bargaining power. Jane, a thirty-two-year-old businesswoman, finds her days as wife, mother, and working woman to be stressful and exhausting. Her predicament resonates with many women across America. Jane's lie, like Angela's, is compassionate in nature.

How can I tell my husband the truth, that after a day of work and coming home to two toddlers, sex with him is the last thing on my mind at ten P.M.? I can't even remember when I was into him or if I was ever into him. I don't see the point of explaining it, but I feel strongly. I'm exhausted. I'm tapped out—I don't want to hurt his ego but I also don't want to sleep with him.

When it comes to sex and love, we see that lies can be purposeful for women. But there are pitfalls to the process as well, and some women have found themselves in over their heads.

The Pretender

Carmen, twenty-four, has always been a slippery one when it comes to monogamy. She wants the relationship with her present boyfriend, but the boundaries are blurred. To preserve the relationships, she hides her true feelings about her own sexuality. Not only is this less demanding, but it serves her well.

> I lie to my boyfriend because there would be too many problems if I told the truth. I lie about where I go, what I do, who I go with. He asks if I flirt with guys when I'm out with my girlfriends. I lie about my ex-boyfriend and what went on, how I miss him. I don't know who said a lie wouldn't help; it's the only way to get through.

According to Susan S. Hendrick, in her book *Understanding Close Relationships,* we place great value on positive illusions with our romantic partners. If these illusions fade and reality kicks in, there's less satisfaction between partners. When a woman defends her lie to her boyfriend or husband, she doesn't see it as detrimental to the relationship; instead, we see it as a way to keep it going. The lie to a romantic partner almost seems inevitable, how else can the mystery be sustained?

The Cheating Heart

In our society, female infidelity remains fascinating. As I mentioned, in the film *Unfaithful,* Diane Lane is a woman whose lie is born of an extramarital affair. Who knows how long Lane's character would guard her secret and lie to her husband about her whereabouts had she not been found out?

How curious that two former lovers of famous women would document their love affairs. According to a former boyfriend of the late Carolyn Bessette Kennedy, she had a secret. In his memoir, *The Other Man: John F. Kennedy, Jr., Carolyn Bessette, and Me,* Michael Bergin recounts how his love affair with Carolyn Bessette, whom he had dated in 1992, lasted beyond her marriage vows, taken in 1996. A memoir written by Captain James Hewitt, *Moving On,* addresses the late Princess Diana's affair with Hewitt and his role in her life during a difficult period.

For celebrities and women everywhere, an affair stirs a forceful lie, one for which women take the leap willingly, as we see in Kathleen's case. Several years ago, when Kathleen was in her late thirties, she found herself attached to a married man who was a close friend and business associate of her husband's.

> I spent all my time with him, every single Saturday while my husband was at his office. Barry had four young kids and a wife who thought he was at work. He was ten years younger and that made it even more fun. I held off on going to bed together. Even though I was willing to spend time with him, which could easily have been discovered, I thought if we had sex the guilt would kick in and we'd somehow be found out for sure. It was a very well kept secret and I lied to be with him. My husband was so married to his business that he never noticed, and for a time it was exciting to have this kind of secret going. I'm certainly not sorry because Barry made my days happier.

Although Kathleen remained married and her husband never found out, trust is the issue once infidelity has affected a marriage or monogamous relationship. So while her affair was the result of feeling neglected by her husband, who she describes as "married to his business," she knew the stakes were high.

> I never wanted my husband to know because he'd never have understood, and wouldn't have trusted me again. I was so careful since this was supposed to be the basis of our marriage.

Sociologist Jessie Bernard reports that marriage is significantly more beneficial and satisfactory to men than it is to women. However, many wives remain in less than happy marriages. Once an extramarital affair is brought into the mix, rather than feel guilt, a woman feels righteous. Kathleen's betterment lie was helpful during the time of the affair and in the aftermath when she decided to keep it a secret.

The Loveless Match

We see women settle into what appears to be happy relationships and marriages, and assume they're set. Yet women say they are missing an emotional connection, as Alexa indicates in her interview. These women describe the laundry list for happiness, without the real thing. For women who remain in these unions, it's a lie lived daily, a pact made for the sake of children, financial stability, and status. Clara, fifty-four and working full-time for a corporation, has grown children and is unhappily married, but she's committed to staying. Her secret is a compassionate lie, she leads her husband to believe she cares.

> I'm not leaving my husband under any circumstances. He's my second husband and we have two children together. They're in college now and I could surely leave. But starting up

with someone new makes me sick and I've found other av-
enues for escape. I travel with girlfriends, and I've learned how
to tolerate him. He even falls for it. I suppose this is the best I
can do at my age. When it comes to romance I pretend that it
still matters with him, if it ever did.

Our romantic lives evoke great secrets.

On April 18, 2006, *The Oprah Winfrey Show* focused on
women living a lie. One of the guests, Holly, spoke of how she felt
distant from her husband despite the fact that, to the outside
world, she had the perfect marriage, with children, a successful
husband, and a beautiful home. She felt her unhappiness was
something she had to keep to herself, that few would understand
her feelings or the basis for not being satisfied. Not being close to
your spouse but having the accoutrements of a happy marriage
can be stressful, and provoke guilt and ingratitude. Based on the
women with whom I've spoken who are in this position, it's a
weighty secret. They describe themselves as being in an out-of-
body experience.

In these situations, it isn't that a woman is doing something
that is blatant; rather, there is a subtextual aspect to her lie. By not
communicating her real feelings toward her husband/boyfriend
about the relationship, she is avoiding the truth. A woman goes
through the motions without meaning it, her secret is her lack of
love for her partner and she holds on to the relationship for the il-
lusion it creates and the perks of that particular life.

Within these three patterns there can be crossovers: a woman
will cover up an affair, which places her in the "cheating heart" slot,
and at the same time will purport happiness in her long-standing
relationship or marriage, placing her in the "pretender" category as
well. When it comes to the loveless match, it's familiar territory.

The Awakening, a novel by Kate Chopin, shows the dangers of *not lying* when it comes to love and desire. When Edna Pontellier, a young wife and mother in late-nineteenth-century New Orleans, sates her passionless marriage with her lover, she chooses to break free of the convention-bound life she leads.

Yet both her husband and her lover would rather she keep her struggle for a moral center a secret and sustain the image of an ideal wife to a wealthy man. Has a new century in the life of a wife and mother rendered us more attune with what works—hypocrisy rather than the raw reality? If the emotional state of a woman's life today resonates with Chopin's heroine of the turn of the century, her ability to lie has been more carefully honed. The decades since have rendered us intelligent enough to use the lie, believing the truth can be overrated. Celine, thirty-four, explains it:

> I haven't the guts to leave my husband or break up our family over how I feel. But I don't love him and I don't know if I ever did. I look at my children and at my husband and I just keep going. So every day is a lie, a lie I tell the world. It works, it's the only solution I've got.

LIES ABOUT SEX

As we witnessed at the start of this chapter, women lie about their sexual encounters and number of partners. It's surprising that so many years after the sexual revolution, this is actually still the case, and that the perception of women-as-pure is at a premium.

Taking it beyond Alexa's confession at the start of this chapter, where she shortened the list of sexual partners she had before she married, is Jessica's dire need to rewrite her sexual history. Jessica, twenty-two, from Arkansas, is the mother of an infant and works

part-time in retail. She describes her "really big secret" as having
been a prostitute when she was younger, as a means to survive.

> At first I was afraid and then I got used to it. My husband
> doesn't know. He's eight years older and he's been around.
> I've never told anyone, it makes me feel really dirty. It was pro-
> tected sex but still I was worried about getting sick. Men were
> kissing me and leaving wet marks, slobbering all over me. I
> made enough money from this to get through and I know this,
> but it's a big secret and it gives me nightmares if I think about
> it. I push it down so I don't have to think about it or remember
> it. Now I have a husband and baby and I'm never mentioning
> my past to anyone. I don't want to explain this to people, and I
> don't want it to have anything to do with my life today.

Listening to Jessica's story, I thought of the glamorized version
of female prostitution that was offered to us in the hit film *Pretty
Woman*. Although Richard Gere's character hires Julia Roberts's
character as a prostitute, this fact is quickly glossed over into a
rags-to-riches Cinderella story. There is one line in the film,
though, that makes it all too clear that prostitution might be a living, but it's not romantic in any shape or form. When Julia
Roberts's character tells Gere's character that he can do anything,
as long as he doesn't kiss her, we all get it—the kiss is too real, too
intimate, and too sacred.

The harrowing experience that Jessica shares with us can be
contrasted with Rebecca's story. At thirty-four, she lives in a small
town in Texas and has never known a man sexually.

> I never had sex, and I pretend that I have. When I was a
> teenager, I would have been the perfect person for casual sex
> and I never got to do it. There was a boy in high school and I
> liked him, but I was so afraid to talk to him. I had a crush on

him for years. I'd believed that one day I'd marry him, but in reality we never even dated. He was the one I would have had sex with. I saw my friends have broken hearts and then I saw them become very loose about it. I somehow lost the chance to date or get to know any man intimately. I don't tell people because in this day and age it's really strange that I missed the boat. It would be embarrassing for anyone to know. Recently I met a man who is similar to me and this has been the only kind of connection I've ever really had, but we've not had sex either. No one can know any of this . . . it would make me too strange.

In these extreme cases, we see two women who at an early age were affected greatly by what happened or didn't happen to them sexually. Both Jessica and Rebecca are ashamed of how their experiences played out and have kept their pasts a secret. And so they are trapped in denial and deceit, where the lies protect them but also keep them from seeking counseling that would help them deal with their previous encounters. A study in the *Journal of Sex Research* reports that for women, sexual behavior is related to societal expectations. This being the case, women might lie about their sexual history when they are surveyed. When we reflect upon this, it's understandable why a woman's sexual experiences can become a secret.

The "Good Girl" Isn't Supposed to Be Sexy

On a lighter note, women are known to lie about orgasms and how enjoyable sex is with their partners. The famous fake orgasm of Meg Ryan in *When Harry Met Sally* underscores how well women pretend. When Nicole Kidman's character in *Eyes Wide Shut* tells her husband, played by her real-life husband (at the time), Tom Cruise, about her intensely sexual feelings toward a sailor, it sets

Cruise off on a sexual escapade all his own. Maybe Kidman's character is playing with her husband, but it has quite an effect on him. This female power, to titillate and seduce through sexual acts and tales, is not encouraged in our society, it isn't "good girl" behavior. Yet for Wanda, thirty-nine, who kept her "really sexual" affair a secret for three years, it was all about the sex.

> I lied to my husband in order to have sex with this guy, to spend time with another man. And I doubt my husband would have ever picked up on it. I was just there to have sex. The sex was so sexy when I was with him. I wasn't worrying whether my son would get home in one piece, by curfew, like I do with my husband. It really made it better. I was in charge. I doubt I'd ever felt this way with my husband, or I've been faking it with him for so long, I don't remember.

When we hear women tell such acceptable lies, we realize our culture's fascination with sex. Proof of this is the hoopla over the sex tape of Pamela Anderson with her husband Tommy Lee in 1998 and the sex tape of Paris Hilton in 2004 that propelled her to fame. According to Lola Ogunnaike in an article she wrote for *The New York Times* on March 19, 2006, "Sex, Lawsuits and Celebrities Caught on Tape," "Sex tapes today seem to juice up careers" and is no longer a destructive force. Ogunnaike reports that both Paris Hilton and Pamela Anderson tried to stop the distribution of their tapes, but the article states that Paris Hilton reportedly receives profits from hers and actually dropped a lawsuit against an Internet company that distributed clips of the tape.

However these two female celebrities felt about their tapes being watched by untold numbers of people, it's a reflection of women viewed as sex objects that their popularity ascended after the tapes were distributed. This, in itself, gives us insight into why women lie about their sex lives and experiences.

LIES ABOUT LOVE

The epic film *Legends of the Fall,* starring Julia Ormond and Brad Pitt, tells of a woman who is romantically involved with three brothers, one at a time. Set in the early 1900s, Susannah (Julia Ormond) is engaged to Samuel, who dies fighting in World War I. When this innocent love ends, Susannah consummates an affair with Tristan (Brad Pitt), whom she does not marry. The ghost of Samuel contaminates their love and Tristan abandons Susannah to travel the globe in order to escape his guilt. Several years after Tristan is gone, Susannah succumbs to marrying the third brother, Alfred (Aidan Quinn), whom she never loved. However, a promise she made to Tristan, that she would "wait forever" for him, becomes a lie when he finally returns and discovers her living a luxurious life with his surviving brother. "Forever was just too long," Susannah tells Tristan before taking her own life. This tragic tale reminds us of the depths of romantic love and the promises we make and cannot keep.

Bianca, forty-four, lives in Montana with her two daughters and teaches grade school. She lied about a man she loved in order to secure the relationship.

I met a man on the Internet after my divorce a few years ago. He told me from the start that he was married but that seeing someone on the side was acceptable to his wife. So I agreed to it. He said that if his wife got better, he'd leave her. But she was sick and she controlled the money and it never happened. I didn't tell anyone that he was married—I was so in love with him. He was the first guy out of my divorce and I miss him to this day. I doubt I'll ever find anyone like him again, but keeping his marriage a secret was wrong. I wanted my girls to think he was a good person, and we come from such a religious background. Unless I lied about his wife, no one would have welcomed him into our family, they would have thought I was crazy. I saw this as a necessary lie and, in the end, I got tired of waiting and lying about it. No matter how much I loved him.

If Bianca gave up a man she loved because he was married, Hanna, thirty-five, living in Maine and working as a nurse's aide, purposely chose a man who was married. As in Bianca's case, the secret was burdensome.

It was a real love relationship, and at first it was on my terms. He couldn't demand anything because he was married. In a way, it wasn't my secret but his secret that became my secret. It was sort of a relief that it was his lie, but then I lied to people about where I was and what I was doing. After a year, I didn't like the way it made me feel, I didn't like having sex with a married man. One day he came over and I said, either you tell your wife it's over or you go home and fix it. And that was the end since he didn't want anything but the lie. I was so tired of being secretive; I wanted the weight lifted from my shoulders.

Both Hanna and Bianca were hoping their lovers would come clean, and they could rid themselves of their designated lies. In these situations, the feelings were in place, but the circumstances were not. In contrast, there are the poignant stories of women who love one man and marry another, keeping the old love a secret for much of their adult lives. Essentially these women are going through the motions of marriage and family while secretly pining for someone else. Oftentimes the search for the old love is triggered by a life event, such as illness, the loss of a parent, a financial loss, or even a big birthday, such as thirty-five, forty, fifty.

Perhaps it occurs at a high school or college reunion or by surfing the Internet, but once a woman rediscovers her old love, she's more than willing to keep it a secret, if required. Donna Hanover's book, *My Boyfriend's Back,* explores how couples have been reunited after years apart, having led separate lives. She also details her reunion and remarriage to her boyfriend from the days before she met and married Rudy Giuliani, former mayor of New York City. While these stories have happy endings, with triumphant second chances, for many women in this position, reconnecting to a long-lost love creates a reason to lie.

Women are willing to lie for a second chance at love.

Although Gayl, thirty-seven, has four children and a comfortable life with her husband, she has missed her high school boyfriend for the past twenty years.

We were from a small town in the Midwest where there was a race to get away. I got out pretty quickly and I married young, someone who was the opposite of my old boyfriend. I heard he was married, too, my sister told me, and that he had a few children. I pretended it didn't matter, since there was nothing I could do. Then I ran into him when he came home for his niece's confirmation and I knew, I just knew that I'd missed him all these years. So now we see each other and we'll end up leaving our spouses as soon as we can, as soon as the kids are a bit older. I remember my mom asked me when I got engaged to my husband if I didn't want to just talk to my old boyfriend. I lied and said no, I said I loved my husband. But I loved my old boyfriend. That's who I loved and still love. I'm lying to sneak out with him.

Affairs of the heart trigger multilayered lies. First there's the lie that you are over your ex (a betterment lie), then the lie to your present partner that you love him enough to make a commitment (a compassionate lie). Next there is the lie that evolves once you are reconnected to the old love. This manifests as the lie for the sake of the affair (a beneficial lie), which now feels, according to my interviewees, spellbinding and justified.

A SHORTAGE OF CHANCES

The importance placed on romance for women only ratchets up the fabrication and deception that comes with the deal. Since women are deeply invested in the results of their sexual and love lives, the lies follow. *The Wall Street Journal* featured a piece on Internet dating on April 1, 2006, by Ellen Gamerman, entitled "Mismatched.com." Gamerman reports that almost two million marriages are the result of Internet match-ups, but the subsequent divorces are now kicking in. Gamerman points out that "some divorce cases . . . highlight false claims made in the online profiles that led to the initial attraction" as well as "the natural perils" of meeting someone "virtually." One example of misrepresentation is a divorce case in which the woman is alleged to have used her younger sister's photo on the Web site. Do the women who have "misrepresented" themselves do it out of desperation, since the competition is steep and the goal a worthy one?

For Kristina, thirty-four, the idea of emphasizing herself as a successful businesswoman to her new boyfriend was very meaningful.

I said I was entrepreneurial when I met my husband on the Internet. I knew from his ad that he wanted to be with someone like that; it was at the top of his list. So I said I was like that, but I wasn't, and I hadn't worked in years. When I met him, I told him I was in media relations now, but had worked in the corporate world in the past. I wouldn't have said so much, but I thought he was so cute and he was the kind of guy I was looking for. I'd had some horrible experiences with guys and I wanted to be with him. I even begged my girlfriend to let me work for her small business on a freelance basis so I could appear to be in the business world. He told everyone he introduced me to that I had this job and I pretended it was a big job. I would describe what she did as if I did it.

After we got married, I suggested taking time off to fix up our home, and get us set, and he seemed surprised. I never went back to work, and after a year it really bothered him. His ex-wife hadn't worked and he hated it. Finally my cover was blown and I was discovered when a friend of mine told him. I wasn't sorry so much that I did it but that I got caught. I explained that I lied because I liked him and he wanted this in his girlfriend or wife. But it really ruined the trust between us. I doubt we'll make it; things are bad right now over my lie to him.

Keep the secret, risk the lie.

What is interesting about Kristina's experience is that she's not lying about her feelings for her husband, as some women do—in order to get the life or to fix things, or to keep an extramarital affair going—she's using an acceptable lie to impress him. And she's impressing him with her beefed-up career, which is a current lie, whereas fifty years ago a woman might have fooled a man with a home-cooked meal that her mother or sister had concocted. That, too, was a misrepresentation of a woman's abilities—as a homemaker. As Wendy, sixty-six, recalls:

My mother made the first six meals when I was married, and I passed it off as my own cooking. But I didn't want him to find out so I took a crash course in the basics and I realized it was no big deal. I do know that if I had told my husband the truth, he'd have been annoyed. He wanted a wife who could cook, and although today it's laughable, this was forty-three years ago.

Another recent cultural phenomenon is when a woman of a certain age seduces a man by feigning her availability, when in fact she appreciates her singlehood. Like Kristina's reason to lie to *get* the guy, these women in midlife are lying to *keep* the guy without really committing. The story that ran in *Newsweek* on February 20, 2006, "Sex & Love: The New World," featured a naked women who appeared to be forty-something standing behind a pair of bifocals. Since it's a woman who showcases the article, it's worth noting that only 14 percent of older single women are hoping to get married or live with a man, while 22 percent of men in this position are looking for marriage or a long-standing relationship. With this discrepancy between the women's and men's hopes when it comes to love and sex, we can only imagine how many women are lying about something—their intentions to be monogamous, marriageable, or available when many women of this age report that marriage is no longer the ultimate goal, nor is an exclusive relationship.

Lying to her husband during her marriage about sex was nothing compared to lying to her boyfriend about romance after she was widowed, according to Lynne, a forty-six-year-old technician who lives in the Midwest.

I'd been married for fifteen years when my husband died. I had always told him how great it was to be with him and we were very connected, emotionally and sexually. Not that it was still so fabulous, but I always told him it was. Then I met a man through friends, a younger man, he became my boyfriend. But he's very possessive and I find it exhausting. I'll make up excuses when I can't see him. If I say it's my girls' night out or a dinner with one of my kids, he goes crazy. I guess I lie to him about my schedule because it's easier than explaining my plans. I lie about how great it is to be with him since he seems to be thrilled to see me every time we're together. I boast to my friends because he's young and hot. I am glad we're together but it isn't the love affair he thinks it is.

Unlike Lynne, who flaunts her young boyfriend and her secret is that she's not smitten with him, Lillie, forty-four, is married to a thirty-five-year-old man to whom she feels committed. Both women have used compassionate lies along the way.

Not only am I older, but I'm the major breadwinner. I run a company while Keith is a writer. But we've worked it all out and I look back on how long I lied to my parents and friends about him, as if it was shameful to be with a younger man, having three kids with a young guy. We love each other and that's what matters. We're really well suited, even in how we are raising the kids. But mostly it's a love relationship and I try hard to keep it alive. Ten years ago our age gap was much more obvious, but as we've both aged, it's lessened.

There's been progress, without a doubt, for women sating their needs when it comes to their love lives. For women who secretly hope for younger men, Madonna's or Demi Moore's choice of younger partners is a stamp of approval. Madonna is married to Guy Ritchie, a film director ten years her junior, and Demi Moore, in a bold move, married Ashton Kutcher, sixteen years younger than she, in the fall of 2005. According to Celebrity

Couples Online, Courteney Cox is seven years older than her husband, David Arquette. Undoubtedly these liaisons have encouraged women with a penchant for younger men to go public with
the relationships.

Whether it's about midlife sex or midlife romance, cradle rob-
bing, false love, or secret trysts, women conjure lies and secrets.
In her book *Women's Sexuality Across the Life Span,* Judith
Daniluk notes that the cultural myths, combined with biological
and psychological influences, cause women to separate themselves from their own needs. Based on my research, it's clear that
secrets about our sexual selves and our romantic longings are a
dicey business. Some women position themselves perilously, others profit from the lie, downing hatchets on relationships while in
search of a better offer, feeling sanctioned in a double life with
the perks of two men. The media and pop culture reinforce this
duplicity; a heady new attitude emerges when it comes to female
lies for love—go for broke and enjoy the rewards.

THREE

Cashing In: Money and Lies

It would be almost impossible to write this book and not take a look at how money affects a woman's truths and lies. We've been taught since we were young girls that money is a motivating factor in many of our decisions, the implicit message is that money is worth lying for. In fact, when lies of another sort might not be excused, a lie for hard green cash will stand out as a benefit all its own. What we do for money isn't always predictable, depending on where our lives take us, but it's often understandable. Consider Kara, twenty-six, who is a former bartender from the Northeast.

> I joined the army for financial reasons. I told everyone I did it for the opportunity, the education. I wouldn't come out and say it's for the money, but it is. Those perks mean a lot; I just don't want people to think it's all about money for me. I've always acted like I do what I like, but I've always needed money. I pretend I don't care about it, but I do. There were choices. I could have looked for a rich husband, but it seemed out of my league. I didn't know how to meet that guy. I couldn't be a model or actress and I needed to get away—I wanted to make something of myself. For that, you need money. So I lied about my plans and I looked very patriotic to people.

When Kara saw other soldiers doing well financially, she felt encouraged, but remained inclined to lie about her intentions.

> There's definitely money to be made here, compared to how I grew up. But I'm not ready to explain that to people. I want to look better than that. In the end I won't be rich but I'll be in a better place. It's not something you shout about, but you can use the army to get there.

What happens when it comes to our financial status can't be predicted, positively or negatively. For Dawn, forty-nine, a social worker from the South, her financial situation was shattered by her husband's unexpected death.

> I was widowed eight years ago and my son never knew about the money his father had left him—I never told him. I was the trustee and I used his money to move us cross-country and start a new life. I promised myself I'd replace it once we were settled. But in seven years I haven't because life is so expensive. I doubt I'll ever tell my son what I did. For years I've alternated between talking myself into thinking what I did is okay and feeling like I could have done better. Raising a child as a single mother isn't easy and I wanted him to have all that we could afford. The problem is that there's no money for college and I'll end up lying about that, too. So I know that one lie causes another. I have two jobs right now and it's still a struggle. . . . I feel there's no choice, really. . . .

Women Lie About Money: Money Is Power

Gina, at thirty-six, is a stay-at-home mom in the Midwest who does community volunteer work. She believes that a moneyed life is the only life, but her husband cannot actually support her preferred lifestyle.

> I always acted as if we were wealthy, my husband and I. We sent our girls to private school, and we indulged ourselves completely all the time. I was taking lots of money from my mother and my husband was taking a little from his father. Although we did it together, I was the one urging my husband to live this way; I was the one who wanted to let everyone in town think we were rich. I'd grown up in this place and our father was known. I felt like we were being judged so I had to live as we live, had to act like I act.
>
> Really, I was carrying the family and the world thought that my husband was successful. It wasn't just a secret, it was a big lie. I don't know what makes me sicker, springing for the truth or keeping up the lie.

Our society emphasizes our financial status, it's part of our self-definition, and those who have it have clout. In fact, 75 percent of the women with whom I've spoken for this book say that financial lies comprise a large part of their secrets, as varied as those moneyed secrets may be. From hiding money to boasting of a lifestyle that isn't affordable to stealing money, women are remarkably hooked into greed and the secrets this sets forth. If, historically, financial lies have been a man's arena, we only have to look at the recent Enron trial to know that women are capable of financial deceit as well. Lea Fastow, the wife of former Enron CFO Andrew Fastow, served a year in prison for falsifying a tax return that neglected to show her husband's illegal income. As reported in USA Today, on July 12, 2004, although Lea Fastow "eventually admitted" to submitting this tax return, her actions revolved around protecting her husband and children.

Young girls are keenly aware of the potency of money, as exhibited in Isabel Rose's novel *The J.A.P. Chronicles*. The story follows seven women, now in their thirties, who years before were bunkmates at an elite summer camp. In their adult lives these women are motivated, to different degrees, to lie for a material life. Similarly, money motivates the three wives of a polygamous Mormon in HBO's television series *Big Love*. Chloë Sevigny's character, Nicki, the second of Bill Paxton's three wives, has racked up a credit card debt to the tune of $60,000. What is implied is that her wealthy mafia-style polygamist father spoiled Nicki. What is also evident is how Nicki's secret shopping addiction is a means to soothe the frustrations in her life, from the competition with the first and third wives to the trials of raising young children. Without a doubt, women tell falsehoods when it comes to their finances.

For example, Carol Ann, fifty, had worked at several jobs over the course of her adult life, always with the intention of being financially secure.

> My husband left me when my youngest child was three. I opened up a woman's dress shop with the help of a friend. That helped, but then a mall was built and no one came to this part of town anymore. I became a store manager at a super store and got us the insurance I needed. When I met my second husband, who had lots of money, I quit. I actually took money from him, in sneaky ways, so that I'd never be poor again. I could have asked outright, but it was better to siphon it, it was my secret. I've become so good at it over the years, I can take large amounts or grocery money, and I do both. I'd rather lie to get it than go through the asking and depending—letting him in.

It's apparent that Carol Ann needed money to survive, but her overall distrust is what makes her more comfortable with her clandestine thieving; she'd prefer that to leveling with her husband about her fears. How can women help but feel this way in a culture where we're keenly aware of money as freedom, if not joy, to counter our problems? Carol Ann's survival lie about money suits her better than baring her soul and presents as a form of self-preservation.

> Recently I convinced my husband to buy a small cottage in a summer resort. I also convinced him that it should be in my name. I was half honest about that, saying if he ever got into trouble, it would be better to have this place out of a creditor's reach. What I wanted in orchestrating this was ownership that was all mine. I don't trust anyone when it comes to money and possessions that translate into money. How can I trust anyone when I can't trust myself?

POSSESSED BY POSSESSIONS

Women fabricate their wardrobes, lifestyles, salaries.

Women are schooled by the media in how to purchase inexpensive new wardrobes that mimic the couture trends, as well as couture itself. Yet the danger of female consumerism is a cautionary tale. So, while "The Art of Spontaneous Shopping" by Rebecca Miller in *Harper's Bazaar* (April 2005), describes how "the thrill of a sudden unplanned purchase can really lift our spirits," Vanessa Geneva Ahern's piece in *Shape*, "Save Yourself from Holiday Debt," recognizes the dangers of overspending. Likewise, Glinda Bridgforth warns against overspending in her piece "When Shopping Is a Sickness" in *Essence* (August 2004). Book titles also address the downside of female consumerism. *I Shop, Therefore I Am: Compulsive Buying & the Search for Self* by April Lane

Benson, *Addicted to Shopping* by Karen O'Connor, and *Overcoming Overspending* by Olivia Mellan each offer ways to work through this issue. Yet based on my research, the problem of being possessed by our possessions remains high on the list of dysfunctions for women.

Whether they make their own money and are single, are primary breadwinners in a marriage, or contributors to their husbands' earnings, women are ambivalent about money, spending, and what kind of financial support they want from their partners. It's common for women to lie about what they spend and what kind of lifestyle they're after, especially if it isn't their reality. Some women admit financial concerns, while others say they only married for financial security. In either of these cases, women don't disclose their motivations to their husbands or partners, rather it's a quiet lie, buried in day-to-day life. When it comes to money, it's often a direct reaction to how much a woman feels she is missing. As Gigi, thirty-six, explains it, her rebellion in her marriage is tied into their finances.

> Some of my friends talk about their husbands withholding money or being controlling about it. But how can I worry about my husband's lies when I lie to him every day about money? His lies don't matter, they're so transparent—about work or why he didn't pick up the kids. For me, I know the exact ways he won't notice that money is being spent and I take advantage. I don't think he'll ever figure it out. If he does, I'll make some excuse, meanwhile I get to use the money and shop.

There are ways women maneuver to get money, using whatever leverage they have. Gigi's designated lie and style make her feel in charge. Conversely, there are women who make their own money and find they lie about this, protecting their earnings. According to my research, women who make an impressive salary and can support themselves still adhere to the traditional view of men supporting women. For Kim, forty-one, being the major breadwinner has been a problem, to the point where she no longer tells her husband about her raises.

> I've always earned more money than my friends, my husband, anyone in our family. I never thought it would bother my husband, but it does. I have learned not to tell him my good news about work or compensation—that's my new MO. I now have a personal bank account and I keep putting money into it, keeping things separate. Somehow I want to lie about how much I earn so I can make it all mine. This lie is worth it, I work hard for my money and I don't see my husband putting in my long hours.

It's little wonder that Kim keeps her salary a secret from her own husband, since husbands can feel threatened by successful wives. To make matters worse, women often feel they aren't respected by male colleagues. "Why not lie" is often the mantra of the achieving woman who confronts sexism and a husband whose confidence is eroded by her success.

These women are in the minority, as in 67 percent of marriages in America today, the husband is the primary breadwinner, according to the U.S. Department of Labor. In these cases, a woman might spend money as a form of rebellion. She has her children to feed, clothe, and educate and a husband who controls the purse strings through earning power. If she is in charge of household finances, an arena relegated to 75 percent of women, according to *American Demographics,* it seems natural to be secretive with the money. Women, feisty creatures when it comes to cold hard cash, whether they are poor, middle class, or wealthy, tell me that they cannot resist the urge to be in charge.

As therapist Brenda Szulman, who treats women with money issues, remarks, "Women believe they don't deserve to be told what to do with money, to have to watch what they spend. They're angry that they make less money than men; it makes them feel they are less. So they spend to get back and it becomes a self-soothing behavior."

Getting away with money secrets is mesmerizing.

Adele, thirty-seven, has just moved to the Midwest with her two small children. Recently she gave up her position at a corporation. She finds that her shopping sprees and acceptable lies about these sprees have increased lately.

> Every time I have a fight with my husband, I go shopping. This has gotten much worse since we moved here. I think because I'm not at work, and in a new place, I'm isolated. We moved here for my husband's job and he's always at that job. I'm stuck in a new part of the country with no friends or family nearby. I gave up my job to do this. I admit I was always a shopper, and I always tried to keep it quiet. The first day the kids left for school, I drove myself to the mall and bought boots. Before I even went food shopping. I wouldn't share this with my husband or my sisters, but I sure felt like doing it.

As Dr. Ronnie Burak, a psychologist whose practice concentrates on women, comments, "Money is a big conflict area for couples and plays out in many forms. A woman who is protecting her children by protecting the family money needs to guard her secret and defend her decision." A woman who, at thirty-five, has hidden money because her husband is unreliable with funds, gets over her guilt fairly soon. In a scenario like this, a survival lie kicks into place and the greater good theory (I do this to protect my children) overrides any other feelings.

The steps women take to hide money, make it, and preserve it, are exceptional. J. Randy Taraborrelli reports in his book, *Jackie Ethel Joan: Women of Camelot*, that Jackie Kennedy made a deal with her formidable father-in-law, Joseph Kennedy, to stay married to Jack if, in return, Joseph would set up trusts for both Caroline and John and any other children she might have.

Two extraordinarily wealthy women who were constantly in the news in their day and who were blemished by their fortunes were Doris Duke and Barbara Hutton. Doris Duke, an American heiress born in 1912, managed not only to hold on to her massive inheritance but to somehow make a scandal disappear. Duke kept her secret—that she "accidentally" gunned her car and ran over her interior decorator, Eduardo Tirella, outside the gates of her Newport mansion—from 1966 until her death in 1993.

A less fortunate heiress was Barbara Hutton, whose emotional issues, anorexia, and addictions were carefully guarded by those closest to her, according to C. David Heymann, in his book *Poor Little Rich Girl: The Life and Legend of Barbara Hutton*. Apparently, the public knew little about Hutton's serious problems (stemming from the stress of her great wealth and unhappy childhood), but was aware that she had seven husbands. Cary Grant was among them (despite the fact that he cared nothing about her inheritance, the couple was dubbed "Cash and Cary"). The travesty of her life is that Hutton died with $3,000 to her name, having squandered more than fifty million dollars during the course of her life.

Another manifestation of money and secrets surrounded Mary Todd Lincoln, who struggled with her spending habits her entire life. When she lobbied Congress for $20,000, a hefty sum in her day, to redecorate the White House during the Civil War, she was criticized for such a frivolous plan. To make matters worse, she was $7,000 over budget. Lincoln offered to pay out of his own pocket rather than reveal his wife's misjudgment, and while he tried to protect his wife from gossip and judgment, the extent of her extravagances weren't even known to him. It was only after Lincoln's assassination that the depths of Mary Todd's debts were discovered.

Surely money is absorbing for women in the twenty-first century, the focus begins early and can last a lifetime. Based on my research, lying over money is a popular female lie, with more than 70 percent of the women with whom I spoke advocating such untruths, with little regret. While Dory Hollander writes in her book *101 Lies Men Tell—And Why Women Believe Them* that men lie to women about money to get their attention, I was surprised to learn how many women are out to impress other women when it comes to wealth. And often it's about a husband who provides the goods rather than about a woman's own success. What I found less surprising is that women hide what they do with money and how much they spend. This makes sense, since women have been taught to lie about money.

For example, although the following four women have postured when it comes to their financial status for a variety of reasons, the common thread is the deliberate decision to lie.

Rory, forty-two, a full-time wife and mother of two, married to a very successful man, is willing to wear her material life on her sleeve.

My husband first began to make money about six years ago. We were so excited, but we kept quiet about it—I didn't want any of my friends to know. We lived in a small town and everyone had about the same amount of money and the same goals for our kids to do well and go to college. Then my husband went into partnership with a few guys and the company grew fast. No one from the company lived near us, so the other women's lifestyles had nothing to do with mine. First I got a fancy car and then we added an addition onto our house. Then we bought a boat. It all was changing and I was basically lying to my closest friends, who I could tell were sort of jealous and also noticing my new ring, new clothes. . . . This went on for years, until a few months ago when we moved to the city, and now I can be who I've become with money. It's not that I flaunt it but it's a relief not to have to pretend to still be sort of poor.

In contrast to Rory is Allison, thirty-five, whose husband lost money over the past several years. She finds herself lying about her finances to her family and friends. Allison works part-time in hospital administration and has one young child.

We always had so much and I assumed it would always be like this. I married my husband for financial stability, but I wouldn't have said that before he lost the money. Now I know what it's like to worry and I resent that this happened. I married him believing he was a great provider and anxious to make loads of money. This setback is something he wants to work through, by selling our house, downsizing, taking our child out of private school. I am refusing, still pushing for the great vacations and the parties we've given in the past. I won't succumb. I expect him to work hard and to fix things so I don't have to lie forever and his work situation isn't this heavy burden I have to have over my head all the time.

Defending her deception when it comes to money is a continual concern for Chloe, a forty-eight-year-old single mother. Chloe lives in San Francisco, where she has worked for the same corporation for sixteen years.

I make money and I give some to my children and keep plenty for me. I use it to keep myself happy and entertained. I've worked hard for money in the past and less hard lately. But I never let my kids, who are out of college, know all that I've got. I keep it a secret because I know they look to me as their failsafe. I shop for myself with my money for necessities. But my idea of necessities is extremely different from other people's. Sometimes I feel I don't have enough to pay after I've gone on a trip or bought something big. Then I'll feel guilty and remind myself that there's plenty of money and I can stop feeling this way. I never let on to the kids that I have guilt or that I spend what I spend. I don't want them to feel so entitled, so I have to keep them from knowing.

Lacey, thirty-nine, works full-time in the media industry and describes her use of money as a secret. She believes her purchases will inform people about her, and then she'll be unfairly judged. She also tells us that she has a proclivity for making and spending money.

It's really about having things, whether it's furniture or clothing, a new car or tickets to a play. Somehow I feel stronger, in charge, when I buy what I want. I say to myself, "I make this money, I want these things." We had no money growing up and I think that makes it harder for me. I used to be really sneaky when it came to money. I was afraid if some guy knew I had money, he'd be after my money—kind of like women treat men. Or if some guy knew my net worth, he'd feel emasculated. Plus my friends were always trying to figure out my lifestyle. That was why I kept it quiet. And my sisters have no money, so that was another reason to lie about it, to make my success seem like less.

Then I decided I only have myself to please, so I'm a bit more open now. Still, I'm on guard, money does strange things to people. It's definitely made me more confident. It's a secret weapon.

Whether a woman is in a traditional marriage or provides her own earning power, there is a cauldron of betterment, beneficial, and compassionate lies to implement at will. Even if women feel their tall tales aid them, it can be exasperating to be positioned this way, causing women in everyday life to lie as a shortcut to satisfaction. Letia, thirty-four, who works a day job as a megastore manager and a night job as a waitress, sums it up:

> It's just easier to lie. I work too hard to tell the truth. I have to take care of myself and it means I've got to lie about money.

For the women who have made money on their own, the secrets surrounding money have not lessened. In fact, their attitudes are similar to women who depend upon men for their source of income. Whatever the circumstance, women aren't prepared to wear their heart on their sleeve when it comes to money.

LOVE AND MONEY

Women have been schooled at lying for the monetary payoff.

The highly publicized tale of Anna Nicole Smith and her marriage to billionaire J. Howard Marshall II, sixty-three years her senior, raised a few eyebrows. Once Marshall died in 1995, a year into the marriage, a legal battle over his estate ensued, and continues today, even after Smith's unexpected death in February 2007. E! Television reported that Smith was rarely with her elderly husband and supposedly saw other men during the marriage. Nonetheless, within weeks of Marshall's death, Smith claimed that she was entitled to one half of his estate, estimated at well over one billion dollars.

Women have done this for centuries, with some having better

luck than others and the majority of them lying about their feelings. We don't scratch our heads and ask why would Anna Nicole marry this elderly man if not for the money. Still, women do claim to be in it for love. If it's a lie, it works because who can dispute matters of the heart?

Lucy, thirty, a model, describes the older man she married as handsome and dashing, despite their age disparity. Lucy's husband is twenty years her senior, with vast resources and wealth.

> I make no bones about why I married my husband. It helped that he was good-looking, but there were plenty of guys who were my age who were better-looking and who I would prefer. I knew, though, that they couldn't take care of me and I wanted a moneyed life. So it was a deal on my part but my husband was smitten. I figured I wouldn't model forever and I wanted insurance, I wanted to have all that he can pay for.
>
> I also act very loving toward him. When we met he was married and I went after him and I got him, and I got the lifestyle. If I had to be sexy and seductive to get that, so what? Is it because I lied to him that he didn't see it? Or was he just blind? Other people were whispering about it but I never said a word. I guess that's sort of a lie. I never even said to my mom or sisters, "Look at what I did." They knew it, though. But then he lies to himself and I just keep it going. Those who wanted to see it, saw it. I never said "no thanks" to a piece of jewelry or to room service. It isn't that I didn't make my own money, it's that he had so much and I wouldn't be spending my money if we were together. If I was going to get married, this is what it should be. I say "I love you" all the time, and I don't mean it. He definitely means it when he says it.

Trading on love or pretending to love for money is a tantalizing subject for films, a theme we know too well and seem to have an insatiable appetite for. In the steamy movie *Body Heat*, starring Kathleen Turner and William Hurt, Turner plays a femme fatale, Matty Walker, so obsessed with inheriting her husband's money that she arranges his murder. Matty Walker seduces Hurt's character, Ned Racine, coaxing him into committing a murder after she's stolen another woman's identity in order to ensure her own escape. Racine, the pathetic attorney who falls for her, is left to take the rap while Turner's Matty escapes with all the money to an island that looks like paradise.

Family money is just as gripping for Liz Taylor's Maggie in Tennessee Williams's *Cat on a Hot Tin Roof*. In this 1958 film, Brick, played by Paul Newman, is a disenfranchised husband, perhaps alcoholic, perhaps homosexual. His wife, Maggie, is desperate for them to inherit her terminally ill father-in-law's money. Brick is the favored son, but in this patriarchal southern family, the problem is that Brick and Maggie are childless. This means that Big Daddy might choose his less favored son for the grandchildren he's provided. Maggie hints to Big Daddy that she is pregnant, a lie that is underscored by the fact that she and Brick no longer have sex. While we don't doubt Maggie's frustrated love for Brick, we also see how love and money inform unhappy marriages and lead to very decisive lies.

The big bucks aren't easy for Demi Moore's character, Diana Murphy, to resist when Robert Redford's character, John Gage, a wealthy enigmatic man, becomes smitten with her in the 1993 feature *Indecent Proposal*. Redford offers to pay one million dollars for one night with her, knowing that she and her husband, David Murphy, played by Woody Harrelson, are in financial straits. Although the couple swears to each other it will change nothing and enable them greatly, Moore's character is smitten after the actual event. Now it isn't just money as a motivation but a moneyed life with this charismatic, unknown man that beckons her. She reveals little to her husband when she leaves him for

Redford, and less to Redford at the very end when she chooses true love over money—plus she does get to keep the million for the one night.

How and why Moore's character chose Redford's character after the "indecent proposal" was consummated is understandable; besides being handsome and mysterious, he offered her everything her husband could not. For some women, Demi Moore's return to Harrelson was not so apparent, but with either man, Harrelson or Redford, Moore's character *had* to be secretive, showing her feelings would not have benefited anyone.

MATERIAL GIRLS

As Madonna so succinctly points out in her 1985 hit song, "Material Girl," Mr. Right is always the man with the cold hard cash. More recently, a 2006 study entitled "What's Love Got to Do with It," conducted by sociologists W. Bradford Wilcox and Steven L. Nock, at the University of Virginia, reported that husbands who make more than 68 percent of the money in a marriage make their wives happy. This is an interesting juxtaposition to the values of the 1970s and 1980s, where women sought their own level of financial success.

By the early eighties, reality set in; it was too difficult to hold it all together, as working women, mothers, and wives. The mantra of "having it all" wasn't an abundance of riches after all, but a new form of misery masquerading as the great female lie of this period. The husbands weren't standing up to the plate—they'd had no training and didn't know what to do. Women no longer needed to keep their secret a secret, that they'd fallen out of love with their lives, including their husbands (partly because the husbands weren't always the primary breadwinners anymore, partly because the women had met men in the workplace, and partly because the women could support themselves). The bubble burst and the divorce rate rose to over 50 percent.

The result was that by the nineties women put their belief into egalitarian marriages, which became the latest form of lying. As usual, materialism reared its head when it came to the reason for the lie. Some women voted for these peer marriages where their husbands and they would both work, and share the responsibilities of childrearing. Others sought more traditional marriages and wanted money for the life it provided. Others clung to the myth of work/life balance and kept their corporate jobs.

Several of my interviewees said they'd stuck with their husbands through every decade of marriage, since 1980 or earlier, for the comfortable life they knew couldn't be duplicated. Agnes, who has been married for forty years, admits:

> I look the other way a lot, I take advantage. I lie when I have to, all for money. It's not a bad way to be, it's a way to have things . . . what else can I do? What were my skills, even back then when I should have had something to fall back on.

Women in the twenty-first century are looking for a material life offered by husbands regardless of female earning power. According to my study, whether women work full-time, part-time, or have given up careers to be available for their children, the honesty is still missing. The U.S. Census Bureau tells us that more women now earn undergraduate and graduate degrees than do men. The latest lie is what young women today plan to do about their careers once they're married. Liza, twenty-six, views her MBA as secondary to securing her marriage.

> Why should I work so hard that I'm too stressed out for my husband and kids? Who cares if I have an MBA—I don't care. I only care when it seems appropriate!

Eva, a thirty-nine-year-old accountant who is partner in a firm, confides:

> How can I admit to anyone that I'd rather stay home with my children than go to my office? But my husband and I both want to live this way, have this lifestyle—we rent a house for the month of August every summer and we have a nanny who cares for the boys. I don't want to give it all up, I just wish secretly that he'd make enough to pay for all of it.

Likewise Deirdre, who lives in a suburb in the Northeast and works part-time in marketing, at thirty-five feels that her financial situation drives her decisions. She admits that the lies in her life are all about money.

> I work for money and money makes it easier for me to have the designer clothes I want. I think I'm obsessed with shoes and purses and there's no way to pay for it unless I work. I would work harder and longer if it weren't for my children's schedules. My husband is always asking where the money goes and I'll tell him it goes to the kids' expenses. But it doesn't—he just believes me and doesn't pay enough attention to figure it out. Every cent I make and every hour I spend making it is for my shopping sprees. My husband makes enough money to pay for everything else. He could pay for this stuff but he won't. So I lie and say what I say, get what I want.

It isn't that only married women are in it for the money or are secretive when it comes to material possessions. In *Sex and the City*, Carrie Bradshaw, played by Sarah Jessica Parker, was constantly purchasing Manolo Blahnik and/or Jimmy Choo shoes. That she was a journalist, working on a laptop from her small apartment, didn't cause us to question how she had the money for such expensive shoes. Her friend Samantha, played by Kim Cattrall, who apparently had a better-paying job than did Carrie, was hell-bent on having an authentic Hermès Birkin bag (according to Wikipedia, the price tag begins at $7,500 for such a purse). Neither of these women had husbands footing the bill for these extravagances. Rather, Samantha, on her own, lied to the salesperson to beat the two-year waiting list, in search of immediate gratification with her Birkin bag, a symbol of wealth and status.

With the cultural message bombarding us that materialism is practically a religion and, according to Catalyst, that women are still being paid seventy-seven cents on the dollar, no wonder they lie to get the goods they want. It seems self-evident that neither Carrie nor Samantha on *Sex and the City* seem likely to give up their guilty pleasures any time soon. The moral here is that it's all within reason, the line between being able to afford the shoes and bag isn't as significant as finessing ownership. It's all in how you tell the tale to achieve your materialistic goals.

LIFELONG SECRETS

From the time women are girls, their consciousness about money as power is raised. At each stage of our lives, money affects our circumstances, if what money can buy changes as we grow older, women are impelled by financial security and the temptation of money remains. It's curious how many women who make money or want it in their lives can be clandestine about it. As Yvonne, a forty-five-year-old physician, confessed:

> My husband took my money six years ago for a business he started, and promised to pay it back. I felt forced to invest in his deal and I never saw a penny. I'm still married to him because

I'm waiting to get paid back. Meanwhile, I now hide the money
I make.

Another issue for women and money plays out when semiretirement begins. With home offices at a premium and technology
prolonging our work lives, semiretirement can last for decades. As
Business Week online reports in its 2006 retirement guide, *Stay
Happy, Together,* the problem with all this new togetherness is
in meshing two separate lives, financially and emotionally. For
women it's especially tricky since they don't always relish retirement as a concept, not financially or in terms of the time commitment to their husbands. Furthermore, a self-imposed cutting
down on spending isn't appealing. Many women will "yes" their
husbands while scheming to protect their own assets, or encouraging their husbands to become consultants.

For Mary, sixty, who is in sales and married to a man twelve
years her senior, her reluctance to give up her career now that her
husband's is winding down has created a series of designated lies.

I tell my husband all the time that it's okay if we're on a budget, but I don't mean it. I just say it so I don't have to listen
anymore to how much he wants to retire. He's had some ups
and some flops and I always act supportive, but I don't forgive
him for the flops. We have four kids and he's put us in a perilous place financially. Twice we sold a house and moved to
smaller quarters. Now he's saying he wants to wind down and
I smile and tell myself it's better than his going downhill
again. But I have just bought some land as an investment and
I'm not telling him, I'm putting it in my name. I work harder
than he cares to admit because someone's got to take care of
the money, stash some away. I guess it has to be me. I always
say I'm fine with his decision and then I put money in my
secret account.

And so the skills we honed as young women impel us into midlife and beyond when it comes to cash. It seems unlikely that women are inclined to move away from materialism and deception to achieve these goals. As a teenager, I remember how my grandmother would praise a man with money. "It's as easy to marry a rich man as a poor man," she instructed me. "And when he stands on his money, he'll be very tall, even if he's a dwarf." How fascinating it is that women today, despite the great gains of the women's movement, will lie, beg, steal if need be, for the right material life.

PART II

THROUGH GLASS DARKLY

FOUR

Mothering as Myth: Ambivalence and Lies

It always comes back to the same story, that motherhood, highly touted, is also a thankless task. No matter how many books are written on mothering, there is no one guide that can save us from stumbling, nor shield us from the inevitable challenges inherent in the role. We each have biological, social, and emotional needs that we incorporate into our responsibilities as mothers. In addition, what our mothers have taught us, by example, catapults us into our "style of mothering."

The bar is held very high when it comes to mothering, and this makes it all the more stressful. So much is expected of us while we're trying to navigate the other parts of our lives—romance, career, finances, friendships. Nothing is so damning as to be labeled "a bad mother," nothing makes us feel as diminished as does a troubled child for whom we've done so much, tried so hard. If our sacrifices don't make us feel joyous and self-less, but lost and disillusioned, they become the dark secrets of motherhood.

Women lie when it comes to their real feelings about mothering.

CONFLICTS OVER MOTHERING

Many of us were raised to believe that without children we are incomplete, and we were encouraged to have children at all costs. There is this sense that childless women have failed, and that they are judged unfavorably by society at large, along with family members and close friends. Then why is it that more than 50 percent of the women with whom I spoke had felt some kind of ambiguity in their role as mothers or in contemplating the process?

The media frenzy over the birth of movie stars' babies, from Julia Roberts's twins in 2004, to Katie Holmes's baby, Suri, with Tom Cruise, to the long-awaited birth of Angelina Jolie and Brad Pitt's daughter, Shiloh, dubbed "Baby Brangelina" during the pregnancy, only ramps up the imperative that motherhood is golden. But what about those of us who don't embrace motherhood, what of women who suffer from postpartum depression, what if our children have special needs, or we find our lives turned upside down for motherhood? What if some of us aren't as happy as we're supposed to be? In these instances, compassionate lies, betterment lies, and survival lies all kick in.

Lina, a thirty-nine-year-old working mother, explained that although she'd kept secrets for her entire adult life without regret, she struggles with her hidden dissatisfaction with mothering.

> I truly hate my role as a mother. I pretend that I enjoy our three sons, but it isn't how I imagined my life. We live in a suburb where everyone is devoted to their kids, bordering on obsessed with them. My way of living my life is a fraud; I leave work early to carpool, I bake cookies for the class, I take the boys to after-school activities when I can, but I'm not into it at all. My husband and I have no time for each other, no intimacy, I wouldn't have had kids if I'd known how draining it

would be, how it would change my marriage for the worse. My husband has no idea I feel this way, and he'd be repelled by my feelings. And I wouldn't have a friend in the entire town. . . . I have to act like this is great . . . like I enjoy being a mom. . . .

What struck me most about Lina's story was when she described her marriage and children as a lie, believing she'd be ostracized if she revealed her innermost feelings, considered downright villainous. That she hasn't signed on for this cultural prescription has become her secret. For some women, other manifestations of unutterable truths exist.

Consider Dolly, thirty-three, a designer who decided to distance her mother from her secret of not wanting a baby.

I won't tell my mother that I had an abortion since it's only going to upset her. Instead I've kept it to myself. It has to do with our religion and how she feels about my boyfriend. It also has to do with how I feel that I've let her down—it has to do with how much she loves being a mother and wants me to be one. I've done the one thing I was raised to never do, get pregnant and have an abortion. So I feel terrible about this, and I can't even go to my mother for comfort. I have to lie to her. What's more horrible than keeping this secret is that I'd probably do it again, if something happened. I'm just not sure I want to have kids. This isn't something I can talk about without being judged.

If a woman isn't certain that she wants to be a mother, the judgment she incurs for her indecision is inescapable. Eyebrows are raised when you say you are married for X number of years without any offspring to show for it. Many women in my study, between the ages of thirty and forty-two, admitted it's easier to say they're "trying" than to say they are unsure, or worse, simply do not want children. Having one baby is a feat, two children garners great respect, and more than three children deserves a badge of honor. For a woman who isn't married or is childless at a certain age, there's pity for her with little thought paid to her personal choice.

It's treasonous to doubt any aspect of motherhood.

When I spoke with women who are married, childless, or on the fence about having children, their concern was how they would manage it in their busy work lives. What is obvious is that if they opt to have a child, an enormous adjustment kicks in. Anything less than euphoria over having a baby is considered a betrayal. We are well aware that ambivalence toward motherhood would appear hedonistic, selfish, and narcissistic.

Generation Y women (born between 1978 and 2000) are not anxious to emulate the working women of the eighties or early nineties who put their careers ahead of marriage and children, only to wake up to their ticking biological clock and a short supply of men. This proved enough of a cautionary tale for Generation Y women for their formula to become "Go to college, go to grad school, have the skills, say yes when asked if you want a career one day (a lie), say no when asked if you'd forfeit your marriage and children for a career (a truth) and glamorize your marriage (even fake it) at all costs." This is why Alexandra, at twenty-seven, believes that the MBA she is now earning is a tool. More important, she tells us, is her belief that marriage and family vanquish any interfering job offer.

I'm all for taking care of my husband and children and I won't work at a company where the hours are too long. I've promised my fiancé this. But I haven't told him that I'm not really ready to have a baby quite yet, I need a bit of time. I know lots of our friends are starting early and so I say yes, of course. I know it's inevitable that we'll have kids much younger than my mom had me because of her work. And I figure I won't be lying to my kids about why I missed a school play or any of that—like she did. She was stuck at the office, she had to be out of town. . . .

I know this degree is a necessary step; it's what I should do. It makes me look serious and smart, which I'm supposed to be. My husband is the one who will work, though, and I'm in grad school so I can buy some time. I don't tell anyone, but that's what it does for me.

So while Alexandra tells an acceptable lie because she isn't sold on getting pregnant immediately, she has signed on for the young mother/martyr/glam marriage, as have her friends. In her righteousness about this path, she seems in denial about her scam: she's already stalling when to have children, keeping her plans a secret from her future husband. Alexandra's approach, that of an accommodating wife who nonetheless schemes, reminds us that even before she's a wife or mother, she recognizes that the role requires secrets.

Can the lies we tell as mothers have value?

New York magazine ran a cover story on July 24, 2006, "Mothers Anonymous" by Emily Nussbaum. The photo on the cover is of a mother holding up her darling baby, smiling broadly, while thinking to herself, "I know my husband is cheating on me. . . . I never wanted this baby. Anyone else in a sexless marriage?" Nussbaum

describes UrbanBaby as an online anonymous Web site, a reposi-
tory for unhappy mothers, and ambivalence about the role is a big
part of their venting. This is where New York City mothers express
their concerns and spill their secrets. Finances, infidelity, marrying for money, marrying to have a baby, envy, and jealousy of other
mothers who seem to have it better are the issues identified on
UrbanBaby.

How do mothers *really* feel about their babies, about motherhood? These are the probing questions asked on UrbanBaby.
These new mothers are ahead of Alexandra, who is speculating on
how her marriage will be, where she'll cut corners, what secrets to
keep in life; these women are already deep into it. There's no
turning back and the irresolution is palpable.

Dee, thirty-six, living in California, identifies strongly with the
concerns raised on UrbanBaby.

> I've been a freelancer since I had kids because I couldn't
> leave work altogether and didn't want to leave them with a
> nanny all day. Plus we need the money I can bring in. But my
> insurance benefits would be better if I'd stayed at my job.
> Some days I miss being at work so much and I don't find my
> children as exciting as other mothers do. Other times, when
> I'm at meetings all day, I miss my kids. I can't say anything to
> my husband, who wanted kids much more than I did. Now
> the boys are two and four and we're really in the thick of it.
> My whole life revolves around the children and I tell myself
> it'll get better. Then I count how many years till they're inde-
> pendent, but then they'll be hateful teenagers. I never
> thought it would be like this. Sometimes I'm depressed, but I
> don't utter a word.

If Dee admits to being depressed on occasion and knows her
survival is predicated on staying silent, Janie, forty-one, feels that

she's come to terms with her secret wish to have more time to herself, away from her small children.

> Sometimes I wonder why I can't say out loud that these kids drain me. I had my last child to please my husband and that's never a good idea. I didn't tell him it was just to keep us going that I popped one more out. That's the truth, though, that's why I did it. I look at these children and I crave sleep and free time. I'm supposed to be infinitely grateful and obsessed with them. They wear me out and make me jealous of working women who have no children, no husbands. I never say, but I'm sure I had postpartum depression. What I suffer from now, since that was over a year ago, is housewife syndrome.

Postpartum depression evokes survival lies.

If what Janie describes as "housewife syndrome" following her postpartum depression isn't readily addressed, it will elicit an unforgiving attitude from family and strangers alike. For this reason, it has been a deep-seated secret long held by women. The shame and guilt associated with anything but euphoria over the birth of a child is looked upon as almost immoral. Yet it is estimated that almost 20 percent of all new mothers experience postpartum depression to a degree, manifesting symptoms from mild to severe, as reported by the Center for Postpartum Adjustment. When we consider the attitudes toward women suffering from postpartum depression, combined with the stats, it's not surprising that these survival lies surface.

Perhaps Brooke Shields's courageous book, *Down Came the Rain,* will dispel postpartum depression as a secret worth keeping and help women face this problem, without fear of being judged harshly. Shields describes her experience as "a bizarre state of mind," and "feelings that ranged from embarrassment to stoicism to melancholy to shock, practically all at once." She tells her readers how she believed that her situation wouldn't improve, had suicidal thoughts, and sought treatment.

Kate, a thirty-nine-year-old first-time mother, noticed that her mother and her aunts were whispering about her at her son's christening.

> "What's wrong with Kate," I heard them say. "Why, she should be head over heels in love with that baby—and at her age. . . . Her moping around is . . . inexcusable . . . she's sick in the head, not fit to be a mother. . . ."

Most of the women with whom I spoke on this subject said their family members weren't supportive or open to their ordeal. While women tell me that they feel absolved of any guilt in lying about it, they feel shame and guilt in suffering from it. This was the case for Charline, thirty-seven, the mother of a baby girl who is now nine months old.

> If I keep it a secret, act like I'm happy, maybe my husband and my mother-in-law will get off my back. If I start describing how I feel, I know I'll be in trouble and they'll talk about me, make it worse. And they won't trust me alone with my baby; my husband will treat me differently. I don't want that. I'll be paranoid on top of down in the dumps and miserable. I know I have a problem, but it's one I'm not sharing with anyone.

Charline has decided it's a lie worth pursuing rather than become disenfranchised from her husband, who she reports is "madly in love" with their baby. For Janie, who initially suffered with postpartum depression (and has shifted into an unhappy mode of being assigned to baby care twenty-four/seven), the feelings linger. She deals with this in the same way Charline does, by not uttering a word. Dane, a thirty-five-year-old mother, describes the first few weeks after her daughter was born as exhausting. Her unpredictable mood swings left her disinterested in her baby. In each woman's predicament, the survival lie is obvious, based on the reactions of those around them.

> I was almost in a state of shock. I had no idea what to expect and my whole life was turned upside down, I had this baby to feed constantly, I was on maternity leave . . . my husband was back at work and thought I was some kind of super-mom. I had no idea what to do and I was inert . . . I couldn't move to even lift my baby. No one knew what was wrong and I wasn't going to tell them, they'd hold it against me.

Like postpartum secrets, the lies of the infertile are shrouded in shame.

Few women with whom I've spoken admit having any fertility problems. The irony is that women who battle postpartum depression are often those who craved motherhood and signed on for fertility treatments to have a child. Often these women, who have been successful at their endeavors from grade school through graduate school, keep their infertility a big secret, having rarely known defeat.

Patsy, forty, was assisted with donor egg and donor sperm and made the decision to not tell her own mother any of this. Nor did she feel like discussing how "blue" she was after she gave birth.

> My mother was so fertile in her day that she never really understood what it was like for me. She kept telling me to relax. My husband and I were obsessed with having a baby and it

became this all-consuming part of our marriage. I'm someone who has always landed the right school, the right job, the
right guy, so this was a shock. We had to jump through hoops
and I didn't find my mother very sympathetic. Then, when I
had my baby, finally, she wasn't keen on my postpartum depression. Her attitude was that I was on overload and the stress
caused all of my problems. That wasn't exactly the case but I
went along with her explanation. When people called me those
first few months I just lied about how happy I was to be home
with my baby. Just like I lied when my girlfriends were pregnant
and I couldn't get pregnant—acting like pregnancy wasn't my
thing. It was easier to not tell anyone what was going on during
any of this.

Similarly, Yolanda, forty-four, an accountant, couldn't tell her
sisters or mother that she was undergoing fertility treatments. No
one in her family had ever encountered such a problem before.

Now that I have my daughter I can talk about it, but for the
years that I was trying and not pregnant and my sisters were
always pregnant, it was torture. I didn't want anyone to know
what I was going through or that the chances looked slim of it
happening. We tried everything, and it was a big secret. Then
the in vitro worked—the third time. I was afraid to even tell
people I was pregnant, I felt so fragile.
    When I was pregnant, I thought it was a nightmare and
when my daughter was born, I was less than thrilled. Now that
she's in school and I've been back at work a few years, I'm
happy. But I wasn't at the start, I was down and no one needed
to know. I was ashamed about my feelings, so I was quiet.

For women whose lives don't go according to plan or are truly
undecided about their level of maternal prowess, it's best to be

cryptic because other people's tolerances are so low. In Ayelet Waldman's novel, *Love and Other Impossible Pursuits,* her protagonist, Emilia, is deeply, understandably depressed after the death of her baby from SIDS (sudden infant death syndrome). She blames herself, secretly believing that she killed her own baby, that it was her fault. Nor does it help matters that she's quit her job as a lawyer and has weekly responsibility for her young, preschooler stepson, William, who is a constant reminder of her loss. Emilia struggles with failure as a mother and as a stepmother, perhaps not believing she's capable of protecting anyone's child, hers or her husband's. Lurking beneath is the question of will she ever get the chance again—Emilia hides from the world and can't emote; her pain is enormous.

Nancy, forty-five, reports that her uncertainty during her first and only pregnancy has resolved over time. Today, she works as a grade school teaching assistant and has met other mothers who, she suspects, had infertility problems as well.

> I was so sad about not being pregnant when all my friends were and I had to pretend it was okay. Then finally, it was a miracle, after a few miscarriages, and some heavy-duty treatments, I was pregnant. I have one child, who is in kindergarten now. Since I work at a nearby school, I'll see a pregnant mother come to pick up her six-year-old and I imagine that some of them wonder why they bought into doing it again since one child is more work than anyone expects. Lots of times they're pregnant with a third child, or twins.
>
> They act like they deserve a medal, like they did something so unique when I know what they went through, it's not that unusual. I know they took the same drugs I took and said the same prayers, but they all pretend it just happened, that they're more fertile than the rest of us, more special somehow . . . they just happened to be pregnant with twins

in their late thirties or early forties. No one dares utter a word. But we all know it; we all know how it's more of a big deal than anyone lets on.

Nancy's secrecy and betterment lie surrounding her own pregnancy are mirrored in the mothers she now meets. In these instances, any problem getting pregnant is swept under the rug, infertility is a dirty word, while pregnancy is joyous. How could women not have secrets when the entire world is allowed to pass judgment, still, today, on a woman's personal choice about pregnancy and mothering? "I will hear mothers boasting about their children, when they're not even enjoying being a mother," remarks Dr. Ronnie Burak. "So how could anyone ever confess to the pressure of infertility or the demands of motherhood? If we aren't falling over our children and giving up our lives for them, it's got to be a secret. No one would approve of that."

ACHIEVING CHILDREN

Women tell whoppers when it comes to their children.

Mothers are invested in their children's success, from their days as preschoolers until they are full-fledged adults with children of their own, instigated by a culture of competitive mothers. As Evelyn, fifty-one, who lives in a Midwest suburb describes her environment, a mother is judged by her children's success. While Evelyn exaggerates how well her three children do, it's all based on fact.

I don't know if I'm as competitive by nature as I've become living here. But my two daughters and one son have been pushed very hard, by me, their father, and by the circumstance. When my first child got into some great colleges, I made it even better; when my second child got a scholarship, I said it was more money than the actual amount. That's how I do it. I always act like everything is great with them, never a problem. I intimidate my neighbor so she'll never tell me how her kids are really doing, she's forced to lie completely. I know her kids have issues. And my kids are learning how to do it—to make all that they do the best. I can't say I'm proud of it, but it's what we do. I doubt I'd get through without this technique.

The pressure to have children who excel, as Evelyn describes, is felt by mothers everywhere, and is not confined to urban or suburban settings. Roberta, forty-seven, a mother living in a small town in the South, lies constantly about her son, who is not working.

My children had every opportunity and when they were small and I was in charge, they did everything right. They were on Little League, they won the science prize, they were known as good boys. But my older son hasn't worked since he got out of school. He almost refuses to work. I sometimes think it's to get back at me. I'm so busy saying he's doing something, hoping I can remember my last lie to the neighbors and to friends, that I don't even worry about him anymore. In this little town, I'm too worried about how he's perceived and how I'm perceived since he has nothing to show for his school years. I'm embarrassed, ashamed, really, and tired of lying about it.

What Evelyn and Roberta experience rings true enough for many mothers once their children are too old to be micromanaged. The secret is that the child is not doing what she's supposed to do, and when children are considered a reflection of the parents, a beneficial lie ensues. In Daphne Pollock's March 2006 article in *More* magazine, "Learning Curve," we realize a mother's initial frustration, sadness, and secret surrounding her high-achieving daughter's decision to not attend college. The problem is compounded for Pollack by her own status as a graduate of the first class of women at Yale University in 1971. Pollack describes her conversations with other mothers, whose children were doing the "right thing"—enrolling in college—while her daughter had opted to work for UPS instead.

> "So what's Alli up to?"
> I sighed inside.
> "Working really hard." (It's the truth.)
> "Did she ever go to college?"
> Perky as possible. "Not yet."

> That first year, I'd mumble something about Alli taking a year off, which seemed acceptable, even trendy. Three years later, the story's tougher to spin.

If women strive to be proud of their children and are willing to hide what is not socially acceptable, what about wicked mothers who posture as caring in their quest for perfection? This was the case for Christina Crawford, the adopted daughter of Joan Crawford, whose memoir, *Mommie Dearest*, exposes her mother's unrelenting abuse, telling the world what really went on with her famous mother. Whether a mother's secret is that she is emotionally abusive, as in Joan Crawford's case, or someone who feigns a deadly illness, as in the case of Jollie's mother, we see how powerfully these secrets affect the daughters.

For those women whose mothers are hiding extreme behavior, shame is often associated with the secret. Brené Brown, author of *Women & Shame,* explains in her interview with Judith Stadtman Tucker in The Mother's Movement Online, "Women most often experience shame as a web of layered, conflicting and competing expectations. At their core, these ideals are products of very rigid social and community expectations." Brown qualifies feelings of shame for women as often connected to our roles as mothers and to our relationship with our own mothers. The guilt that accompanies this shame seems inevitable, for as mothers we tend to question ourselves, to second-guess our efforts and decisions.

It follows that if mothers feel they have to be more than they are, children have to be more than they are as well. I saw this when the mothers who answered my ad for *Little White Lies, Deep Dark Secrets* confided that they weren't proud of their insincerity when it came to their children but found little recourse. The kind of secret that deals with motherhood is keenly female, especially the she-wolf aspect. Consider Luisa, a forty-two-year-old mother of three who has lied for her nineteen-year-old daughter for the past three years.

> I would do anything to protect my daughter. . . . I've been like this since she was small. Now she's nineteen and I'm not sure that all the times I wasn't honest over the years have helped. I mean, they helped in the moment, but she has serious problems. She used to become hysterical when she was five over canceled plans and I defended her, rearranged things for her. When she got older, it got worse, she was out of control. She drank for a long time but I think that has recently stopped. Since I always acted like it wasn't happening, it's hard to know what's real. She never finished high school and can't hold down any kind of job. I lie to my friends, my mother, my husband, and say she's fine, because everyone else's daughter is great, just great. So my secret is that my daughter

isn't really okay. The lie is that she is okay, that her life is better than it is.

What is so painful in Luisa's interview is her blind defense of her daughter. She has kept her daughter's problems to herself, which isn't helpful to either her daughter or to herself. If not so much was expected of Luisa as a mother, let alone for her daughter, to be on the right track, she might not need to closet the true story.

It can be harmful to both mother and child when lies are told about children of any age.

Since, in our culture, mothers feel judged by their children's achievements, they'll push their children for the sake of a superficial recognition. A mother insists that her son play soccer when he's not the least bit inclined, or pushes a daughter to be on the chess team when she would prefer another activity altogether. The underlying problem is that these mothers are overly concerned with their children's lives and how they compare to others. As Dr. Ronnie Burak notes, "There is this shame associated with children who are less than optimal. So we live through our children's successes and the secret becomes when a child is not so smart, or not doing so well."

For instance, Meredith, fifty, an emergency room nurse, tells us how long and drawn out her issues have been with her youngest child, now twenty-four.

What should I do about my daughter, who has been in rehab twice and has finally stopped using drugs but drinks too much? I've done really well in my job and my husband is a doctor and has loyal patients and lots of respect in our community. So here I am with this daughter who I can't escape. My other kids I will tell the truth about, but when people ask me about her, I just make it up. Sometimes I say she's getting a teaching degree, sometimes I say she's working freelance jobs. I always lie, I never tell my secret, that she needs help. She won't listen to me or to my husband. We wish we could be prouder of her, but we're not proud. We make up these stories—I feel like I'm a big liar. But in our neighborhood, nothing is more embarrassing than to have a kid who fails.

Agatha, forty-five, who has recently moved cross-country, has been so disappointed by her son that she's chosen not to tell any new acquaintance that she even has a child.

I'm in a second marriage and my husband has no kids. My son has been so difficult and we are estranged. I don't see the point in telling anyone at my new job or socially about my son. He won't be coming here and he's not kind to me. If he had a great life, if he'd done well, I'd say something. But he's basically a slacker and I don't try to do for him anymore. Years ago I made all these gestures, and I made excuses for him. Not now. Now I'm finished. It's almost better this way. When people bring up their kids, I say, how nice. They pity me for being childless, but if they knew the story, they'd pity me more for who my son is.

In Meredith's and Agatha's survival lies, we witness two mothers who have taken their children's lack of success to extreme measures. This disservice is evident: it's unfortunate that they aren't more accepting of their children and more comfortable with themselves. What is even more disturbing is how much the expectation from other mothers contributes to their secrets and lies about their children.

The perpetual mommy wars create sparring mothers and endless lies.

Women's rivalry and subsequent lying over their young children's accomplishments is a scenario we're all familiar with as of late, with the media attention paid to the "mommy wars." Beyond aggression on the mother's part for her children to outrank others is the division between the two factions of mothers; stay-at-home mothers and working mothers. These factions compete through their children, locked in a constant contest and underlying duplicity. The children often become extensions of the parents, and must be outstanding, at the very least. Based on this attitude, a story is embellished when your child can't possibly be that fabulous, even in your own eyes, let alone the eyes of the world.

On *Good Morning America* on February 22 and 23, 2006, Diane Sawyer aired a series on the mommy wars, highlighting how working and nonworking mothers are locked in an unhealthy competition, where deception and blatant lies are rampant. In her book *Perfect Madness: Motherhood in the Age of Anxiety,* Judith Warner explores the way that motherhood is perceived today, how mothers feel inadequate, disappointed by marriage and children. All the while the working mothers and the stay-at-home mothers are at a standoff. Says forty-four-year-old Gail, an attorney with three small children:

> It's self defense—that's why I lie about my kids. I go on and
> on about my children's talents even with my sister. You should

hear me when someone makes noise like I'm not doing the right thing. I think I'm part of the mommy wars because I feel defensive and worried that my children are missing out. I also feel competitive with the nonworking mothers and about how my kids measure up. On top of this I have a job to do each day in my office. So it's a lot, and the only way I can feel better is to take sides with the working mothers and force my children to be stars, or at least say they are. Partly I feel guilty when I miss time with them, that too.

Stay-at-home mothers defend their position as well, ironically using similar tactics to the working mothers. The measure is always about how well the child does, but the parents want recognition for the commitment they've made and the time invested in their prodigy. In the case of Dennie, thirty-four, when work in a local hospital kept her away from her children, she shifted to a part-time schedule, then left the job altogether. She presently lies about not missing work, about being a full-time mother, acting as if it's a happy way of life, when in fact she misses her job and feels overwhelmed.

What am I supposed to do? My children are small and they need me and I couldn't take the pressure from my husband, my mom, and my friends who quit their jobs years ago. Now I do all this mother-at-home stuff and there are days when I really miss work. I feel I have no choice, I have to get my kids where they need to be, even if it means sacrificing my work. I say this is a great thing—but really I'm home all day with my kids in grade school and then I drive them around for hours after school. But I sure am more popular with the other mothers who are at home. Except they can't be trusted. I bought my daughter the wrong ballet slippers last spring and everyone talked about me. I heard one woman say I made the mistake because I used to be a working mom. My secret is that I'm friendly to these awful mothers, that I suck up to them so my girls get invited to the right birthday parties.

The ongoing nature of motherhood instills conflict and often evokes survival and betterment lies. The fabrication may seem relatively simple, such as saying your daughter got an A when if fact she got a B−, or it may be a serious ordeal, lying about your son's drinking problem and time in rehab, or about your child's learning disability. Ultimately, women can become so caught up in these lies that they lack introspection. The pros of lying in this arena are that it's a method to get through the challenges of mothering and of interacting with the other mothers. The cons are that a woman can feel compromised and misunderstood if she doesn't conform. The lies told, mainly survival and betterment, are driven by a constant focus on advancing one's goals.

FIVE

Family Matters: Shattering Secrets

Our families define us; they propel us into the world through a certain slant of light. A combination of cultural and family influences can endanger a woman, and she doesn't always have the courage or insight to question this. Of all the types of secrets women have and the lies they tell to guard their secrets, the shadowy side of family matters stands alone. In fact, more than 70 percent of the women in my study had some kind of family secret at some point in their lives. For women of all ages, there is a backlash in these deceptions, and until a woman sorts out what has occurred, she can be traumatized. Sexual abuse, incest, domestic violence, questions of paternity, adoption, mental and physical health are the issues that are cloaked and rewritten in families. Again, these secrets are female-driven, with women often fronting for a family member. In this way, these survival lies overlap with compassionate lies, but the women are also second-guessing their actions and have an ongoing sense of shame and isolation.

Although it may be perilous to do so, women fiercely protect a family secret.

Family secrets are stratified, making them more intricate. The tragedy in *not* telling anyone is that a survival lie bordering on an unsafe secret is perpetuated. Both mother and daughters (who are touched by these secrets more than sons) suffer in silence. Evan Imber-Black, in her book *The Secret Life of Families*, writes, "How do secrets affect the boundary . . . between your household and the outside world? . . . Do secrets prevent you from using necessary resources to solve problems? How have these secrets affected the development of individuals and relationships in your family?"

DISAPPEARING ACTS

The women who confessed to family secrets concerning domestic abuse and incest say they kept the secret in order not to disrupt the family. Furthermore, the women made excuses for the perpetrator, or failed to tell a mother, sister, or teacher, what had transpired. This makes it easier for the woman, as the victim, to blame herself rather than blow a whistle on a husband, stepfather, uncle, or older brother or family friend who appears incapable of the abuse he inflicts. A young woman who takes on this burden is losing herself, her self-esteem, and her self-confidence; she's disappearing for the sake of an invasive family lie.

Consider Dina, who at twenty-five has one child and lives in Utah, where she volunteers in a library. She describes her family secret as something she'll never reveal. As Dina puts it, she was very much alone in her hellish experience, "My sisters know that something happened . . . but I'm the one who is scarred."

I was sexually abused by someone I knew when I was very young, somewhere between four and six. It was a family friend and no one in our family knew, so they couldn't do anything to save me. I come from a pretty religious family, but everyone had their back turned. I don't know what they knew but I felt destroyed. My sisters know that something happened . . . but I'm the one who is scarred. They sort of kept the secret, too, from our strict parents. I've never been able to tell my husband everything . . . I keep it from him because I want to forget it, to be in this life with him where I can forget the past.

But I feel marked, like maybe underneath my family life and my being a mother, you can see what happened. You can see that it's something I can't escape even if I lie about it by never saying a word. . . .

Sadly enough, a majority of women's secrets and lies entail physical or emotional abuse (and may be compounded with another kind of secret, such as a financial secret or a mothering secret). According to the Gabe Kapler Foundation, in America, a woman is abused every nine seconds. As reported by Sunshine for Women, violent acts against females occur ever eighteen seconds, three to four million women are battered yearly, and three out of four women end up being victims of a violent crime during their life span. These acts include sexual abuse, physical abuse, and psychological abuse. Thirty percent of woman in emergency rooms are there because they've been abused, almost always by someone they know—most often a family member.

Bessie, twenty-two, married with a baby, living in the Midwest, believes her family's betrayal affected her entire life.

I ran away from home because my cousin molested me when I was in junior high. He's a few years older and my parents acted like they didn't believe me when I told them. Once my cousin broke my arm and my mom didn't even take me to the emergency room. She knew and she said to me that she didn't want to go to jail. They made me sleep on the floor and never

confronted my cousin. It made me feel dirty. I was emanci-
pated at sixteen and then I met my husband, who's in the
navy. I pretended it didn't happen once something good had
finally happened to me. I put it all behind me and tried for a
new start, getting married, denying what it was like. . . .

For Heather, fifty-three, who was abused by her former husband, there is a nagging sense that had she come forward and
told her sister or her mother, she might have left her marriage
years ago.

My husband was so cruel to me with words at first and then
physically. I stayed for years and told no one. Really, I had
nowhere to go and I liked where we lived in Virginia, and I
didn't want to lose all that. I told no one. I figured if I faced it,
I'd be running back to my family as a middle-aged battered
woman. It would be another sort of hell, so I just kept trying
not to upset my husband. Until one day it was too unbearable.
I took a bus cross-country back to my hometown and confessed. I felt so beaten down, so ruined. My mother was supportive and my sister did the "I told you so" routine. I don't
want anyone else to know. I rack my brain wondering why I
stood for it for so long.

Sarie, thirty-eight, works in a nursing home in North Dakota.
She believes that her secrets were the result of poor choices she
made as a young woman.

I made some big mistakes when I was younger and was in a
physically and emotionally abusive relationship in my twenties. I thought I could get away with it until I ran into a neighbor who convinced me to move out. I was keeping it from
everyone. After that, I just lied to the guys I dated; even guys

who could have been good ones, I faked loving them. I'd say I loved them but I didn't, it was my secret. I pretend that I come from a healthy family and I pretend that it's all gone well. I even tell strangers that if they ask. My intention is to lie for as long as I have to about whatever comes up since it works better for me.

Janna, a forty-eight-year-old journalist, found that her secret sufficed until it became a problem in her relationship with her children:

I thought it was best not to tell my children why I divorced their father. I actually thought I was best serving my children by not disclosing the real reasons why I wanted a divorce, not dragging them into it. One reason was that my father-in-law made advances toward me, and my husband didn't want to hear about it. I felt he wasn't supporting me, and it added to all my unhappiness in the marriage. There was also a lot of drinking and I didn't want the kids to be a part of that, either. So I made it look like my divorce was some sort of personal decision and not about the bad stuff that went on with my husband, about his treatment of me. I never said a word about that.

In the end I took the rap and let their father look good. I looked like the bad guy for asking for a divorce and for not sticking it out. He used that against me over and over, for years. Still, I told the kids he'd take good care of them because I wanted that. I'm the one who's lost out since my kids are brainwashed. I'm the one who suffers. . . .

Although the first four women rely on survival lies in their attempt to bury the past, Janna uses a compassionate lie in order to make it easier for her children. Yet today she feels punished for her secret and regrets that her children are misinformed. So while the lie may have started out as a better choice than the truth, it's only while it works in one's favor that a woman can count on it.

In reviewing these interviews I realized there are two ways that women handle family secrets. First, they hide the truth from everyone, make excuses, and try to get by. The second approach is to face the facts, a result of an inciting incident that causes the woman to be strong enough to start fresh. Still, if these women are able to leave, it doesn't put the problem behind them. Being able to confront the abuse is another story, as Dr. Claire Owen sees it. Keeping a secret of childhood molestation until adulthood is devastating to the woman. "If a young woman or girl is able to get help right away, she will be much better off. If it's a secret, and the family covers it up, it becomes internalized for this woman and comes out in adult maladaptive behavior of some kind. The women can become alcoholic, drug users, find themselves in abusive relationships or will be inappropriately sexually active," Dr. Owen explains.

Personal Velocity: Three Portraits, Rebecca Miller's book and subsequent film, deals with women who have suffered at the hands of those closest to them and have found the courage to leave. In the "Delia" section of the book, a working-class woman and her three children escape her abusive husband after a particularly brutal beating. Although Delia and her children find refuge in a women's shelter, they eventually move to another town and start fresh. Slowly she comes back to life and reclaims herself, becoming the sexual woman she was before she met her husband.

The Burning Bed, the 1984 television film starring Farrah Fawcett, is about a disappearing act. The film is based on the true story of Francine Hughes, a battered wife from the Midwest who was prosecuted in 1977 for setting the bed on fire, with her husband still in it, after she had been attacked one too many times. Hughes's fight to the finish occurred because no authorities provided assistance despite her repeated requests. Thus, the problem is twofold: (1) women are initially quiet about being abused by a family member, spouse, or boyfriend, and (2) once the cry for help is uttered, they are not believed and not taken seriously, putting them in great danger.

Domestic abuse envelopes women in shame, guilt, and denial.

In defining the three ingredients that enter into a female lie, all three work against a woman seeking help for domestic abuse. Clearly in these interviews we see a woman who feels shame, as if somehow it's her fault, *she didn't measure up.* Guilt is also an emotion used here, because the woman feels *she did the wrong thing,* and denial, the third piece of it, is about how *powerless* these women feel about their lives and the way they are treated. In the interviews that follow, we see how three women were able to come to terms with their experiences.

Audrey, thirty-four, pregnant for a second time, works in the catering business. While not exactly denying what happened to her, she's chosen to diminish how it affects her present and future.

> My husband knows very little about my upbringing and what happened with my stepfather. I don't see why I need to tell him everything. I don't want to end up like my mother, divorced, then married to a man like that. I don't want my daughter to have such a terrible life as I had. Yes, we should have gotten help when it was going on, when I was a teenager, it kept us from getting better because we didn't. But when I married my husband, I swore it'd be better, and I found a good man. I'm very grateful to him. So I say nothing and move on . . .

For Myrna, forty-five, it was a repeat performance after she divorced her physically abusive husband and married a man who had the same traits.

> I covered up everything in my first marriage, then I went into therapy and I got out. I started dating, I was only thirty-five, and I was in a hurry to get it right. So even with a therapist and my friends warning me, I ended up marrying the same kind of guy. And I pretended that it was just fine, like I did in my first marriage. I acted like it was a good relationship when I was covering up bruises with heavy makeup. I lied because I felt rotten about myself and my mistakes, two big mistakes. I wouldn't tell anyone who I meet now what happened, that I'm twice divorced and twice an abused wife, but it's a different kind of secret now.

Brianna, thirty-nine, a nurse practitioner who has moved to another part of the country, feels she's ready to improve her life.

> I've read a lot of books and I've gone to support groups. I've tried to educate myself and it's helping. I understand what went on in our family and why it had to be so hush-hush. My children and my husband aren't a part of this. What I'll never get over is how my family appeared in our small town compared to what went on behind closed doors. But now I know we weren't freaks, we were part of something terrible that happens to women and girls, and not everyone has the guts to talk about it.

When Teri Hatcher's story of sexual abuse at the hands of her uncle, Richard Hayes Stone, ran as the lead article in *Vanity Fair* in April 2006, it was both shocking and a relief to thousands of women who have suffered the same. Hatcher told journalist Leslie

Bennetts that this started when she was five years old until she was eight or nine, when her mother intervened, "she removed me from the situation, but she never asked me about it," says Hatcher. Then close to more than thirty years later, Hatcher learned that her uncle had been charged with molesting a young girl, Sarah Van Cleemput. The story hit the news when Van Cleemput, in 2002, at the age of fourteen, committed suicide, leaving a note behind that read, "You're probably thinking a normal teenager doesn't do this, well ask Dick." Hatcher told Bennetts, "I don't want to pretend it never happened anymore. Now everyone is going to know." At this point Hatcher came forward to testify against Stone.

A mother can save or sabotage her daughter's secret.

If a mother suspects that something is awry, or she knows but refuses to act on the secret, there is the perpetrating of a lie that harms her daughter. Frequently a mother makes the decision not to seek help because she fears it will break up the family. Or she fears it will cause a rift between herself and her husband, and she can't afford this financially or emotionally. Then she, too, carries the weight of the secret and lies. Tess, forty-seven, describes her mother's alignment with her molester.

> My mom made up lies about me so my dad would hate me. I got used to it. She said so many lies about me that I believed it. She told him I was sleeping around and he thought I was a dirty little whore and he didn't want to touch me. The truth was my mom's nephew was hurting me physically— violently. . . . My mom told these lies to cover up for my cousin. So I never felt safe . . . even now, now that my dad's learned that my mom was lying, I'll never feel safe.

As Annie, thirty-five, recalls it, her sister's anxiety throughout her life is the result of their father's molestation of both his daughters. Although her sister sought solace with Annie, Annie had her own problems with their father and her own secret to protect.

> When my father turned from me to my younger sister, I knew it was time to take charge. I told the school nurse, who believed me but didn't want the responsibility. She took this to the social worker, who was called in on special occasions. The social worker also seemed reluctant to get help, but finally she filed some complaints. Then my parents lied and we ended up lying, too, sort of, not really telling anyone what my father had done, what my mother had let happen. No one got help, everyone had the same lie. I got through better than my sister; I got out of town and took her with me as soon as I could. But this has always affected her. I think I did better because I'm the one who tried to do something about it.

The most distressing aspect of women's secrets and lies about domestic abuse is how ruined the women feel, outcasts at the hands of the perpetrators. Some of the women with whom I spoke had found a way to begin a new life, but not without serious repercussions and emotional destruction. Our patriarchal culture *causes* women to lie about this abuse, discouraging them from coming forward. Tess tells us, "My mom told these lies to cover up for my cousin . . ."; Audrey recalls, "Yes, we should have gotten help . . . it kept us from getting better because we didn't . . ."; and Brianna, today, understands that "We weren't freaks, we were part of something terrible that happens to women and girls. . . ."

Despite the fact that some women are able to improve their lives, their survival lies are fundamentally unhealthy, and any heightened awareness or social vigilance paid to the situation hasn't had enough impact. Although Julia Roberts's character,

Laura Burney, in the 1991 film *Sleeping with the Enemy*, brought domestic violence to the foreground, its dramatic content places it in a thriller genre more than as a cautionary tale. Still, when Roberts's character desperately stages her own death in order to escape her brutally abusive and violent husband, it brings home how a woman who has it all—a husband, stunning beach house, looks, and lifestyle—can be living a lie.

HIDING ILLNESS/UNSETTLING COVER-UPS

When it comes to illness, mental and physical, the secrets and scars can go as deep as it does for women who have been sexually abused. In Pat Conroy's disconcerting novel *The Prince of Tides,* a family shares a terrible secret of rape, molestation, and murder. Two brothers, a sister, and mother are bound by the pain, suffering, and secrecy surrounding a violent act and aftermath. The family covenant would have stood the test of time, except that Savannah, the sister, traumatized by the event and mentally unstable, attempts suicide many years later. The therapist who treats Savannah insists that this survival lie, a lie of omission, has to be confronted in order for the healing process to begin.

A brother's struggle with schizophrenia becomes the burden of two adult sisters in the television series *Once and Again* (1999–2002). In this show about romance and family life after divorce, another theme is how two sisters, played by Sela Ward and Marin Hinkle, deal with their family secret—their brother's mental illness. What kind of excuses they made throughout their childhood, how their parents covered up the problem, makes it all the harder for them to be responsible to their brother as adult siblings.

Another kind of story altogether shows us the value of telling all and removing the invisible cloud that hangs over a family in

The Mermaid's Chair by Sue Monk Kidd. Although both Jessie Sullivan and her mother, Nelle, lead full lives thirty years after the death of Jessie's father/Nelle's husband, each woman keeps her own secret about his death. When Jessie is summoned to Egret Island, where she grew up, to aid Nelle who has recently taken to self-mutilation, their emotions surface. At last Nelle confesses to her daughter that her husband, Jessie's father, had an incurable illness and died of an assisted suicide, not a boating accident. Nelle's self-inflictions are a result of her own remorse for having aided her husband in this decision. Jessie, since childhood, had believed that the accident was her fault and this delayed truth sets both women free.

The above dramas show us the impact of a survival lie for a family and how much we try to look away, hoping these tarnished truths will disappear rather than reemerge. The experiences women described while enmeshed in a family member's mental illness or checkered past has a resonance that women say affects them deeply.

The stigma of mental illness is a huge burden for female family members.

In Becca's case; it is her own mental illness that has been at the center of the family's lie. At thirty-four, a theater producer from Texas, Rebecca believes that she's been ostracized her entire life. Yet she feels separated from the family secret at the same time that she feels she has caused the secrecy. She views herself as having clouded her siblings' and her parents' lives.

When you have a mental illness, people show no sympathy. My parents were embarrassed by my behavior and had trouble with social acceptance themselves. My older twin sisters were living the right life, and the family rejected me. They were so mortified by me . . . they made my problem worse . . . no one acknowledged my mental state—we all hid it. I have a bipolar disorder, and it's screwed up my life. I have a job now, and I'm doing better, but for a long time, I never could have relationships with anyone. I did weird things and sometimes I went crazy, manic, but when someone is mentally ill, there's no real support, there's just shame and everyone seems very tired. I know I wasn't very rational and I had problems with friendships.

My sisters were prettier and then I had this problem, so they were always embarrassed. To make it worse, I wouldn't sign myself into an institution sometimes, and that was really upsetting for my sisters and parents. This went on for a long time. My family was so unsupportive that they're toxic to me. Their shame of me makes me ashamed . . . and I needed to escape them . . . to find my own way, even with my problems.

Becca is the perpetrator in her family's eyes, the reason they all have a secret to hide and a lie to tell. Laine, at fifty-two, a teacher, is the sister who watched her younger sister grapple with mental illness and made the decision not to reveal her sister's condition.

When we were in our twenties, we all wanted her to go away so that our lives would be normal. We would go through these periods when we thought we could do something, my brothers and I, and other times when we just wanted her to live somewhere else. And our little sister did move away, into a community where she could be cared for. But then I had this feeling we were shunning her and we sure weren't willing to say much to our friends or neighbors about her, not her condition and nothing about her at all if possible—unless

someone asks me how many siblings I have. I keep it quiet
and don't go to see her very much. I know through her caregivers that she seems happy enough and the finances are
taken care of, but I know I don't do enough. We don't visit her
and we don't show her the love she deserves. I tell myself that
when I do visit her, she hardly knows it's me sometimes.

*The shame surrounding a woman's mental illness is profound—
all the more reason for secrets and lies.*

The National Mental Health Association tells us that in a
given year, fewer than 8 million people seek treatment for mental
illness, although 54 million Americans experience some kind of
mental disorder. Of these illnesses, depression and anxiety are
the most common, affecting 19 million Americans annually. The
National Institute of Mental Health states that women are twice
as likely as men to develop depression and that depression is a
leading cause of disability in women. Yet in our culture, mental
illness is frowned upon, stigmatized by our society. Women are
supposed to be happy, they're *supposed* to be content. Why not lie
about being depressed, as one interviewee explained it, because
there's a low tolerance for the truth.

Gloria Steinem's essay "Ruth's Song (Because She Could Not
Sing It)" depicts her mother's mental illness during the 1940s.
Steinem describes how her mother's family was unable to accept
the condition of this once "spirited, adventurous young woman
who struggled out of a working-class family and into college." After her mother's nervous breakdown, "she was never again completely without the spells of depression, anxiety, and visions into
some other world . . ." writes Steinem. What is so disturbing,
Steinem points out, is that a woman with a mental illness was

essentially dismissed and not treated properly. Not only was this a family secret, with an obvious shame factor, but there was also a societal disregard for a woman whose "functioning was not that necessary to the world."

If we fast-forward to July 2005, we find Jane Pauley, a television anchor on *The Today Show* during the 1980s, divulging that she'd been struggling with bipolar disorder. In fact, she was doing so poorly in 2001 that, according to her book, *Skywriting: A Life Out of the Blue*, she was in a psychiatric hospital for three weeks. In an interview with Jennifer Barrett for Newsweek.com, Pauley explained why she disclosed her secret, "To hide the most significant fact of my current life . . . and to pretend otherwise would have been unreal." However, she also admits that "if the price was so high that I didn't have a career anymore, I was fifty-something then, I could probably live with that." This latter quote reinforces ageism as another lie and secret when it comes to women, underscoring how Pauley came forward when she had little at stake in doing so. She also points out how "we have all been so quiet about it [mental illness]," that "we don't know the extent of common suffering."

So while Gloria Steinem saw the horror magnified for her mother because she was a woman, and Jane Pauley was able to reach out to comfort others by revealing her own illness, women have been stigmatized for years for their behavior, even called "crazy" and "not all there." The fact that girls and women suffer at a higher percent when it comes to mental illness combined with how they are expected to be "healthy," only makes the condition worse, especially since the National Institutes of Health reported in 2000 that teenage girls are more likely to develop depression than teenage boys, and that major depression is the "leading cause of disease burden among females five and older worldwide."

According to Deda, thirty-one, her depression was treated as a burden by her parents and grandparents. Oddly enough, Deda used a compassionate lie while in the midst of her own health problems in order to assuage the pressure of the family.

> I think my parents just wanted me to be normal, to cut them some slack. They vacillated between getting me into treatment and feeling like they'd done all they could. They acted as if I was resistant on purpose. So I had this very real depression and then I had these concerns that my parents and my brother couldn't handle me. I had to be okay—I wasn't allowed to have any kind of problem. So we all pretended it wasn't there and I would be left alone with these demons.

Mental health as a family secret affects women of all ages, including elderly women. On September 1, 2006, an unsettling report from Reuters stated that a prominent society family, the Astors, were involved in an elder-care scandal. Reuters reported that a judge had ordered "immediate improvements" in the care of 104-year-old Brooke Astor, a famous socialite and philanthropist. The order arose out of a complaint filed by Philip Marshall, Mrs. Astor's grandson, alleging that his father (Mrs. Astor's only son), Anthony Marshall, had caused Mrs. Astor, who is bedridden, to live in "squalid, abusive conditions." As Reuters described it, the lawsuit contended that Mrs. Astor had been "forced to live in tatters after a life of luxury" and that there had been ongoing financial mismanagement of her assets. In one example cited in the press, Anthony Marshall had apparently arranged for the sale of one of his mother's favorite paintings, a Childe Hassam, in 2001, for which she received ten million dollars while he pocketed a fee of two million dollars.

Anthony Marshall denied the allegations, and a State

Supreme Court judge ultimately found the charge of "intentional elder abuse" was not substantiated, according to Serge Kovaleski and William Rashbaum in their December 6, 2006, *New York Times* article, "Astor Son Claims Vindication Over Words in Judge's Rulling." But, in a settlement of the dispute, Anthony Marshall relinquished the right to make health-care and financial decisions for his mother.

Some mid-age women confide that they've entertained the notion of using their afflicted parents' money for their own needs, and apparently this way of thinking is on the rise. An article that ran in *The Wall Street Journal* on August 30, 2006, entitled "Intimate Betrayal: When the Elderly Are Robbed by Their Family Members," by Jeff Opdyke, informs us that "financial swindles are one of the fastest growing forms of elder abuse." The National Center on Elder Abuse reports that five million elderly people are affected on a yearly basis.

Lauren, fifty-four, explains that it was tempting to take money from her father, who was afflicted with Alzheimer's. Yet it was her father's fall from grace in the eyes of the family and the community that made them keep his illness a secret.

> In the town where I grew up, it wasn't about money but about pride and being respected. Once my father had Alzheimer's, we felt we had to hide it. It would have been better if he'd just died, that's how demoralizing it was for us. He had been such a presence; it was horrible for all of us. We basically hid him and then moved him to another part of the country. We also fiddled with his finances, because it was so easy and hard to resist. But it wasn't in any way a problem for him financially, it was his poor health and how he was so unlike himself that was so awful. No money could help with that. I feel like we could have done better, but on the other hand, we had to do something.

While Lauren seems to be both defensive and remorseful over hiding her failing father, many women say that how the family is perceived and any loss of prestige is worth a family lie. Certainly Beth, forty-two, an office manager in northern Vermont, suffered greatly for her husband's health problems. She anticipated that his illness and death would affect her and her sons socially and emotionally.

I kept my husband's disease a secret as long as I could, because he wanted it that way. He was a drug user and he was so careful that until he became really ill, no one knew. Once he started to become really sick and it was a presence in our lives, we told our younger sons. But my oldest son knew all along and he resents that he had to live with the secret while the younger boys didn't. And my youngest son tells me he resents that he didn't know. My husband is dead but now my boys and I are angry—angry that we had to carry around the secret of how he died. Plus we have to live the rest of our lives with people knowing, those family friends and neighbors who knew toward the end, they think about it when I'm with them, I'm sure of it.

People don't forget what goes on with a family and we didn't move out of town, so four years later, it's there, hanging over us. It's like you're marked for your bad luck and there's nothing to say to change it. I wanted to tell new friends the truth but I know now that it isn't worth it. Men don't like to hear it and women aren't sympathetic. I've learned to just say nothing and one of my sons tells a complete fib about how his father died.

Robin, forty-eight, an accountant who lives in North Carolina, has an older brother who has been ill her entire life.

I remember feeling ashamed of my brother from the time I was eight or nine. He is nine years older than I am, and in those days people didn't have any information. My parents looked at him as disappointing, as if he never measured up. If they'd known then what they learned later, I believe they would have been more generous and kind to him. Since he was a pariah in our family, my parents sent him away, out of sight. It was a temporary relief and always hanging over us that he would return, and be an embarrassment. My parents made it so that my brother was like a stranger to me and I had no contact with him growing up and I didn't really know him.

Today, I'm the caretaker. It's been left to me. His life has been a long disaster while I've raised three children. I'm married and I have a solid base. But my family gave up on him and made him into the shadowy pathetic person he is. So I carry this around with me and now is my chance to redeem him—and myself. I finally tell people about how many health problems he has and how he's now institutionalized. I can't make up for all the years when my parents were alive that I distanced myself, but at least from today onward I can be there for him and I can speak about it—it's no longer some big lie. What I used to say if people asked was that I had a brother who was living overseas and divorced. Now I tell what happened, and it's much better.

While Lauren has endured shame, using a beneficial and a survival lie to get by, Robin has faced her shame and stopped the falsehoods. Misty, who we met in Chapter 1, once troubled by her physical illness and her mother's designated lie about her condition, has made the decision to take care of herself and dispel the family lore.

In my thirties I overheard my mom and the doctor saying
that I'd never be married and that I was a problem. They
made me feel this way; their view of me became my burden.
And I never did get married, I believed their lies. Either it was
the illness or the way I was raised to not tell a soul that
made me think I couldn't have married and had a family.
Only now, in the last five years, in my mid-fifties, have I been
able to let this go. I'm doing some healing energy and facing
how I had to live my life until now. I know how much this secret hurt me and made things a bigger deal because it set
me apart.

If women weren't compelled to have flawless family members,
or be flawless themselves, perhaps the shame and necessity of
family lies wouldn't be so prevalent. Because women feel disgraced and responsible as mothers, daughters, sisters, bystanders,
or victims, *not* lying is almost out of the question. Yet the com-
promises made by lying or by attempting to distance ourselves
from a family matter plays into our psyche. For Beth, Laine, and
Rebecca, each wearing a different hat as principals in the family
drama, the compromising, cryptic route has been a temporary solution. The catharsis that Robin finds in facing her brother's problems and caring for him comes as a huge relief, and she tells us
she "finally has nothing to hide."

ADOPTION AND PATERNITY LIES

In *The Secret Life of Families,* Imber-Black notes that when adoptions took place as recently as twenty-five years ago, both the
adoptive mother and the biological mother were taught to guard
the secret. Court records were sealed and there was little re-

course to find one's birth mother. The third party in the adoption secret and accompanying lie, the adopted child, was told she was special, but carried the weight of the secret with her, without any information available to her. "Adoption of an infant began with secrecy and was expected to remain a secret," writes Imber-Black, who explains that this secrecy was intended to protect children from being stigmatized as illegitimate.

Ann Fessler's book, *The Girls Who Went Away: The Hidden History of Women Who Surrendered Children for Adoption in the Decades Before Roe v. Wade,* consists of interviews with young mothers who gave up their babies in the 1950s and 1960s, mostly because a pregnant single woman had no place in society in those days, and was ostracized. In postwar America, until 1973 when *Roe v. Wade* made abortion a viable choice for women, 1.5 million babies were given up for adoption. Parents went to great lengths to hide their daughters' shame, mortified to have daughters in trouble. From 1987 to 2001, despite today's option of single motherhood and high-tech fertility treatments, adoptions have remained at a steady level, according to the National Adoption Foundation Clearing House, hovering at approximately 120,000 adoptions per year.

Women involved with adoption vehemently guard the secret.

For Allie, forty-five, living in the Midwest where she works for a corporation, adopting her son fifteen years ago was a long process after years of infertility.

I was in the corporate world where women would leave after they had a kid, half the time at least. I looked like someone who had nothing but work in her life. I wanted as few people as possible to know what was really going on. It's taken me years to be able to talk about how my son is adopted. I talk about it now because he can be so difficult. I sort of told people my secret, that he wasn't my biological child, when there were problems. But my son wants to keep his adoption a secret; he doesn't want his friends to know. So I have to respect that, too. Our life is filled with secrets—my husband and I wonder what our son's genetic background is, but say nothing to him about our concerns; our son wants his friends to think he's our biological child. I think it's only going to get harder to keep up the charade as he gets older.

Nadine, forty, a designer, was adopted as an infant and began to actively search for her birth mother a year ago.

When I was adopted the records were sealed, and later, when I wanted to know more, my adoptive mother made it clear to me that the sealed records were better for her. My older brother is also adopted and he didn't want to find his birth mother, he felt that life was fine as it is. But I'm hoping to learn about my birth mother, and I don't see how anyone can object to this. I always felt like an outsider; even with our mother telling us how special we are, I know I don't fit in. I told friends when I was eighteen that I wanted to find my birth mother and our mother was unhappy. It made her feel like she hadn't done a good job, I guess, and I was also making her look like a liar. I mean, she never ran around offering information that we were adopted and there I was this loudmouthed teenager, ungrateful enough to want to search for my birth mother. I'm still working on it and it's not easy. That's why open adoption today is such a good idea. There would have been so many less phony moments if I could have just cleared this up when I was in high school, when it became so important to me.

It is interesting that the mother and child are troubled with the same family secret, from different perspectives. Both are locked in the lie, particularly when the adoption is closed and the records sealed. Marni, forty-six, married with children, confides:

> I wonder if I look like my real mother. I've always wondered about this, and about my real mother's genetic makeup. It's a great mystery to me and I doubt I'll ever know.

When Kathleen Silber and Phylis Speedlin wrote their book *Dear Birthmother: Thank You for Our Baby,* it seemed as if adoption could be about openness and trust between the birth mother and adoptive mother. Yet the theory was more manageable than the reality—the reality is filled with secrets that begin with the birth mother, who can be ambivalent about giving her child up and not up for disclosing this. She lies about her commitment to the adoptive mother because the deal has been made, and the adoptive mother harbors her worst fears—that the baby won't ultimately be hers.

Adoption secrets have an urgency about them because each family member's take on the necessity of the secret has its own angle. Often a mother chooses to keep it under wraps because she feels, as Nadine describes her mother, threatened by the truth. Meanwhile, the child who knows she is adopted and feels she doesn't fit in, and would like to learn about her adoptive parent as a way to understand herself—at the same time, keeps it quiet. The birth mother may have regrets about giving up her child and yearns to connect, yet is guarded. In the life she establishes for herself after she's given up her child, she lies by omission, reticent to share her past.

Paternity lies are no longer easy for women to tell.

As with adoption lies, paternity lies for women demand lies of omission, lies of necessity. The caution and secrecy play out in several ways. It may be that the father's identity can harm a woman—perhaps she is married to another man, perhaps the father of her child is married and she isn't, perhaps the person is known in her community and it would injure the family should the secret be divulged. These are serious issues that require serious lies. A paternity lie falls into the category of a survival secret and a compassionate lie.

Long before DNA testing with its tell-all consequences, there was *The Scarlet Letter,* Nathaniel Hawthorne's classic novel that many of us read in high school. When the film version came out in 1995 starring Demi Moore as Hester Prynne and Gary Oldman as the Reverend Arthur Dimmesdale, the romantic slice of what becomes a paternity secret is shown to us. Since having an affair in 1666 in the Massachusetts Bay colony was unheard of by Puritans, Hester Prynne pays dearly for her sin, discovered through her pregnancy. It hardly mattered that Hester's husband, an older man, played by Robert Duvall, was presumed dead. Hester was treated harshly by the colonists, but she refused to name the father. She gives birth to her daughter, Pearl, in jail, and lives the life she is sentenced to for her sin. Pearl's father's identity remains a secret until the day Dimmesdale dies. Hester Prynne pays twice for her sin, first through her daughter's birth, as evidence, and then through her silence.

Colleen McCullough's panoramic novel *The Thorn Birds* is another tale of a paternity lie and lifelong secret. Set in 1920s

Australia, the love story of Meggie Cleary and Ralph de Bricassart has an eerie, inescapable quality to it. Although Ralph chooses the priesthood over his love for Meggie, and Meggie marries Luke O'Neill, a brute, Meggie and Ralph do consummate their passion. Not until years later, after Meggie's son Dane has tragically died, does Meggie reveal to Ralph that Dane was their son. The implication was that Ralph was too caught up with the glory of being a priest and seeking a higher position in the church to consider a nonsecular life. Still, Meggie's decision to withhold the truth about Dane caused tremendous suffering and loss.

When DNA proved Stephen Bing, real estate heir, the father of model/actress Elizabeth Hurley's baby, Damian Charles, in June 2002, it was no surprise to Hurley. According to CBS-newsonline, Hurley was "deeply distraught" at Bing's doubts. What is interesting in this case is that Elizabeth Hurley was so open about the father's identity while Bing was reluctant to be named.

Most women with whom I spoke concerning a paternity secret preferred to not disclose who the father is. As Julie, thirty-eight, a designer living in a Midwest suburb, views it, there was little question that she'd keep her son's father's identity from her husband.

> I was already married when I ran into an old boyfriend and we began to see each other. My husband was traveling for work a lot in those days and I knew when I found out that I was pregnant it was a problem. I managed to sleep with my husband as soon as I could, and he never suspected. I know that the old boyfriend knew, or at least thought it was his baby. But I distanced myself from him right away. I lied to him and said I didn't want to see him anymore. It's like the pregnancy shut down the affair and forced me to lie to be safe.
>
> If I hadn't gotten pregnant, who knows, maybe I would have left my husband for this man. But it became so bizarre

and I had no family and no one to guide me, help me. I had to distance myself from the boyfriend, I had to keep this to myself. I was desperate, I couldn't play with fire, I couldn't do it any other way.

Although Julie feels that she acted in despair, a paternity lie can suffice for a woman who will suffer *without* the lie. Charlene, forty-eight, learned her mother's secret quite recently.

Recently, when my father died, my mother told me that he was not my biological father, that another man had been my father. I don't know what possessed my mother to tell me, and I couldn't imagine how she had kept it from him all these years. I was so shocked but I also wanted to meet my real father. I think that upset my mother but it wasn't my lie, it was my mother's lie.

I'm planning to meet my real father, but I have mixed feelings. I feel such gratitude for the man I thought was my father. Mostly it's been confusing and it makes me wonder about my mother. What kind of life has she had, lying to me all these years and to her husband who raised me? I understand that in her day, she couldn't have had a husband if she had told the truth. I see that what she did was in order to protect me and to protect herself. But I don't know how she got through each day.

Charlene's mother's decision resonates with the recent film *Volver*, starring Penélope Cruz. When Cruz's character, Raimunda, discovers that her husband has molested her daughter, she reveals to her daughter that he wasn't her real father. However, Raimunda's secret goes much deeper than that, since it was her own father who molested her, and her daughter is also her sister. And while there can be justification for family lies (we understand why Cruz's character did better lying with such a story than being honest), Charlene points out how difficult it can be, too.

From Dina's experience with sexual abuse when she was a small girl, to Audrey's decision not to tell her husband what transpired with her stepfather, to Laine, who hid her sister's mental illness, there is evidence that women are victims of family secrets. Whatever part a woman plays, it's a delicate balance between the raw truth and the tainted tale, and few family secrets are light of heart. As murky and burdensome as these lies are, women are fluent at telling them, instinctively recognizing the parts that are useful.

SIX

Facing Our Lies: Addictions

Carmen, a twenty-four-year-old bartender from Wisconsin, has wrestled with her mother's drinking problem for years. What is so disquieting is that her mother's ability to function as an alcoholic makes it worse. For women like Carmen, who are drawn into someone else's addiction and denial, there is the layering of the secret. In Carmen's situation, her mother's lie is also her lie, every step she takes at her mother's behest aids her mother's excessive drinking.

> I know what my mother does. She lies to me, in a subtle way. She says she has to work late, and asks me to watch my little sister. She acts like it's noble, but she ends up just drinking . . . she drinks with her coworkers, she drinks and denies it. . . .
>
> I wish she would clean up her act and make it easier for all of us. I wish she would listen to me. I know that whenever I stay with my sister, which I do because she's my little sister, my mother is drinking too much. I think it's too big a problem for me to know what to do about it. We need her to not drink, to not have it as part of our life . . . to stop pretending it's okay when it's not. . . .

What family secrets and addiction lies have in common is that they're both grim secrets in a woman's life. For women whose secrets surround an addiction, these addiction lies can *become* family lies, part of the family lore. Their secrets exist in a world without much advantage. In both categories, the women's experiences often become shameful secrets blended with survival lies. As I listened to women confide their own addictions or those of their children or spouses, it echoed the confessions of abuse and domestic violence.

There were women who spent their weekly paychecks buying lottery tickets or gambling online, women adamantly denying an eating disorder, wives telling their husbands untruths for the sake of their addictions. One woman told me that her addiction to painkillers was the only way to get through the day with her husband and children. Another woman shared her sexual addiction, a problem often attributed exclusively to men. In each of these cases the women disavowed their habits and the wreckage it caused those closest to them.

Women lie and deny the gravity of their addictions.

According to Dr. Ronnie Burak, these addictions are a method of being passive-aggressive. "A woman who spends money or takes pills is often rebelling. She feels that she's highly responsible to her husband, family, or boss, but she feels trapped and miserable. The addictions are an adolescent rebellion, even if she's a grown woman. The terrible part is that she's addicted and hiding it."

The National Center of Addictions and Substance Abuse reports that more than eleven million women collectively abuse alcohol, illicit drugs, and prescribed medications. Their statistics show that 70 percent of women substance abusers who sought treatment had been sexually abused as young girls. Female gamblers comprise more than 40 percent of the gambling population according to gamblersanonymous.org, and while no statistics have been reported for "retail therapy/shopaholicism," it is fast becoming recognized as an issue for women. The lie told for addiction is often a multilayered lie, including denial, shame, guilt, and survival techniques. These secrets require a great effort on the part of the woman to hold it together.

An addiction is a dangerous secret because for women who have an addiction, or have loved ones with an addiction, help is needed: denying the problem only exacerbates the condition.

ASSUAGING PAIN

After hearing about women who had no intention of shaking their addiction and kept it hidden as long as possible, I realized that a lie surrounding an addiction has a pathology all its own. The interviewees in this chapter seem immobilized by the cultural expectations placed upon them: an addiction lie is a bleak secret with a moral taboo. As Dr. Donald Cohen explains it, women often lack self-worth. "These women want to be acknowledged somehow," he remarks, "and to come to terms with their problems." Unfortunately, the cry for help is frequently unheard by those closest to the women, and the pressure to pretend that all is well is tremendous. This brings to mind Sandra Bullock's character in the film *28 Days* who approaches rehab with a snide sense of humor and enormous denial.

For Aurora, thirty-eight, her secrets surrounding her drinking appear as a betterment lie, but more important, it's a serious cry for help.

> I drank to get through my father's mistreatment of me. His mistreatment was my first secret, since we seemed like such a healthy family. The shopping sprees were my second secret and

it numbed me. I lied about him—to myself and to everybody who was around. He wasn't on my side, he favored my older sister. I was so hurt and rejected, I drank wine, mostly, and I shopped crazily—I still do."

Sixty percent of the women with whom I spoke for this chapter confessed to addiction as a means to get through an ordeal in their lives. When Angelina describes her primary secret, that her father treated her unfairly, which falls into the chapter on family secrets, she quickly adds her addiction secret, a form of self-medication for the pain.

How else could I get through the day when I felt so terrible? I used my Visa card, I binged on booze and junk food. But I needed something I couldn't have, that's why I did all this stuff secretly.

This attitude is common with women addicts, and I'm hearing about two styles of behavior from my interviewees:

1. *Act self-righteous while escaping your pain.* For women, a fall from grace in terms of status is an extremely painful experience and often manifests in drinking, taking pills, or gambling to diminish the anguish. Although it's obvious that these women need help, they're often resistant, even insistent that they're well. Yet unlike the women in Chapter 2 who lie about their love life and sexual selves, or those in Chapter 3 who lie about their finances, these women have no agency; their secrets and lies only worsen their situation, and aren't advisable.

2. *Use your addiction as a means of controlling your universe.* When it comes to shopaholics, plastic surgery

junkies, women with eating disorders, the women who suffer are not in control of their lives. Any of these addictions provide a sense of some authority. As several interviewees describe it, binging, starving, or planning a third tummy tuck makes a woman feel in charge of her own destiny.

THE MIND/BODY SECRET: EATING DISORDERS

Many of us remember Karen Carpenter, the talented musician who became famous in the seventies and eighties along with her brother, Richard, as the brother/sister duo The Carpenters. Although she was awarded three Grammys and had ten gold singles and eight gold and five platinum albums, Karen Carpenter suffered from anorexia nervosa, and fought the eating disorder while at the height of her fame. In 1983, having sought help and while in therapy, she died from cardiac arrest triggered by her illness. Her tragic death raised the awareness for physicians and parents about anorexia and bulimia that, until that time, were relatively unknown.

Despite the fact that Karen Carpenter's death was highly publicized and resulted in articles and media attention to this disease, according to a National Institute of Mental Health statistic, 42 percent of first- to third-grade girls want to be thinner, 81 percent of ten-year-olds are worried about being fat, and 91 percent of women on a college campus wanted to diet to control their weight. According to the Renfrew Center Foundation for Eating Disorders, eight million people have eating disorders and seven million of them are women. Although anorexia is sometimes considered a "rich woman's disease," it's actually about control and often stems from family life and parental influence.

Female addicts nullify the hazards of their addiction.

As a female's eating disorder gets out of hand, she will frequently hide the truth about her problem. The common wisdom is that the cause is in part cultural and in part due to media influences. If a mother encourages her daughter to be thinner, this can have an effect, as can a hypercritical brother or father.

Jade, twenty-four, tells us that her mother made her feel fat when she was in grade school, although her mother denies this ever happened. Today Jade lives and works in the South and feels that she is coming to terms with the betterment lies she told for years in the name of an eating disorder.

I would go up and down in weight and my mother loved it when I was thin. When I was heavy, she chided me and said things like how would I get a boyfriend, how could I compete with the other girls? My father had left us and my mom raised us alone. She's very pretty and she was busy dating and working but she still had time to push my older sisters and me. She wanted us to have lots of chances, but she saw that the chances would only come if we looked good. I think she was too extreme about it. I still had a boyfriend, I still got into college and got a job. But I went up and down with my weight and I kept my habits a secret from everyone. Sometimes I didn't even want a boyfriend—I didn't want to be found out.

I knew I had to escape her and the way she always talked about my weight. She acted like it wasn't a problem, like she could just say all these things to me and I'd just go and lose weight. So she lied about how she didn't upset me and I lied about how bad the problem was. Once I faced that this was a bad part of my life and that my mother wasn't right to carry on so, I did better. I found a decent weight for myself and switched jobs. Now I live with a friend in another city, and that helps, too. I don't confide in my mom that I'm okay—it just opens the door to her tirade about weight and looks. So I'm sort of keeping it quiet that I'm fine, just like I keep it quiet when I'm binge eating and vomiting.

In comparison to Jade is Nassa, forty-nine, a mother of two daughters, who watched her younger daughter, sixteen, battle anorexia for the past three years. Although Nassa and her husband have sought counseling for their daughter, Nassa is reluctant to tell her daughter's teachers, family, and friends the facts. To compound matters, Nassa herself has struggled with anorexia her entire adult life and chooses a designated lie for herself and for her daughter.

I really can't face what goes on with my daughter. Sometimes she'll be okay and other days I know by early morning that there will be an episode. I see how her schoolwork has slipped and how she tries to hold on to friends. Other times she's a wreck over an assignment. She's consumed with her weight. I've always been thin and my older daughter is naturally thin. This daughter isn't and I think she feels pushed by us to be thinner. But in truth, if she didn't have an issue, she would be happy, because she's happier when she is thin, when she gets her weight down. This has become a mess and I've spoken with a few close friends, swearing them to secrecy. They really can't do anything but offer support. I don't know if things will get better any time soon, and I don't want her teachers to know because they'll treat her like she has a psychological problem. Mostly I try to help her and still respect her privacy.

I identify with her secret because of my own struggles with

an eating disorder, something I don't acknowledge really, but it's been a part of my life since I was her age. It makes it worse for me, not better. I feel like I'm hiding my story and my daughter's. That's why I say so little, it's too loaded.

A part of the anorexia/bulimia secret can manifest as the mother's denial of her involvement in her daughter's issue. Nassa is unwilling to take responsibility and becomes complicit in the secret and lie by minimizing her daughter's addiction. Based on her own history, Nassa goes as far as to comment that her daughter looks best when she is thin, and therein is the problem. In a society such as ours, where women are valued for being thin and little regard for a woman's body type and natural weight is taken into consideration, mothers are caught up in their own appearances and their daughters' appearances. As Diane Guernsey writes in her April 2006 special report on eating disorders—"The Dark Side of Weight Control," in *Town & Country*—as important as intervention is, the success rates vary, with roughly 40 percent of anorexics recovering fully and 40 percent recovering partially. For bulimia, she reports a 50 percent success rate with intervention.

There are some success stories with these percentages, where women are able to shed the secrecy and come clean with what was once a negative force in their lives. An actress who disclosed her own battle with food disorders, and her triumph in overcoming this demon, is Faye Dunaway. Having had a "driven, dream-deprived mother and distant, alcoholic father," she writes in her memoir, *Looking for Gatsby: My Life*, that she used food "to counter the stress of filmmaking. I've never stopped guarding against a return to that kind of emotional reliance on food. . . ." Fortunately, Dunaway offers us hope, declaring that she is "finally beyond that now, but it was the pendulum I would swing on for years." As Barb, forty, explains her own personal odyssey with an eating disorder, having children and working at a rewarding career has made it less of a focus.

> I know that during college I was obsessed with my weight, and then when I was first married. I cared so much how I appeared to people, what I ate. Slowly, I've gotten over it. Now that I'm on to other things, I'm not into this anymore. I don't have to be sneaking around with food and my weight. It's such a relief.

THE ROLL OF THE DICE: GAMBLING ADDICTIONS

Gambling is usually considered a male behavior, and for this reason we don't hear much about women with gambling addictions. With the advent of online gambling in the 1990s, however, the percentage of women gamblers has increased dramatically. Gamblers anonymous.org reports that women now make up 40 percent of all gambling addicts, whereas in the past, 90 percent of gambling addicts were men. According to Jerry Kennard for http://menshealth .about.com, men gamble to make money but also for the emotional high—entwined with depression and drug and alcohol use. In my research on female gamblers, I found similarities and differences with male gambling patterns. Like women, men gamble in secret, and when found out, it strains family relationships.

The ability to be covert is better honed in women; they described how careful they were not to allow the gambling to interfere with family time or their work. The women believed that this addiction was manageable, even boasting that if the addiction causes money problems through a streak of losses, the women still keep the secret, lying about why they need money. One woman's husband believed that she used their savings for the high cost of after-school activities for their children, while another confided that her husband believed her medication was no longer covered by insurance. In the case of Nicola, thirty-one, a newly married secretary, her persistent purchase of lottery tickets defines her as a gambler.

> This started as a whim with a few friends. I just wanted to win the lottery and saw that someone, somewhere could do it. But then I was even going across the state line to get a few tickets. And while I was there, I thought I might as well get a few extra. After a while it became a part of what I did each week, buy lottery tickets, and the stakes got higher. I lied to my husband once when I needed money to buy these tickets. I told him the refrigerator had broken, we needed extra food money, things like that. He's an in-charge kind of guy and would be angry if he knew. So I made up stories and took some cash from his stash on the dresser a few times. I can't give up the idea that I might win the lottery.

Nicola's story concurs with the conclusion of a study reported through the Ontario Substance Abuse Bureau that most women start gambling as adults. The study also informs us that a majority of the women are in "pink collar" jobs, meaning they are secondary breadwinners without as much access to funds as their partners or husbands have. For these reasons, women are in debt more quickly than their male counterparts, and run out of money. Notwithstanding the hole that a female gambler falls into, few women express guilt (since guilt would signify that they believe they did the wrong thing). Instead, women like Nicola become intent on what their future could be if they gamble until they win. Consider Laurie, fifty-three, a designer who is a recovering drug addict but still finds herself gambling.

> I'm just glad that I gamble instead of drink or snort drugs. I know that sounds like I'm making an excuse, but this doesn't

hurt anyone and I have the money to do it. I don't see why I need treatment, but I knew I needed treatment for drugs. Maybe I'm making up excuses, but I know my husband hasn't quite caught on. He's suspicious but I tell him he's wrong, I'm not doing it. I guess I'm just an addict at heart and this vice seems easier than being strung out or high. When I used drugs, I was more open about the gambling. Now that I'm in recovery, I have to cover up the gambling, so I do. Especially since I go to meetings for the drugs and I can't exactly tell them that I'm doing this little bit of gambling.

Although Laurie was able to overcome her drug habit, the gambling is now her secret. According to the Minnesota state-funded compulsive gambling treatment program's final report, one third of problem gamblers who seek treatment for compulsive gambling also have a chemical dependency. As with any addiction, it isn't only the addict who suffers, but family members and close friends. Laurie is dismissive of her husband's questioning, putting her secret addiction ahead of his caring. For Judith, thirty-nine, her mother's gambling addiction has affected her and her two sisters for years.

Our father left us enough money that we all looked forward to it, but our mother gambled it away. We knew she had a problem, but we are grown women and live thousands of miles from her. How could we control it? Whenever any of us has come to visit her, we've tried to get her to not go to the casinos. It's her whole life, gambling and drinks at the casino. Some women her age play cards for a few dollars, but she is always at the casinos, at the tables. Maybe she's just a lonely woman. . . . I've put all this energy into getting her focused on another life. I've even invited her to live with me. And that would have been horrible, because I've never told anyone that she has this problem. I just say she

has a busy life when my friends and I talk about our mothers. I
talk to my sisters about it, but it doesn't go beyond that. It feels
so dirty to have a mother who is addicted.

Judith's experience has no upside since she and her sisters
stand by while their mother gambles away family money, as if it's a
sport. Judith is powerless to change her mother's behavior, and has
decided to keep it quiet, although she might benefit from a support group herself. In contrast, Nicola and Laurie each view their
gambling addiction as having not interfered with their lives. Since
Laurie has battled a drug addiction in the past and is in recovery,
her denial quotient when it comes to gambling is high. This is how
she distances herself from her guilt and shame. And as I define the
denial quotient in Chapter 1, it's almost as if both Nicola and Laurie feel empowered by the fact that no one has caught on. Although women may be adept at hiding their gambling addictions,
these designated lies are fundamentally unhealthy.

Lisee, forty-four, explained that she decided to find help for
her excessive gambling because she was afraid of getting caught.

I have two boys and I didn't want them to know. For some reason that bothered me more than if my husband found out. I
ended up going to a support group and it was what I needed.
But in the beginning I never worried about lying because no one
knew. At first I thought I'd always rationalize what I did. Then
my thinking changed, I thought I could be discovered. What
would happen then made me stop—how awful I'd feel about
myself. I am really impulsive, so the gambling sort of worked for
me. I'm doing better now, but no one knows I'm in a support
group—I go to meetings during the day, when no one is home.

The good news for Lisee is that she has come to terms with
her problem, ditched her acceptable lie, and sought treatment.

Yet the shame factor contributes to her choice to keep her recovery a secret. As more literature and information on women and gambling addictions become a part of our culture and an awareness is raised, more women will be able to dispel their secrets in order to help other women.

PARTY TIME: SUBSTANCE ABUSE

In the 1994 film *When a Man Loves a Woman,* starring Meg Ryan and Andy Garcia, a marriage and a family are put in jeopardy by a wife's alcoholism. Ryan's character is so lost to her addiction that she can't take care of herself, let alone her children. Garcia plays the long-suffering husband, a codependent to her behavior. But as with many addiction secrets, until Ryan's character commits to sobriety, the husband and children are dragged into the dishonesty, hoping against hope for a miracle. Every time Meg Ryan's character insists that her drinking is not out of hand, the problem gets bigger, the hole she's digging gets deeper. Almost always, as in this case, women need the guise of appearing healthy and functional.

The National Center of Addictions and Substance Abuse reports that 4.5 million women are alcoholics, 3.5 million women misuse prescription drugs, and 3.1 million women use illicit drugs. Furthermore, 70 percent of women substance abusers who seek treatment have been sexually abused as children, while only 12 percent of the male population have this history. The study also found that working women are 89 percent more likely to drink heavily than nonworking women.

The gravity of the problem is confused for women by a world that not only encourages but endorses drinking. How else do we acknowledge a raise, an engagement, the birth of a baby but with a champagne toast? If we remember *The Bachelorette,* on ABC, Trista drank wine (a lighter alcoholic beverage but alcoholic all the same) while her potential suitors drank liquor. In *High School Reunion*, cocktail parties are very popular, and on *Ally McBeal*, each episode closed with the cast at a bar, drinking. It appears to be what women are *supposed* to do.

What begins as a rite of passage for many women in their teen years ends up being a lifelong problem and deep secret. For this topic, women felt burdened by their role of integrating another person's secret into their daily existence. Merry, forty-five, a teacher in the Northwest, has covered up her sister's drinking problem, using a compassionate lie, since they were in high school.

> When I married my husband twelve years ago, I made the decision not to tell him about my sister. She appears perfectly fine and is never drunk. She's just always has alcohol in her system and can't be without it. She works, she functions, but I won't let my kids in the car with her. I make excuses to be the one driving, and since we live nearby, it works out. But I don't trust she won't leave a cigarette somewhere and the house will burn down while my children are visiting her kids. I don't say anything since it will look like I'm stirring up trouble in the family, and I notice that everyone else acts like it's fine, and so we all enable her to drink. She needs help and isn't getting it and I won't even tell my husband the real story. The funny thing is, my brother also drinks and everyone seems to know it. He's excused for it—it's not this big secret. I just go along about my sister, like our mother did about our dad, like I've always done. I resent that this is how it's set up, but I'm not the one who can do anything about it.

Merry raises some important points about women and drinking. The cultural taboo for women contributes to keeping this a secret, while a man is allowed leeway with his drinking. Frequently there is the family's tacit consent of his "excesses." If drinking is hidden for women, drug use is tolerated even less. My interviewees tell me that it's been helpful to know of female celebrities who have struggled with substance abuse. This includes Carrie Fisher, who writes in her autobiographical novel, *Postcards from the Edge,* that she had taken as many as thirty Percodan a day and at twenty-eight overdosed. Tatum O'Neal, who won an Oscar when she was ten years old, wrote in her autobiography, *A Paper Life,* that her mother was emotionally unstable and her father was not dependable, and that she was mentally abused. By the time she was twenty, she was addicted to cocaine. And Jamie Lee Curtis told Amy Wallace in a famously honest article in *More* magazine, September 2002, that she had "quit drinking and ended a lengthy addiction to painkillers that she said began when she was recovering from plastic surgery."

When Melanie Griffith committed herself to rehab in the fall of 2001 for her addiction to painkillers, she let her fans know through her Web site, www.melaniegriffith.com. "Before you hear it anywhere else," Griffith wrote, "I want to be the first to let you know that my doctor has referred me to the Daniel Freeman Hospital in California. I'm in a step-down program for the prescribed medication that I have been taking for a neck injury." The fact that Griffith shared her addiction with her public and didn't hide it is a step in the right direction and comforting to women who struggle with a similar problem.

With these unveiled secrets of female movie stars, we see the nature/nurture influences in substance abuse. While much of developing this addiction can be traced to how a woman was raised, genetics are a part of the outcome as well. *The Archives of General Psychiatry* report that if one parent is an alcoholic, it increases the likelihood for the offspring. The "environmental risk" of not growing up in an alcoholic family decreases a woman's chance of becoming an alcoholic, even if she is genetically predisposed to alcoholism. There are women who have been able to resist their genetic predisposition, and their environment. For example, Casey, twenty-three, recalls how her mother's using affected her entire childhood.

> My mom has been drinking and using drugs since before I was born. She's using now but she's been in and out of rehab. My sisters, my dad, and I, we never told anyone what was really going on. We made up excuses all the time. We acted like she was sick or like she was out of town, visiting someone. It was easier than telling the truth. I think my mom used because my father is so controlling, it's hard to get along with him. Even though she's been in rehab, she pretends she never had an addiction.
>
> When I was thirteen I figured out what was wrong with my mom, though no one said anything. It was like I was being lied to by everyone, especially my mom. At thirteen you think that using drugs is funny and cool. My mom would be hallucinating and I'd laugh. I also knew, even then, that she was shirking her responsibilities and that I'd become the responsible one. That was ten years ago and I was ashamed, now I can tell the truth about what happened, although I don't really. And I'm not a user. I've escaped.

Casey's story is sad and filled with misfortune—she was submerged in her mother's designated lie and her own survival lie. That she has the ability to overcome what is inevitable for some women is impressive. Similarly, Lexie, twenty-five, a young mother, was able to avoid her mother's drinking and drug problem and has no issues with using, regardless of her childhood experience.

> It's been a burden my whole life. Everyone was in on this secret, this secret about our mother. I married young to get away from the family, and I'm lucky that I've improved my life. I have one sister who I'm close with and she had anxiety issues and a hard time because of our mom. When I started dating,

it was hard for her. She's doing better now but she can't get away like I did; she's stuck. She's always been so afraid because of our mother—I took care of both my mom and this sister. I love my mom but she's missed out on life, and I've watched her do it.

The hardest thing for me was when I was having my first baby and she couldn't come for the birth. My friends were all with their mothers when they had babies and she couldn't be there. I knew not to have her—I couldn't take care of her and the baby. I said she had to work, I made up some excuse, as usual.

When it comes to women substance abusers, the lies told for the sake of one's respectability—as a mother, wife, working woman—carry weight. As Dale, forty-eight, a dress designer living in rural Georgia, explains it, her present husband and his ex-wife waded through their substance abuse almost like a form of parallel play.

My husband ended up joining AA and is doing well with the drinking, but he's not able to work and has no friends. So here I am with a man who has no friends and no work. And I'm supposed to act like it's normal—I can't say a word. I feel like I inherited his whole secret past. For years he'd miss work and it was because he used and drank. His wife at the time was also into drinking and drugs, but she dealt with it differently. She'd manage to get their kids to school and to make dinner. She would sort of binge drink a few times a week, pass out, and come back to being a mother and to getting by. Not that she didn't have a problem. My husband would always be drinking, she would be planning her next time, but could sort of hold it together a few days a week. She was the one who could cover up better out of the two of them and she didn't always drink too much at once. Part of the lie is that she drank socially and she had a good front, she was raising children, running a household. She had a reason to get up every day and perform. So it was her secret, she was an addict. They had to hide the reality, it was shameful, it wasn't acceptable.

This was ten years ago, and since I've been on the scene, the kids have grown up and one of the girls has a problem with drinking. I've been married to their father for four years and no one mentions the mother's problem, all I hear is that she has a new job. She needs help and it's not going to happen. I don't say much about this, but it's worrisome to me. Her problem sure affects us through the kids. I always have the feeling there's an elephant in the room.

Women are remarkably clever at secrets when it comes to substance abuse.

How curious that from every angle, when it comes to substance abuse, women tell a lie. Dale's life is polluted by the secrecy of her husband's addiction, his ex-wife's ghost, and herself as the nonuser in the triangle. Casey and Lexie are not falling prey to what might have been their destiny with their mothers' histories. But they lie about their pasts in their brave new lives. Lexie admits her decision not to have her mother visit when her child was born, "I knew not to have her—I couldn't take care of her and the baby. I said she had to work, I made up some excuse, as usual." And Merry tells us that little is said about her sister who drinks.

As we've seen repeatedly in this chapter, whether a woman has an addiction or is close to someone who does, how they are perceived by others only enhances the need for the lie. Although women seek counseling and treatment, their take on recovery is separate from how men with this serious problem react. Research conducted at the Kaiser Pemanente Medical Care Program in Oakland, California, monitored men and women in treatment for substance abuse. Interestingly, their findings showed that women who were married were more committed to treatment and men were more motivated when their bosses insisted on it. Examples of two-layered female lies are noted below; these two women have a need to keep their recovery to themselves, just as their addiction was a secret.

Lea, thirty-three, a professional actor living in Virginia, explains:

I've been a member of AA since I was very young. I keep it a secret. I don't want people to know and I've gotten good at not telling. In college it was heresy not to drink with friends, but it's something I've always covered up. I cared what people thought in those days, but still, I told no one that I'd had a big problem. No one. My friends say, why don't you drink, and they pressure me, but I won't drink and I won't say what I've been through. I've gone to training seminars where I'm the only one not drinking. I wouldn't dare explain to anyone at work what my past is.

For women, more than men, there is tremendous demand to blend in and conform. Lea is invested in her progress but keenly aware of the daily challenges of not being part of the crowd.

Going to the meetings keeps it together for me. And they're anonymous for a reason, there is so much attached to a drinking addiction and to not being able to drink because you had an addiction. It's like you can't win, if you don't drink you're thought of in a certain way, and if you've had a problem and people learn about it, you're thought of another way. And if you don't drink, you're a social outcast. You have to be very strong.

I know the group helps me and the longer I'm in the program, the more I understand how it works. It's a part of my life and I choose not to share it unless the person will understand. I haven't found many people who can really identify with what I've gone through. So I keep making excuses to go to meetings, and I've stopped talking about what happened to me before, how I was so far gone or what I do now. Even my siblings don't know, they think I'm a teetotaler and I leave it at that. It would be nice to share with someone outside of the meetings, but I can't. This is my main secret and it rules my life.

Similarly, Carolyn, thirty, explains her history of rehab as a teenager and her need to keep this secondary secret. She has told no one about her recovery, and despite her personal victory, she is guarded.

I just don't want anyone to know what I went through, and I'm okay now, so what's the point. I never say a word. I sort of act like it never happened. I know guys who talk about what happened to them with drinking or drugs, and today they have big jobs, real lives. . . . I also pulled it together, but I don't want anyone to know, period. My addiction required a huge cover-up and so does not using, my not being a part of that.

FASHIONISTAS INTO SHOPAHOLICS

Obviously our culture encourages women to be materialistic, and the sense of deprivation if one doesn't have certain things is acute. Everywhere we look, be it clothing, accessories, or appliances, we feel we are valued if we are wearing a Ralph Lauren jacket, carrying a Prada bag, or cooking on a Viking stove. Women are taught that owning a certain brand will enhance them, make life better, buy happiness. Few women consider shopping an indulgence; rather, they see it as a recreation. When it comes to women who shop, it becomes an addiction because they feel in command; the shopping temporarily alleviates depression and offers a quick escape. A relatively new form of addiction, female shopaholism might seem nothing more than major shopping sprees, but these women suffer, as do all addicts, from the downside of addiction.

Women tell me they keep it very quiet, a secret protected for the sake of relationships, debt, and the judgments of others. Young women with whom I spoke confided that they'd felt pressured by what is expected of them since they were in high school. Angelina, twenty-five, has shopped frantically for the high since eighth grade.

> Partly my mom was a shopper and partly my friends were all shoppers and partly I loved it, loved the excitement, loved the way I could forget everything but what sweater to choose, when to wear it. I remember when I was waiting to be accepted at colleges, I shopped all the time. And lied to my father about how much I got. My mom told me that was fine, I needed to do it that way.

Angelina latched on to the beneficial lie for her shopping sprees at an early age, as a vehicle for warding off stress. Adult women say the tensions of marriage, childrearing, work, and financial strains are alleviated by shopping as well, making shopaholism a crutch for women of all ages. Consider Justine, forty-one, and her rationale for her addiction:

> I do this because it's an immediate gratification. I don't drink, I don't get high, but shopping makes me feel like I'm in charge. Buying what I like, without any boss or mother or husband telling me what I'm supposed to do is heavenly.

Shopping holds a magic for women, it's a way to control our lives.

A mother of three boys, Gretchen, thirty-two, has been a serious shopper since grade school. Working in the fashion industry seemed a solution to her preoccupation with clothing, but she has found it does little to sate her addiction.

I know I'm a shopping addict because I can't go past a store without walking in. I could shop in CVS or Wal-Mart and run up a bill. It's the thrill of purchasing that gets me going, the excitement of having something new. I see my shopping as an expensive habit. It's not like a drug addiction, but it's a big thing and I tell no one. I mean, I lie to my husband all the time, I'll say I bought less than I did or that I got it on sale. I'll say how I needed it. Sometimes I give things away that still have the price tags on them because it's not exciting or sexy once I bring it home. If I really like what I've bought, it lasts a little longer, the high. But I'm on to the next purchase right away.

Claire, fifty, divorced, works part-time for a corporation located in San Francisco. She doesn't view the situation as a problem because it hasn't ruined her life.

I shop for necessities, but my idea of necessities is extremely different from other people's. I feel like I don't have enough money to pay and always I feel guilty. Of course I still shop, and shop at a level I'm entitled to. I have all these rules, like you can shop semiannually and then fill in between, or you can justify certain purchases and not others. My problem is more about having no control over what I buy and how much I spend. I've made money and I've always spent it on material goods. Maybe it's a guilty pleasure, maybe it's just a pleasure. But lately, since I've been feeling blue and alone, I've managed to shop every day. Every day I buy something new. I don't even tell my daughter anymore. She calls me a shopaholic. So when she asks if I've been shopping, I say no.

After Andrea, thirty-nine, gave birth to her daughter, she became a constant shopper. Having taken maternity leave, she found herself wandering into stores with her baby in a stroller, unable to stop.

I think I was depressed after this baby, and I wasn't quite that way the first time. I felt like I didn't fit into the work world anymore and I didn't fit into life at home, watching a baby all day, either. I would walk the streets in town, looking for sweaters and scarves, gloves, anything I could find. I had always loved shopping but hadn't had the time in years. I could see my savings dwindling and still there was this push to do it. I'd wake up and wonder what stores I'd go to that day. It made being with my baby better, and I bought her stuff, too. I would tell my mother I couldn't meet her for lunch because I knew she'd be unhappy with what I did. I feel too guilty, even if I understand why I do it. If I'd put the same energy into food shopping or fixing up our place, she'd be happy. But sweater shopping, I don't think so. I had work to do from the office, too, e-mails, faxes, and I began to neglect that. My only high was buying something to get me through my day.

Used as a numbing agent, shopaholism resonates with other female addictions, but the lies and justifications are a bit different. The denial quotient seems to be at a lower level than with substance abusers, and the guilt is more prevalent. Shopping addictions are rationalized more easily by women who have been known to shop and have now crossed the line, such as Andrea. The stereotypical woman likes to shop, it's a pastime, and not something men do with quite the same zest, and appears a benign female addiction, one worth making excuses for.

Toni, thirty-seven, mother of one small child, remarks:

It beats taking antidepressants. I'd take it any day over what some of my friends do. It's not dishonest, it's an escape. And women need something like this in their lives. It isn't anything I can't confess to, I suppose.

This cycle of material longing, acquisition, and conquest is worth lying for according to Mindy, thirty-five, who is single and works for a corporation.

I feel so good when I shop. I will tell my aunt that I want a purse for my birthday and my mother that I want a purse as well. When they say something like, why do you need two new bags this season, I say I need to look good for work and that I have a lot of business meetings. I'm sure they think I'm spoiled, but how did I get this way if not from shopping with my mom when I was in grade school? So by the time I was in junior high, I knew that shopping made me feel better. Now I do it because I love it and there are so many things to buy— shoes, purses, skirts, sweaters, coats. . . . I can't stop, and I don't want to stop. I have borrowed money and I've manipulated siblings and family members to shop. I do it when I fight with my boyfriend, if I am out and about, if I'm celebrating something, if I'm depressed . . . for any reason . . . I shop.

For female shopaholics, the concentration required to shop, and the thrill of the purchase removes them from their daily lives and has a calming effect. Mindy tells us she shops after arguing with boyfriend, and that her introduction to retail therapy was through her mother. It's clear that shopping provides equilibrium and a quick fix for Andrea, Toni, and Gretchen, who have have signed on for the designated lie. Claire, who defends her acceptable lie, chooses not to be introspective; even her lies to her daughter have little effect. Rather, she shops because this is what she does and can do.

Shoplifting is the dark side of female shopping addictions.

In completing this section, I want to mention another addiction that is affiliated with shopping in our minds, although it has a dishonest base of another order. That is shoplifting, which is an addiction that is rarely discussed openly and is considered highly inappropriate behavior for women. Someone might refer to a friend as a "shopaholic," and there would be a level of forgiveness, of familiarity. If a woman is recognized as a "shoplifter," the social taboo is very real. Unfortunately for Winona Ryder, her 2001 episode of shoplifting at a Saks Fifth Avenue in southern California was widely publicized, as was her trial. According to Nick Madigan's article on December 7, 2002, in *The New York Times*, "Actress Sentenced to Probation for Shoplifting," Ryder was sentenced to three years' probation, 480 hours of community service, fined $3,700, and ordered to pay $6,355 in restitution to the store.

Samara, thirty-seven, mother of two, confides that her shoplifting has been a secret for several years.

> I do it for the thrill, I do it since my husband has cut down on my spending money. I do it because my friends have more, I do it because no one knows and I like that. I'm not worried about being caught except that it will ruin my reputation. Now I'm this good mother and I have a part-time job. If I'm found out, I'm doing something very wrong. I'll go into all sorts of

stores and I always come away with something. Maybe it's just makeup or clothes, but I'm doing it whenever I'm in any shop. Maybe it's because I'm off painkillers—for a while I was addicted to them. And I love to shop. But I'd lie if I ever got caught, I'd lie and lie about it.

If depression plays into this female behavior, and the National Institute of Mental Health reports that women are twice as depressed as men, lifestyle is a contributing factor in the outcome. The connection to depression and drug use and shoplifting is worth consideration. When Winona Ryder was arrested by the police for her shoplifting, they found seven drugs in her possession, including Vicodin, Valium, liquid Demerol, morphine sulphate, and a syringe, according to Madigan's article. In Samara's interview, she tells us that her addiction to painkillers preceded her shoplifting addiction, and in describing her designated lie, was disenfranchised from her own life.

NIP/TUCK FOSTERED LIES

In the past ten years, the American Society for Aesthetic Plastic Surgery has documented a 465 percent increase in the amount of cosmetic procedures. The most popular procedures in 2004 were liposuction, breast augmentation, eyelid surgery, rhinoplasty, and face-lifts. Of the 11.9 million procedures that took place in 2004, 10.7 were performed on women—this translates into 90 percent of the clientele. The popular television show *Nip/Tuck*, set in south Florida at a plastic surgery center, gives us an up-close look at the underside of plastic surgery. Although plastic surgery can seem an easy fix for a woman's unhappy life, women can become obsessed with their appearance, and this is a very real problem. Once again, our culture feeds the furor, placing an emphasis on beauty, looks, and age, so that women will go to great lengths, emotionally and financially, to attain the standard. As Vivian, fifty-four, living on the West Coast, contemplates her long history of plastic surgery, the secretive part was necessary.

I began with a bump in my nose, and when I saw the results I knew I wanted to continue. That was over twenty years ago. I said nothing to my friends, it was so subtle and I felt it was my secret. I did my eyes a few years later, and then my breasts the next year. I kept looking better and I got hooked. I did lipo after that. Then my eyes needed to be done again, so I did a mini-lift—I was in my forties. I denied any work when people said I looked good. I felt like it was a stigma, like I would be found out. But I couldn't stop. Between surgeries I'd get Botox and collagen, then Restylane, which you need to do a couple of times a year. I see that I need more work—I'm ready for another lift now. I doubt I'll tell even my sisters and I'll act like nothing was done. I admit to the injections but when people say I look good, I say I was on vacation.

In the 1996 movie *The First Wives Club*, Goldie Hawn's character receives so much collagen in her lips that she's barely recognizable. Her doctor warns her that it's more than enough, the implication being as a first wife who has been dumped, her beauty secrets rule her life and become addictions. Alex Kuczynski's article "A Woman's Work Is Never Done," in the September 2006 issue of *Vanity Fair*, reveals how far an obsession with one's looks can go. Kuczynski details her chilling foray into the world of plastic surgery junkies, including her recovery from liposuction, ashamed of her choice of self-inflicted pain. However, once the bruising vanished, all unpleasantness was forgotten.

After her lipo she went on to have her eyes done, explaining how she got hooked: "What could I do next? What about some more liposuction? What about having a washboard stomach? What about a fantastic nipped-in waist? Why were my upper arms always just a little too fleshy, even when I was at my lowest weight? What about that? Was I getting something resembling a bulb on the tip of my nose?" she writes. Many women, according to my interviewees, identify strongly with Kuczynski's concerns, and are completely comfortable with a preoccupation with procedures to perfect one's appearance.

Women lie about their treatments, age, and plans for cosmetic surgery.

Annette, at thirty-six, a mother who works part-time in fashion, has had her eyes done and receives Botox several times a year.

> I'm in an industry where everyone is young and hip and attractive. I don't want to be at a disadvantage. I do obsess over my looks, I buy so many creams that promise to firm your skin, make your skin glow. I will do whatever it takes to remain young-looking. I'm already worried about it because my mother is like that. She's had several face-lifts and will do it until she's eighty. And I agree. It's something you think about . . . plan for . . . it requires guts but it is worse to not have this option, to be someone who doesn't go to a plastic surgeon to improve herself. I'd rather go without a vacation and put money away for my next procedure . . . I wouldn't tell anyone at work about this, or my real age, I want to seem young and natural, so it's not something I'd tell a soul.

With plastic surgery addicts, including those women who go to plastic surgeons for noninvasive procedures, such as Botox and

Restylane, there is a high level of denial and an inability to see themselves as addicts. They might admit to being vain or selfish, but they distance themselves from the possibility that this could be an addiction or that they're telling betterment lies rather than admitting to any treatments.

The MO on plastic surgery is that women are seeking it out at earlier and earlier ages, and admit to few that this is the plan. Since it's a female-driven trend, competition among women, meaning the "she's had work done" syndrome, can be part of why women lie about any procedure they've chosen. Other women lie because plastic surgery is perceived as indulgent. Several women confided that they didn't want to appear as someone who would choose plastic surgery, although they had. This is the pretense, which fosters the lie.

Thus is the case with Terri, forty-seven, who decided to keep her mini-face-lift a secret.

> I figured why not lie to everyone about where I'd be? I think most colleagues thought I was traveling and had left the country. People just say I look fresher, and that's good. I had been so worried about this surgery that I could barely concentrate at work or with my family for months before. All I thought about was how much I needed it and how much it was a secret. Now that it's worked out so well, I'd consider lipo, definitely.

The Web site Talk Surgery noted on February 5, 2002, that Greta Van Susteren, a TV anchorwoman, surprised the media industry when she had an eye lift after leaving CNN to go to Fox television. What was more surprising was her decision to announce the surgery and her honesty about feeling that she needed it. Van Susteren was able to advise women to learn as much about plastic surgery and possible side effects before enlisting. What is promising about her story is not only her honesty but that her decision was appropriate, there was no need for secrecy and no hidden agenda.

SEDUCTION OR OBSESSION:
SEX ADDICTION LIES

Sex addiction, long considered a male disorder, has not actually been defined by our society. We recognize the male standard: porn on the Internet, a lack of connection with one's partner, obsession over the act, unnatural urges. We've read about male stars—Michael Douglas, Rob Lowe, and Billy Bob Thornton—who have reportedly sought help for sex addiction. When Thornton attempted to seduce his sex therapist, according to *The Daily Telegraph*, his then wife, Angelina Jolie, left him. Sienna Miller reportedly asserted that Jude Law was a sex addict when it was discovered that he was cheating on her with his children's nanny.

Sex addiction is synonymous with male behavior: women do it in secret.

All of this centers around male sex addiction, meaning the public would be astonished if a female celebrity revealed a pornographic secret. It's not that women don't fall into this category of addiction. When it comes to cyberspace pornography, 70 percent of women say they do it in secret, as reported by TopTenREVIEWS, an Internet site. Chat rooms offer a woman a fantasy life if she is unhappy with her partner, or single, and so, in many cases, the addiction begins. Women know how to cover this shameful secret and guilty act, because if the stigma against sex addiction for men is strong, for women the taboo is stronger—the cover-up is greater. TopTenREVIEWS reports that 17 percent of women struggle with pornography addiction, women favor chat rooms twice as much as do men, and 9.4 million women access adult Web sites on a monthly basis.

Although she might have been labeled a sex addict, there's the possibility that *Sex and the City's* Samantha, played by Kim Cattrall, just had an appetite for sex. Her sex-for-sport attitude was reminiscent of male behavior, and in our puritanical society, heightened sexual activity on a woman's part is met with skepticism. We all know the jokes about sex in monogamous relationships—exemplified in Woody Allen's 1977 film *Annie Hall,* in the famous scene where Allen's character complains that he gets no sex and Diane Keaton's character complains that there's sex all the time. The implicit message is about good girls again; good girls don't go after sex the way Samantha does, not even close. Yet in real life, women do obsess over sex, and it can become an addiction. Women lie because they aren't even supposed to *like* sex, let alone be addicted to it. The shame factor kicks in with this addiction, women cover their paths carefully. As Bea, thirty-seven, views her preoccupation with sex on the Internet, her entire life would fall apart if she were discovered.

> I've got kids and a job, and I have this past. I turned tricks when I left home years ago, I was a kid. I did it to survive and I think it had an effect on me. I hated sex for a while, and then I wanted it again, much kinkier than I can get in a marriage. I cleaned up my act and I have this normal life and it matters to me. So I do this on the sly, on the Internet and it isn't healthy, probably. But it beats some other things I could be doing wrong. I don't want my family or friends to know, but I don't want them to know about my past, either.

When Bea mentions her hidden past, it makes me think of *The Banger Sisters,* starring Goldie Hawn and Susan Sarandon.

What *Banger* stands for is the number of men these two women "banged" as groupies in their heyday of the sixties. Decades later, when they are reunited, Hawn's character is still a sexy, free spirit while Sarandon has become a conservative housewife, married with two teenage daughters and a comfortable life. She hasn't revealed her past—but instead has guarded her secret for years, ashamed of what went on. Undoubtedly her lies about how many sexual partners she's had suited her perfectly before Goldie Hawn appears on the scene and blows her cover.

Being hooked on sex is often shameful for women, not liberating.

Consider Lorraine, forty-four, who has been with her partner for sixteen years and wants sex on a constant basis. Since this pattern is taboo in traditional relationships, she keeps her desire a secret.

Sex is a huge part of this relationship, it's really the glue. It was like that in the beginning and it's lasted, which I can't believe. But if I don't have enough sex, I demand it or I'll use a dildo, watch the sex channel. It's just what I have to have. I'm available twenty-four/seven but both of us have to go to work. So we have sex more than we do anything else in our spare time. I wouldn't tell my friends this, and my partner and I appear to be very straitlaced from the outside. No one would get it, they'd think I was a sex addict and that he was just a guy who likes sex, amazingly enough, with the same woman for years. I'm not sure how to categorize myself, but I know I'm crazy for this sex life. I think about sex when I'm not having it. And I'm not young anymore, it's just how I am.

Not only do women want sex, they'll even break their marriage vows for this satisfaction and tell designated lies for the cause. And

women are better at keeping the secret than are their male counterparts. This in itself is an engrossing theme, perpetually beguiling
because women aren't supposed to be capable of such deceit.

The last word in older women seducing younger men for sex is
Mrs. Robinson in the classic film *The Graduate*, starring Dustin
Hoffman and Anne Bancroft. When the movie was released in
1967, it raised issues about intergenerational sex and about a
woman's sexuality. As long as the tryst remains a secret all is well,
but once discovered by Mrs. Robinson's daughter, Elaine, the
damage is set in motion. Elaine ends up with Ben (Hoffman) and
her mother's secret becomes hers, since she is now with the man
her mother desired.

In the film *Notes on a Scandal*, Cate Blanchett plays Sheba
Hart, a married women who cannot resist her fifteen-year-old student and engages in a sexual affair with him. Her secret is discovered by Judi Dench's character, Barbara Covett, another teacher
at the school who harbors a crush on Sheba. At first Barbara as-
sures Sheba that her secret is safe with her and that she'd lie for
her, but in the end, when she realizes she cannot have Sheba, she
reveals all, causing a terrific scandal.

If such stories are titillating on screen, in real life there is a sor-
did quality to these affairs. *USA Today* reported on February 11,
2005, in an article by Charisse Jones, that a female teacher in Tennessee, Pamela Turner, twenty-seven, was charged with having sex
with a thirteen-year-old male student, while in Florida, a female
teacher, Debra Lafave, twenty-three, was arrested on charges that
she had sex with a fourteen-year-old male student. A famous case
was that of Mary Kay Letourneau, who taught grade school in
Seattle and served seven years in federal prison for her relationship
with her former student, Vili Fualaau. Today they have two children together. The uncovering of these women's secrets and lies
categorizes them as female sex offenders, which exists at a ratio of
five hundred men to one woman, according to Dale Bespalec, a

chief psychologist at the Milwaukee Secure Detention Facility with whom Jones spoke in researching her article.

Kay, thirty-four, tells us that in her relationship with a young man whom she knew through family members, sex was the commonality and the secret, a designated lie for the initial excitement.

> I never thought of myself as someone who was obsessed with sex until I had this illicit relationship with someone much younger. Then I thought I was a sex addict. He was someone I knew and it worried me that we were together, but it didn't stop me. I knew to never tell anyone, to not let anyone become suspicious. It was this attraction, this sex that was taking over my life and I couldn't believe he'd want to be with someone my age, with my body starting to go downhill.
>
> Today I have such regrets. I might have wanted sex but getting hooked on it with a boy was a big mistake. I was out of it, separate from what was going on, during the sex. Sometimes I think I was so afraid someone would find out and that it made me removed. Sometimes I think it was just nothing but sex and so I wasn't close to him, not really. . . . I lied to all of my friends about my plans, what I was up to. I was so afraid of what they'd think of me, of what I was doing.

Although Kay doesn't announce that she was addicted to the sex with this young man, her description of what occurred raises red flags. She describes herself as being detached from the act itself, which happens with sex addicts, just as being too involved in every aspect of the act is the flip side. She also liked the conquest, as did Sheba in *Notes on a Scandal* and Mrs. Robinson in *The Graduate*.

Today, with media influences, Internet sources, and the reality of a woman's prescribed role in society, sexual addiction is both foreign and a dirty secret. The lies told in the name of a

sexual addiction, as with all addiction lies, have very little upside. If the woman is involved in Internet porn, her lies protect
her; if she's involved with someone, then the lie protects not only
the woman but her lover. Either way, danger is found in lies told
about fundamentally unhealthy behavior.

LOVE INHALATION: RELATIONSHIP ADDICTION

Carla, forty-five, single, works in finance and has been "love addicted" since high school. She feels she has no recourse but to repeat the fate of her last failed relationship and the unhappy
circumstances of the last thirty years. In each instance, she tells
an acceptable lie.

> I have no luck with men. I wanted to be married just like my
> friends and cousins, but instead I'm in one long downward
> spiral. I almost do it to myself, I think, and this really worries
> me. I've been in counseling and I've read all the books. I've
> tried life without a boyfriend and I've tried to please boyfriends
> I've had. I've been with guys who were never married, guys
> with ex-wives and kids, widowers, and it doesn't matter. It's al-
> most like it all becomes the same. The last advice I got was
> from a friend who told me that I was the problem and she so
> offended me. Maybe I'd told her too many details, but she
> seemed really harsh. She criticized me for going from one
> man to the next, without a breather. I never tell men why I've
> never been married. I never say how it's all ended so badly,
> how I obsess. I always think I'm in love with whatever guy I'm
> dating.

Although Carla is wise to not disclose her past to a new con-
tender for love, she hasn't much introspection, nor does she take

responsibility for her actions. It's unlikely she recognizes her own love addiction. Amazon.com lists 1,398 books on love addiction and 700 advice books on love and romance. Titles such as *Is It Love or Is It Addiction, Obsessive Love: When It Hurts Too Much to Let Go, Facing Love Addiction: Giving Yourself the Power to Change the Way You Love,* and *Love Sick: One Woman's Journey Through Sexual Addiction* give us insight into how prevalent this addiction is. The denial quotient runs high when it comes to love addiction because women lean toward repeat patterns in love relationships. So if you were a love addict at sixteen, at forty you'll have the same tendencies. Susan Peabody notes in her book *Addiction to Love: Overcoming Obsession and Dependency in Relationships,* as a disorder love addiction can manifest in someone remaining in a poor relationship to being obsessed with a partner.

Women use the Internet to seduce, keeping their real stories a secret.

What women have said to me regarding this addiction is that they are often dependent on their partner, as dissatisfying as the relationship is. The Internet only increases the odds of a woman fantasizing about the man she meets, since what one presents about herself/himself online can prove very different from the reality. That means the couple is operating on false premises. By definition, joining a Web site such as Match.com or eHarmony, can be both a positive and negative experience. For some subscribers, it's a healthy way to meet a potential mate; for others, it's a way to hook someone before he learns too much, if he ever does. In this way, there is a provision for female lies and deception, which can be perpetuated once the couple meets.

Maureen, forty-three, divorced with two boys and working in the medical field, confesses that she lied about her age and used an old photo when she registered with an Internet dating service. Motivated by her beneficial lie, Maureen is almost a chameleon for whomever she dates.

> I thought a bit of fixing myself up was a good thing. I'd been in several unsuccessful relationships but I wanted another boyfriend so much. I was on this mission to find "the one." I would say whatever the guy wanted to hear on the phone. I would pick up on his tone through his e-mails. I'd write back what I imagined he wanted to hear. I didn't advertise that I'm broke, that my kids are demanding, that my ex-husband stiffs me for child support. I lie about that stuff, act like it's all fine. I just need to get the guy, to get another romance going. I'm unhappy without an object of my affection. I can be whoever they want me to be.

The notorious film *Fatal Attraction*, starring Glenn Close and Michael Douglas, is an unforgettable example of a woman who will go too far to have a relationship, tantalized by the possibility of love at last. Glenn Close's character, Alex Forrest, exaggerates a one-night stand with Michael Douglas's character, Dan Gallagher, into a full-fledged romance. To this end, she follows him, wheedles him, threatens him, lies about being pregnant (perhaps), and then sets out to destroy his family. Likewise, Woody Allen's 2005 film, *Match Point*, deals with a woman as sexual predator and the lies she'll tell to land the object of her affection. Scarlett Johansson plays Nola Rice, a struggling actress who seduces Jonathan Rhys Meyers's character, Chris Wilton, newly married and trading up through his well-connected wife. The torrid affair that follows is hampered by Nola's announcement that she's pregnant (whether it's true or not we don't know) and her threat to reveal her news to Chris's wife and in-laws. Both movies delve into the plight of the other woman and the reckless rage that a fatal attraction evokes.

PERPETUAL ADDICTION/PERPETUAL LIES

Will women continue to conceal their addictions rather than seek treatment and come clean? Is there any way that the enabling lies of female addicts can be blown wide open? The genesis of the disorder is often mingled with the very nature of a female addict. A woman's early experiences, the model her mother set for her, the cultural influences and her own personality all contribute to how and why she lies as an addict.

Addiction lies for women are about control issues and self-esteem.

Although we occasionally see a betterment lie for female addictions, the survival aspect doesn't cut it, and the lies themselves are discredited, despite any woman's rationale. Compassionate lies may fall into this category in a codependency situation (crossing over into the family lies category) be it a child, adult sibling, parent, spouse, or boyfriend—and this, too, takes its toll in duplicity and falsehoods.

The secrets and lies told by a female addict, whether an alcoholic, sexaholic, or shopaholic, are partially a reaction to the bar held so high for women, which only drives them deeper into the abyss. The personal experiences that diminish a woman's self-worth push her closer to the addiction as a crutch. The sense of shame varies, depending upon the addiction and degree of denial, but what remains constant is the splintering effect that these lies have on a woman's life.

A support network, treatment, and counseling provide women with the courage to confront their addictions and to recognize how much of the problem is about self-image, interactions with

men, and female role models. Addictions for women are embedded in lies and secrets: it takes its toll on family and friends, who
vacillate between confronting the problem and pretending it
doesn't exist. Addiction lies are used as anesthesia for a woman's
encumbered life, but serve her poorly. As Rianna, thirty-four, an
administrative assistant, remarks,

> The heaviness of my being a secret drinker for fourteen years
> is finally melting away. I'm working the twelve steps and it
> really has brought me back to life. Sometimes, after a meet-
> ing, I'll call my sister and remember how she had to lie for me,
> she had to help me hide my problem. And how I lied to every-
> one, all the time. I know what I've put everyone through and
> I'm finally on the other side. I feel good about myself—I've
> been sober for six years.

PART III

LIVING THE LIE

SEVEN

Lying to Win: Competitive Lies

When I interviewed women for my book *Tripping the Prom Queen: The Truth About Women and Rivalry*, I realized how much competition, envy, and jealousy factor into behavior and attitudes. After all, we were raised on *Cinderella* and *Snow White*, where wicked, jealous stepmothers mistreated or attempted to destroy honest, pure young women. These were our early paradigms of scheming competitors, willing to lie for the cause. Since female competition is so totalizing today and extends to every aspect of a woman's life—work, sports, beauty, status, men, children—the surrounding lies are inevitable. Women act as if they are supportive of one another, all the while competing and lying to perpetuate a rivalry they feign is nonexistent.

In the hit film *Mean Girls*, the teenage girls who belong to the clique aptly named The Plastics are ruled by Rachel McAdams's character. These girls lie to one another on a constant basis, about boys, friendships, weight, grades. Adult women relate to this because it's so familiar; after all, female rivalry isn't solved by the end of high school. To the contrary, the rivalry continues, only the circumstances change. Again, the HBO series *Big Love* comes to mind, where a polygamous family is fodder for rivalry and secrets, with its own creed of husband sharing and family management. Chloë Sevigny's character, Nicki, the second wife of Bill, played by Bill Paxton, the polygamist husband, tells Jeanne Tripplehorn's character, Barb, the first wife, that she needs to sleep with Bill on Barb's night because she's trying to get pregnant. Barb consents and we see Nicki not only triumphant at beating one of her rivals (there's a third wife) out of a night, but she's also taking birth control pills. Nicki outright lies to Barb, her secret is that she has no intention of having more children.

Female rivalry breeds deception and secrets.

In *Big Love,* it's evident that each of the three wives lies about her true feelings toward one another and denies her secret agenda. In *Mean Girls,* The Plastics disintegrate when their lies and secrets implode, These dramas are examples of how competitive lies are based on an investment/return factor. If by lying to her rival or by secretly undermining her, a woman gets what she wants, she finds her actions justifiable.

Women get caught at a rate that exceeds other lies, whether the competitive lie is over a man, a job, or a friendship. The lies are often obvious, and the disingenuous quality is palpable. In fact, it's a woman's acute sense of limited goods that catapults her into a rivalry with other women, and the lie conceals her tracks. If we look at the three scenarios that follow, we see that the covert aspect of female rivalry fosters myriad ways for women to lie to one another.

The lies attached to female rivalry may appear superficial but are detrimental.

Emily, twenty-seven, is a Ph.D. candidate who lives in the Midwest.

I actually lied to my friends when I got a stipend for my degree. I felt like they'd had enough of me getting what I want. Even though they said they were happy that I'd reached my goal, I thought any more good news on my part and they'd hate me. So I just said my dad was paying for school when my friends asked if my scholarship had come through.

Patti, forty-eight, a pharmacist, is from upstate New York.

I would never admit that I've had work done, not even Botox, let alone my eyes and neck. I just say I'm using great skin creams, I even offer the name of the skin care that I like, but I won't tell the truth. It would make me seem like a vain person. So I pretend I'm not into plastic surgery and that I'm just aging better than my friends.

Rita, sixty-two, from Louisiana, is not working at present.

I never told anyone that my youngest granddaughter is learning disabled. Instead I talk about my other two granddaughters, and boast about all their fabulous awards. I sometimes make it better than it is because my friends are always saying how amazing their own grandchildren are. That's why I can never say anything about the youngest—that's why I have to lie about how my one granddaughter could be a concert pianist. She's only twelve.

Nanette, twenty-nine, regrets that lies are a part of female interactions.

No one should lie to me, especially my best friends. If I lie, it's because there's no other way. I'm really conscious of how I lie, and I also know who lies to me out of my circle of friends.

Soozy, forty, tells us that for female colleagues, lying on the job is pro forma.

> I've been at this hospital working as a nurse for fifteen years. The other nurses, all women, dump on one another all day long, and lie about it. No one even pays attention to the men, who are doctors here. We're too busy with the other women on the job.

What's transfixing about these women's secrets is that they lie *because* of their competitive spirit, including Emily, who has reason to share her academic achievements. Instead she minimizes them, choosing a compassionate lie to avoid any negativity. Knowing that she is locked in a rivalry with her closest friends, she realizes that lying is the easier way to keep these friendships in balance than to share her good fortune and hope they'll cheer for her. Rita prefers to focus on her "perfect" grandchildren than divulge that one has issues, while Patti only wants to be the youngest-looking of her group without the aid of a surgeon's knife. In the these cases, we see women embroiled in a competition with friends to the point where they choose to hide their reality with betterment lies.

DOUBLE-EDGED SWORDS

Rivalrous lies beget more rivalrous lies; some women spend a lifetime at it.

Women convince themselves and others that they are *not* jealous, not even close. And so competitive lies are cloaked in the pretense; the denial quotient is strong. May, thirty-five, a nurse living in Southern California, tells us:

I'm not someone who ever gets competitive with friends, I don't even know what it's like. I'm really just trying to get through. But sometimes I'm so resentful that I hold down two jobs and don't have enough time with my kid. I wouldn't call it competition, but I see that some of my friends are doing better. I try not to pay any attention. The only time it gets to me is when I'm working two shifts and my friends have better jobs. We all work but they have better hours. Or on a weekend, when I'm so tired from the week and have so much to catch up on. I see my friends are out shopping and they seem so carefree. Or they are thinner, or have no money problems and are less tired from their jobs. Or their kids are easier. Maybe someone thinks my life is great . . . I don't know. I tell myself I'm okay, but compared to them, I'm not. I wish I had it easier, and sometimes I want them to understand. Other times, I don't want anyone to know how it is for me.

May is immersed in comparing herself to her friends and coming up wanting. This underscores how competition is considered a positive force in modern-day America, yet women aren't good at competing in a healthy way. May's competition is part of the secret; it isn't as if she and her friends sat down and decided they would compete with one another over who has the preferred life, larger home, more successful husband, perfect children. Rather it's implicit that whatever one of the women in her circle has, May wishes she had, and vice versa. When May tells us that she wishes her friends understood her endurance, and almost begrudges them the lives they lead, it's clear she is envious. Envy for women, as I define it in *Tripping the Prom Queen,* means "I want what you have." Jealousy means, "I want what you have and I want you dead." Competition, where May's female rivalry begins, and the most benign of these three emotions, means, "I'll fight you for what I want."

Female competition breeds mostly betterment and designated lies; women are secretive about their feelings and their actions, or embellish their own lives to appear happier or more successful. With Donna, thirty-nine, a caretaker who disavows any competition that she feels toward her friends, there is the concession that one friend is jealous of her through the children.

> I try not to be all over my friends' lives, I just try to accomplish everything on my own. Everyone struggles and I know that we all want more than we have. I do have one friend who is always watching me and my daughter. Our girls are a few months apart and we were pregnant together. This was five years ago. Now her daughter has special needs and my daughter is doing really well. I think she's jealous but she doesn't show it. This is still a friendship but we don't discuss how our kids are doing at school. We aren't as close anymore but we don't get into it—we both act like this feeling between us isn't there, but it is. I say nothing, I say nothing about my daughter's progress—she's good at school and I push her ahead—but I'm quiet about it.

The lies told in the name of rivalry among women have few redeeming qualities. There is little to commend lies born of female competition, yet 90 percent of my interviewees said that envy and jealousy toward other women colors their lives, 80 percent said they had encountered jealousy in other women since they were in grade school and 70 percent reported they were familiar with the concept of women stealing a friend's husband.

It's unsettling when accomplished women are positioned in this way, as evidenced in an article in nymag.com on June 6, 2005. Entitled "Duel at Sunrise," the caption reads, "Diane Sawyer and *Good Morning America* have all but closed the ratings gap with Katie Couric and *Today*. How the former Ice Queen left

America's Sweetheart in a meltdown." Author Meryl Gordon positions the women as archrivals when she writes:

> Sawyer and Couric, the opposing poles of morning-TV stardom—Sawyer has been called the Ice Queen; Couric, America's Sweetheart—are the lead combatants in the battle.... If *Today* or *GMA* were to cover the story, they'd be virtually bound by the dictates of morning-TV-speak to call it a catfight, a characterization they both, of course, would resist.

It's unlikely that journalists would write about male celebrities in the same way, nor would it elicit the same effect. Nor would men pretend they weren't competing—they would be open and at ease with it. No secrets needed there, but for women, it's the friendly gesture that's often the lie, and the churning competition perpetuates the deception.

The Devil Wears Prada hit the screens in a big way because it was so salacious to watch Meryl Streep in her role as Miranda Priestly, where she alternately iced or ran ragged her two assistants. The pretense that it was a happy sorority at *Runway* magazine where Miranda was the editor in chief wasn't even slightly convincing. It was a cutthroat, vicious work climate, where female employees scurried around, petrified that they'd be undermined by a female coworker or ousted at any minute by Miranda Priestly herself.

The "good girl" image is virtually worthless in a world run by the likes of a Miranda Priestly; the message being it's wiser to sabotage other females than be supportive. Survival lies work best in this environment.

The Rules of Engagement

Always lie when it comes to your competitive feelings toward other women. How can women not lie about jealousy and envy when they are expected to be empathetic and giving? Carol Gilligan, author of *In a Different Voice*, views women as caring more about having connections and aiding other people than do men. No wonder we have to avoid the truth when we are actually as jealous as we are connected. Remember *Joe Millionaire*, the 2003 ABC primer on how one woman should be rewarded with the prize, Joe himself? Although the twenty-five women acted happy to be in a Cinderella-like setting, each was secretly praying she'd be the one and the shoe would fit her alone. The setup was fodder for intense, unacknowledged female competition.

Appear supportive and open-minded while you are secretly prepared to go to great lengths to keep another female from an opportunity. Since women have to keep their ambition a secret, many relationships with other women are on shaky ground from the start. The posturing that's required only makes it more secretive. Then the women lie because the dichotomy is too great between being cooperative and being competitive. In the 1998 film *Stepmom*, starring Julia Roberts and Susan Sarandon, the two women are set up to compete by virtue of their roles: Roberts as the future stepmother and Sarandon as the mother. Although there is a semblance of cooperation, beneath the surface the women subvert each other until Sarandon's character becomes gravely ill and they team up for the children's sake.

No wonder 70 percent of the women in my study on female rivalry said they'd rather work for a male boss than a female boss. But what a disservice women do to one another, not just in the work arena, by being catty and jealous. *Me Without You*, a film about two best friends growing up in England during the seventies, offers us Holly, played by Michelle Williams, and Marina, played by Anna Friel. Marina, the beautiful one, is deceptive and jealous, keeping Nat, her older brother, away from Holly, who is intellectual and soft-spoken. That Holly tolerates Marina's manipulations is troubling, especially since she's loved Nat since she.

was a young girl. To add to the mix, Trudie Styler plays the vampy mother of Marina and Nat; she is competitive and absent at the same time. The rivalry always includes secrets, precipitated by Marina. It's Marina's lack of self-esteem, in contrast to Holly's quiet self-esteem, that creates the triangles. When Holly dates a college professor, played by Kyle MacLachlan, Marina makes sure to seduce him. The movie shows how far a woman will go to deceive her best friend.

Women not only hurt their friends, they can be manipulated and victimized themselves. For example, Caroline, forty-five, who lives in northern California and works in fashion, believes that her ex-boyfriend's sister and cousin both convinced him to break off his relationship with her.

I was with my boyfriend for seven years and we were engaged. But his sister and this one cousin wouldn't let it go. They were so unkind to me and I think he had a lot of respect for both of them. In the end I didn't get to marry him, he broke it off. I know he had some issues, but he had no issue with me. They saw me as the competition—he comes from a close family and he's done so much with these two women for years. Then I came along and he couldn't stand it. He really was torn, and in the end he wasn't strong enough. I wanted so much for it to work out and I feel like they won. Of course, when I confronted them, they said nothing; they really lied, standing there, acting like I was the crazy one.

THE SPORTS ARENA

On Saturday, September 9, 2006, the women's finals at the U.S. Open was a sold-out affair. Not only did Maria Sharapova beat Justine Henin-Hardenne, a five-time major champion, 6–4, 6–4, but the competitors had such disparate styles. Sharapova wore a glittery tennis dress that resembled an evening gown and dangle earrings, while Henin-Hardenne sported a simple tennis outfit that made no statement whatsoever and little jewelry. When the Sunday *New York Times* Sports section reported the match the next day, I was surprised by Selena Roberts's headline, "The Beauty and the Burden," and her use of the words "jealousy" and "envy" peppered throughout the article. Thus in sports, where women have been known to compete in a better way than elsewhere, it seems that we can't escape the dark side of female rivalry.

Even sports for women are grounds for secrets and foul play.

In the 2005 film *Ice Princess,* Joan Cusack and Kim Cattrall are mothers to two daughters who are rival ice skaters. Cattrall's character, Tina Harwood, is a single mother and skating coach whose hopes are pinned to her teenage daughter, Gen, to win the competition. Cusack's character, Joan Carlyle, also a single mother whose hopes are pinned to her daughter, Casey, dreams of her daughter's acceptance to an Ivy League college. The two mothers, from opposite worlds, collide when Tina coaches Casey, who is smitten with the sport. Although Tina encourages Casey to skate, she doesn't want her to beat Gen, and is driven to deception for her daughter's sake.

As Jamie, twenty-three, who lives in a midwestern city where she works as an administrative assistant, describes her years of competitive skating, much of the messaging comes from the mother.

> I think my mother wasn't that into my skating and that's why I
> didn't get so caught up in it myself. I just saw my old chore-
> ographer and she told me the mothers live through their girls,

but my mom didn't do that. I didn't find it catty but I was old when I started and the girls I skated with had been at it since they were really little. They were cliquish and some of them were very competitive. I was amazed by how some of the mothers acted. They would even lie to get their daughters into competitions.

The mothers watched everything their daughters did. These girls were always fighting over how they looked, the guys, their clothes, and their skating. They did mean things, the "group"—they said one thing to one girl and something different to another. It was gossipy, a kind of closed community. Skating attracts girls who treat it like high school, it's highly competitive and there are all kinds of secrets.

Although Jamie enjoyed skating, she avoided any interactions where survival lies proliferated. Perhaps a dirth of female role models causes women to not only be competitive, but sneaky when it comes to team sports. Consider Miranda, forty-four, who coaches a woman's softball team.

I've been at this for so long and nothing improves. I'll try to be upfront with the team, but I think they're basically awful to one another. And some women trick the others, including lying about when the practice is scheduled. Then everyone acts like it's a huge misunderstanding. I'm so busy trying to hold it all together, I say very little. But I see it all, even women saying they can't pick up certain other women on the way to practice, making up some excuse, when it's really just unfriendly and cruel. How can we win when we can't even act like a team?

My goal is to get the women to work together, to know that this is a chance to make friends, get exercise, and win. It's not another way to say one thing to a friend and mean something else.

Another film that exemplifies female rivalry in sports and the secrecy it evokes is the 1992 film *A League of Their Own*. The film is based on the true story of the All-American Girls Professional Baseball League that was formed in 1943 while the male teams were fighting World War II. The story centers around the competition between two sisters, Dottie Hinson, played by Geena Davis, and Kit Keller, played by Lori Petty, and is understandable, since Dottie had always been the star. It's only when Dottie allows Kit to win in the final game that we see how a lie (although we can't prove that Dottie let it happen) can right the wrongs of the past. Although the film is about team spirit and competition among female team players, it's also about how sisters rectify a long-standing rivalry. The good news is that repressed emotions are examined, improved, and the secrecy is shed.

BEAUTY AND DECEPTION

Women pretend they're not jealous of the prettiest woman, but they are.

Nancy Etcoff, in her book *Survival of the Prettiest,* points out that beauty is very much at the center of our experience and has great value. With beauty, looks, and youth so highly touted, it's just a blatant lie to act as if we aren't keyed in on some level. Nothing churns up female envy and jealousy quite like another woman's impeccable appearance and sex appeal. For women who perceive themselves as beautiful, it plays out in several ways. A woman might pretend that she isn't aware of her looks and the advantage she has, or she might be cruel and demanding, heady with the potency of her beauty.

Cameron, fifty-six, who works in retail and lives a suburban life, is quick to point out that her own lifelong edge—being beautiful, wasn't her fault. Nonetheless, it caused her to tell compassionate lies to her girlfriends about her life.

Can I help that people consider me great-looking? It made me nicer to everyone, ever since grade school. I could have been awful and a phony, like some of the other pretty girls, but I was too afraid I'd have no girlfriends. So I always bent over backward, invited the ugly girls over, tried to understand their lives. It worked and it didn't work. They were faking it because they hated me but needed me for guys, for popularity. I was faking it because I didn't need to be with them to have dates, or go to parties. But I needed friends and I wanted friends, so I had to do this.

My secret was how dreary their stories were while I had to act like I cared. Their secret was how much they kissed up to me because I looked the way I did. They were jealous but they couldn't say it. If I had been less friendly, they would have found fault. Everyone compared themselves to me in my small town. And now, halfway across the country, at my age, they still do. I befriend women to get what I want, to win the game.

For a woman who was not the beauty, her MO since grade school has been to befriend the prettiest, most popular girl for how it positions her. Or perhaps she'll posture that the "prom queen" is not her style and be disdainful of her, all the while wishing she could be her. Either way, it's surely a competition. The best of everything is awarded to the beauty and it creates tension and dishonesty on the part of the other females in the circle. This applies whether it's junior high school, college, women in their thirties, or women in their sixties; the dynamic rarely changes and beauty is placed at a premium.

Cat's Eye, a novel by Margaret Atwood, shows an incessant cruelty between two supposed best friends that begins in childhood. Cordelia, the beautiful, maniacal one, is cruel and disingenuous toward Atwood's narrator, Elaine Risley. Although one day the tables turn and Elaine is the stronger of the two, she is affected her entire life by what she endured at the hands of Cordelia. What I keep hearing in the stories of women of all ages when it comes to competition and secrecy over beauty is a partly compliant, partly fearful reaction to someone such as Cordelia. As Shelley, thirty-nine, recalls, for the "ordinary girl," the beautiful one was magnetic.

> I followed my best friend, Claudia, around for years. I thought maybe something would rub off on me since everyone loved her and wanted to be her friend. In the end, I was two-faced, and I used her, to be with guys, to be with the right crowd. People would complain about how spoiled she was, but I was using her without anyone knowing it.

Lies around beauty have several common themes:

Beauty equals power. In our beauty-obsessed culture, female friendships are fodder for female lies and secrets. Women use their looks to get ahead, all the while pretending that they aren't competing and aren't at an advantage because they are considered attractive. Their secret is the very power that beauty commands.

Beauty exudes confidence. Confident beautiful women are not as ubiquitous as we think. Ironically, they posture at having self-esteem, but much of their behavior is based on feeling insecure. A pretty woman is just as competitive and willing to lie about her beauty secrets, from a nose job to breast enhancement to a brow lift, as anyone else. The common wisdom is that sharing a beauty tip will increase the competition and give other women a way to judge them.

Beauty churns up rivalry. It's hard work being the prettiest, and assessing the competition is almost instinctive. What usually threatens the "beauty" is the woman who operates on another plane—having a great personality, being athletic, having a brilliant mind. It is not beneath the beauty to create situations that exclude the competition, all the while seeming open and inclusive.

Female competition over our appearances starts at home, with our mothers. If our mothers are obsessed with aging, it works both ways for the daughters. As Pamela Weiler Grayson reports in her piece in *Harper's Bazaar*, "Will Your Mother Soon Look Younger Than You?," "Far from being our childhood visions of the stooped, wrinkled grandmother in a hand-knit cardigan, our mothers are toned, tight and sexy—more likely to look better in a leather skirt than we do." Do mothers exude more confidence than their adult daughters? Do they have better beauty secrets? Clearly there's no place to hide from the relentless rivalry among all women over looks. Linda, seventy, believes that her latest cosmetic procedure has rendered her younger-looking than her forty-nine-year-old daughter. She utilizes an acceptable lie, steeped in her competitive nature, when she urges her daughter to not disclose her face-lift.

I didn't have this lift to outdo my daughter, but I do think I look as good as some of her friends. Not many of my friends have had anything done, so I know I look younger than they do and they wouldn't dare say a word to me. But when I sit with my daughter and her peers, I realize how well this has turned out. Still, I admit I'm very vain and I never say a word, I act like this is me, naturally. I say to my daughter, don't tell your friends that I've had work.

Appearances and ageism are huge issues for women.

The women who are larger than life, who rise above competition in terms of beauty and success, offer us hope. Such a woman is Susan Sarandon, who, as Meryl Gordon reports in *More* magazine in her article "What Susan Knows," has it all. "When you're approaching your sixtieth birthday with a major modeling contract, three great kids, four new roles and a sexier-than-ever relationship, life is good. Susan Sarandon talks about what's kept her centered, serene, and—she swears—surgery free." Gordon points out that since Sarandon began her Revlon ads two years ago, Christie Brinkley, at fifty-two, has signed with CoverGirl and Sharon Stone, at forty-eight, with Dior. "And I do think it's actually influenced other campaigns to use women who are older," Sarandon tells Gordon. With such women setting the example, there is hope for more self-esteem, therefore less competition among women, and less beauty secrets created by female competition over looks.

ANOTHER GREAT LIE: MEN DON'T COUNT

Female competition over a man can evoke secrets that might not exist elsewhere in a woman's life. While some view someone else's ex as spoiled goods and some imagine that they wouldn't touch a friend's old flame, others say that a potential boyfriend or future husband trumps a friendship. For the woman drawn into this triangle, the concept of being with your friend's ex is a tricky matter, even in the world of betrayal and lies. When it comes to this kind of competition—over a man—few boundaries exist.

For instance, Blythe, forty-seven, tells us how her closest female friendship broke up once she confessed to dating her close friend's ex-partner.

> My friend Natalie had dated this guy Jack for eight years. She never had anything good to say about him and then they broke up. She complained about him for weeks and I listened. I called Jack a deadbeat, I said he was rotten, anything to make her feel better. Then he asked me out and I went, lying to Natalie from the start, breaking dates with her to be with him. I'd have kept it a secret for longer but a mutual friend ran into us. He wants to marry me and he never wanted to marry her. She'll call sometimes still, even though we don't really talk anymore, and I'll say that Jack and I aren't serious. I do that because it's easier and I don't want to be in a contest for who won Jack. But I'm going to be with Jack—I just don't feel like telling Natalie.

Blythe's deception raises the question of the shelf life of a competitive secret. Like Blythe, Susanna, thirty-four, puts her relationship with her best friend's ex ahead of the friendship and knows the lie must come to an end.

> It just happened unexpectedly. Maybe we were always attracted to each other, but it was a secret. I think it's better this way, it's there for everyone to know. I'd prefer to make it known to everyone so I can stop the running around on the sly.

Women will betray one another for the sake of a man.

When an ex-boyfriend or ex-husband is snapped up by your supposed best friend, the genesis of the relationship is often part of the lie. Adriada, thirty-seven, admits that her best friend's ex-live-in-partner was fair game for her.

> We had known each other as couples and I was sort of envious of this friend. She had a big apartment, a boyfriend who was very successful. She was pretty and smart and had this fairy-tale life. I thought her boyfriend was terrific and I suspected she wasn't that happy with him. I heard through someone we both knew that they were splitting up. I figured it was my chance, so I left my boyfriend. I told her I was leaving him to meet someone else, I didn't say it was her ex. I didn't care if she found out or not—I say that, but I did try to keep it quiet as long as I could.
>
> I was definitely not pristine—she was complaining about him and I was secretly seeing him. I'd have lunch with her and then see him that night. When she found out, she dropped me.

As with Adriada, who employed a beneficial lie in order to secure her friend's ex, Monica, forty-four, was told a beneficial lie by the friend who stole Monica's husband.

> This friend isn't someone who has close girlfriends, and I think that explains why she seduced my husband. She didn't care that he was mine, it was another form of competition and he was what she wanted. Yes, we were more than acquaintances, but in her mind, we weren't connected. She told herself I didn't matter and she outright lied to me. She was taking him from me, and still meeting me for lunch. She even asked if I thought she needed plastic surgery. She pretends this isn't enough to ruin a friendship; she acts like this just came upon her, as if we hardly knew each other. I figure she's been keeping it from me for months. She always wanted what I had.

The Truth About Cats and Dogs, the 1996 film starring Uma Thurman and Janeane Garofalo, portrays a very real picture of female friendship, competition, and charade when it comes to a man. Although Thurman's character is supposed to get the guy— she's the beauty while Garofalo's character is the girl with the great personality—it's not without repercussions. It's the age-old scenario where the two friends stop being honest with each other over the guy they both fall for. And it's doubtful that stealing a friend's or sister's object of affection will change anytime soon, as long as female rivalry is alive and well. But so are the lies women tell one another when embroiled in this kind of competition—the secretive behavior seems justified when it comes to a woman's intentions and betrayals. In fact, we're taught to lie to our friends when it comes to a man; how much we like him, if we have secret designs on our best friend's new squeeze, what we really think of him.

It isn't only for love relationships that women compete, however, and the workplace conjures up female rivalry and secrets as well. Corey, forty-one, a supervisor in a management position, tells us that she and her female colleagues compete over a male boss.

> I'm always trying to please my boss, it takes much more energy than a boyfriend or husband. I think this woman at work competes with me because it's over a man, more than because he's the boss. It wouldn't be happening this way if it was a woman boss. It feels like being in high school. I act like I'm not doing it at work, like it's beneath me, but it's not. I scheme and plan and act like I'm not doing a thing to curry favor, but I am.

The majority of women with whom I spoke for this section had little shame that they were dishonest with their female friends over men. The lies told in the name of this competition seem vital and imperative. The perpetrator's rationale is that it works for them; hoping their lies facilitate a win/win result.

ARCHRIVALS: STATUS LIARS

According to *The Journal of Happiness Studies*, schadenfreude (defined by *HarperCollins German-English Dictionary* as "enjoyment obtained from the troubles of others") is necessary to our happiness. After studying Americans for more than thirty years in terms of the connection between money and happiness, this research concluded that while people with money are happier, one's income is not the only factor, another is how one's peers are doing. In other words, the competitive edge makes it all the more important to have more money than your friends, more enticing and more rewarding. Then, when we measure ourselves against our friends and we have the best deal, this makes us happier.

My only question about this study is how the pretense of happiness manifests if people are secretly jealous of their friends' wealth and status. And for women, how does it differ? Female competition, status, and secrets are all rolled into one in the film *Friends with Money*. Jennifer Aniston's character is a former schoolteacher who has become a maid. We observe her as she visits cosmetic counters in every department store, asking each salesperson for the advertised free sample of a face cream—and comes away with an impressive collection. She then steals a full-size jar of the same cream while cleaning a client's house, and slathers it on her feet. Aniston's apparent unhappiness, compared to her friends' easier lives, has become a secret competition for her, where any and all possessions represent the disparity.

My interviewees describe their preoccupation with materialism and social standing, which explains why lying over one's lifestyle is prevalent among women. For instance, Lolly, forty-nine, a socialite, tells us that she was dropped by a very wealthy friend when her finances dipped .

> I've been dropped by one of my wealthiest friends because I'm not wealthy enough for her anymore. If she didn't know my net worth, I wonder if she'd have done this? But she knows and it matters to her, even if she denies it. I remember when money wasn't all that she cared about, and when we both had less, and our husbands made less, but that was ages ago. Now her wealth is at an all-time high and I'll never get to that level. So she's not interested in the friendship and she's giving me the cold shoulder. And lying about it.

In contrast, Delia, forty-five, living in the suburb of a southern city where she works as a marketing consultant, has for years told stories about her material possessions. The competition in her inner circle has influenced her to keep her limited spending quiet.

> I can't afford the real things and I have friends who can. They are always carrying the latest pocketbook, wearing the newest earrings, and traveling first class on some exotic trip. I want to be in their league—they're the in-crowd around here. I've learned ways to buy the clothes and jewelry cheaply and that's what I do. I never say that my husband can't afford this and wouldn't do it if he could. I never say that we need my paycheck so I can't spend the money and have to buy a copy. Maybe I should shop at Ann Taylor or Banana Republic, but I don't want to. I'd rather have the copies or the real thing on sale. It makes me feel better and I lie about all of it, all my

stuff. I even color my hair myself, but show up at the salon
they all use once in a while, for appearances.

We're keenly aware of other kinds of status besides money
and possessions. At an early age, women are impressed by
lifestyle, looks, and accomplishments, including education and
workplace experience. For many women, it becomes a lifelong series of designated lies, even survival lies, to sustain an image. As
reported by the Josephson Institute of Ethics, 71 percent of high
school students said they cheated on an exam at least once.
Young women tell me that the grade is of utmost importance to
them, they view cheating as fine, as long as you aren't caught.
This mentality, acquired in high school, can be found in the attitudes of adult women when it comes to their performance at
work, socially, as wives, and as mothers. In part, this way of
thinking addresses the nature of having a voice as a woman, to
be recognized, appreciated, and to be heard. Competition among
women contributes to female lies that are viewed as a way to get
ahead.

Some women, though, shrewdly choose one of two ways of lying over status:

Playing It Down. In the world of female rivalry there's an edge
to keeping mum, and women know this. The wisdom is that you
can avoid the negativity of female friends and colleagues by not
sharing your good news and success. When friends ask pointedly
about some aspect of your life, say less not more. A lie of omission
can save you from being engulfed in a woman's jealousy and ill
wishes.

Embellishing Assets. Women who are adept at social lies are
competitive by nature. These women are willing to exaggerate any
good news (any news at all) in order to look richer, worthier, happier
than they are. While we will see this kind of lying in Chapter 8,

which concentrates on wishful thinking, it applies here to material goods.

As Jacqueline, forty-six, living in northern California, perceives herself, she isn't at all socially competitive or socially secretive.

> I'm becoming interested in a spiritual life. I don't choose my friends based on what they have or what they do. I'm interested in people, not in how they live. But I do have more friends who live like I do than friends who don't have as much as I have. I think it happens over time. I'm fortunate, my husband has done well—I'm not saying I'm hypocritical by acting low key, and my lifestyle if probably obvious to people anyway, but I don't say much, I try not to show off.

Jacqueline not only lies to herself, but acts one way and lives another. While she fits into the category of playing it down, it's not without conflicted feelings. In a materialistic world such as ours, having the goods can take you far. That applies if you're secretly miserable, as Ellen, thirty-eight, working part-time in fashion, has been.

> I'm ready to put all my energy into good causes and stop being so caught up in who does what. I've been with a sort of slick group of women for a long time and we all keep things from one another. There's too much jealousy and everyone is unhealthy about what they say and do. Everyone sizes the next person up. It's all about how we look and what we have. Socially I want to be accepted, but I also worry about being liked for just being me. I don't talk to people about this but it's hard sometimes. I'm trying not to let what I have rule my life.

Status is a broad sweep, including the categories I've explored—work, sports, beauty, and men—with money remaining a part of the mix. Women believe that money is pivotal in attaining other forms of status; what money does, besides ease the friction of daily life, is to define them. To this end, betterment and designated lies are used handily. Amelia, a forty-eight-year-old mother of three, tells us:

> It's about being recognized, being a part of everything. Without money in this town I couldn't have the right things. I couldn't have the right house or clothes or cars. Everyone competes over this and everyone wants the same stuff. And I'm for real, I don't have to fake it.

If it's up to the individual to get the goods herself, not through an inheritance or a spouse, a survival lie can come into play. Consider Kelly, twenty-nine, living in Santa Barbara, California, where she is single and works in marketing:

> I lied to my parents about my vacations and how I got the tickets and money to go because I wanted to go so much. Those vacations would get me to the right people and my parents wouldn't have understood. So after I lied about that kind of thing, I lied about where I was from when I moved to California. I'm from Wisconsin and I came to California and struggled to fit in. So to boost myself, I had to lie, I had to say I was from New York, not Wisconsin. When I did, there was a difference in people's eyes, they looked at me another way, they had another impression. It's gotten me closer to where I want to be and if I'd been honest about being a nice girl from the Midwest, I wouldn't meet the guys I meet, date them, have the jobs I've had, make the money I've made.

Similarly, Bobbie, in her early thirties, having grown up in a small town, kept her background a secret when she arrived in Philadelphia.

I only have one life to live and people believe lies. They like lies better than the truth. It makes me think more of myself when I say I'm from around here, and everyone believes it. For women to get ahead, they have to say these things. If I said I was from a small town, that my family was poor, no one would like it or pay any attention to me. It can be brutal, so I tell these lies to get ahead. There's all this competition at work and part of it is about your background, how did it go for you . . . what was your advantage? So if you have none, you make it up.

DUELING MOTHERS: LIES OVER CHILDREN/LIES FOR CHILDREN

From the lies we tell for our children to the lies we tell about our children, as discussed in Chapter 4, motherhood can be devouring. Children are a status symbol, not only for middle- and upper-middle-class mothers, but for mothers across the board. We look to our children to live out our dreams, as emblematic of ourselves. We live in such a competitive environment that if our children are unable to meet the standard of excellence, it triggers our lies and secrets. Mothers poured their hearts out to me when it came to this section of the book.

Whether it's academics, sports, beauty, or popularity, we want our children to have it all. When they don't and your neighbor's child does, it can be lie-provoking. Women say they've actually steered their children toward specific goals, sacrificing their individuality for an end product. For instance, Talia, fifty-five, has raised four children and takes great pride in the results. She confesses that along the way there was cajoling, wheedling, and a few beneficial lies in the name of her children's progress.

> There are people who have criticized me for being too hands-on with my children, no question. I doubt I ever completely allowed them to think for themselves, but always made plans for them. Now that they're adults, they've done much better than my friends' kids, where the parents sort of let them be. I might have been too controlling but I'm satisfied that it worked out for the best. My two daughters are married and have babies already, which was a goal of mine. Everyone went to college and everyone got their degree. The boys make good money and are on the right track. Should I have said less, been more open to their ideas? I don't really care as much about that. At least I can say to any of my friends, look at my kids. And if they say to me, well you never let them do a thing on their own, I'd say, that's not true at all—I'd deny anything said about being controlling and competitive.

Although being involved in our children's lives has been a precept of motherhood for centuries, the current method of competition over children and the subsequent cover-ups were familiar to almost every mother with whom I spoke. According to journalist Stephanie Rosenbloom in her *New York Times* piece, which ran on January 5, 2006, entitled "Honk If You Adore My Child Too," "bragging becomes competitive, making parents feel as if they are being drawn into a game of one-upmanship. . . . The mother who bragged about her child's gift is but one example of what some parents call an annoying trend: parents who brag about their children's accomplishments with an aggression befitting a contestant on *The Apprentice*."

A mother's immersion in her child's life is common today.

In my research, I heard women of all socioeconomic spheres deeply concerned with how their children measured up to others; these women showed a nervousness and preoccupation with how their children would get ahead in the world. When my children were younger, I was surprised by how many of the mothers would say, "We have homework. We have a science project." I wondered who the "we" included, the mother and child, the whole family? What was most shocking was how many of the mothers practically did the homework for their children, a trend that continues, and seems to be more popular today than ever before. Daisy, forty-four, a restaurant manager who has decided to change her hours in order to be home at night with her children, remarks:

> So what if I do my son's math homework? He's not good at math, and I can help. He's learning, he's sitting with me and I'm showing him. I do some of the assignments for him, just to help out. I doubt the teacher would like it but my son has so much work every night, some of the kids get math naturally.

If the competition was restrained, perhaps women would be more honest about their children's achievements. Instead, mothers rationalize their designated lies, but it's a disservice to the children who are kept from sharpening their own skills. The mothers raise the level of competition by enabling their children and making it a secret.

Felicity, fifty-one, a mother of three, a bookkeeper who lives in a southern city, tells us that she pushed her children very hard when they were in grade school and high school in order to get them into the "right colleges." Although her friends knew she was a hands-on mother, she didn't "advertise" the extent to which she was involved with their lives, including after-school activities and school schedules.

> I've charted my children's careers since they were really little. I knew they had to do well in school and I hired tutors. But one can't afford a tutor every night, so I ended up having to do a big chunk of it myself. I did it gladly because I wanted successful children. I wanted them better than everyone else's kids. In the end they were bright enough to do well, but I always had this nagging doubt, per child, that I never told anyone. What nagged at me was that if they couldn't cut it on their own, what would they do without me?

Rochelle, forty-seven, a nurse living in a small town, also describes herself as a very involved mother. She made special arrangements for her daughter so that she would struggle less with her high school curriculum.

> I would have done anything for my daughter to do better than her own speed. I wanted her to do well, to do better than anyone in our family, any of our friends' kids. So I moved her to another school, got her through the tough spots. She was learning disabled and I said little to my friends about it. I made excuses for her while I was trying to fix it. Then I had to listen to my friends boasting about their kids in AP classes and early acceptances at colleges. I was dragging my daughter along.

These deceptions and manipulations can span a child's lifetime, as we've seen. Interviewees say that it's a serious business by the time the nursery school rejections and acceptances roll out, keeping the bad news a secret from family and friends. Samantha, thirty-eight, makes up the story for her own mother when her daughter is rejected from the preschool that she herself attended.

> I didn't apply to my alma mater nursery school is what I told my mother. I said I wanted my daughter to have something all her own, to try another school. I never told her that it hadn't worked out. I was too mortified, too upset.

When women lie about their children, the issues are loaded; of course it involves status, yet what sets these lies apart is how compassionate lies and betterment lies factor in. Women may be motivated by prestige regarding their children, but it's also about having children who excel. It's not easy for mothers, as Dr. Ronnie Burak notes, "We're embarrassed and there is shame associated with how our children are if they're not so smart, or not doing so well in school. So women lie about how their children are faring, how they measure up."

Is there any righteousness in competitive secrets?

The principle of competitive lies remains in question; what virtue is there in this type of female lie, driven by a woman's own psyche and the competitive universe at large? Not only do women fight for the glittering prizes, as evidenced earlier, but the ingenuity surrounding the rivalry only worsens the situation. Whether it's about beauty, children, men, or success, the absence of advocacy from other women, coupled with the *pretense* of support, makes this a convoluted issue. As long as female competition is covert and unacknowledged, women will continue to lie to one another, in the guise of friendship and caring.

EIGHT

Born Again: Lying to Ourselves

My childhood friend Jacintha, who lives in northern California, has lied to herself about much of her life. Whether we talk about our careers, children, marriages, friendships and how we compete in the world, she puts a spin on it that makes it work for her. When I point out that she's always finding a way to fool herself, or to be half-honest, she has said to me, "Well, how else can I get through, Susan? What do you expect me to do?" The reason that Jacintha has little regret is that she isn't only lying to herself, she's lying to those around her on an as-need basis.

Having observed her over the years, I'm stunned by how well this technique works. Then again, I don't view her as content or comfortable, I view her as having found a solution. At forty-nine, Jacintha is entrenched in her method of dealing with the world.

> Every time my husband gets fired, I say to myself that he'll rally, he's a player. I don't say, wow, he's such a loser, I should have lost him years ago. I don't say to myself, why am I still here? I can't think that way, I'm in too deep, I'm too old, it's too late. Every time I run into someone in our hometown and they ask about things, I smile and say things are fine. I honestly believe that if I smile, it makes it a possibility.

I smile when my fourteen-year-son is torturing me. I tell him he looks handsome when he needs to lose thirty pounds. I tell him to do his schoolwork and I'm helping him, I'm helping me.

When I sit at some luncheon and listen to all the women complaining and the other ones acting as if they're living with a prince in a castle, I say little, or I boast when there's nothing to boast about. I never tell the truth: that my husband is a huge disappointment, that when I sit in a room with him, it makes me sick, that my daughter can't get noticed and wants to be a ballerina. Meanwhile, I don't entertain fantasies of leaving my husband, I entertain fantasies that he'll get a great job.

DAMAGE CONTROL

Wishful thinking, as defined in *Webster's Collegiate Dictionary*, is "the attribution of reality to what one wishes to be true or the tenuous justification of what one wants to believe." Self-deception, which goes arm in arm with wishful thinking, can work to a woman's advantage, up to a point. Jacintha's approach to female lying includes societal lies and survival secrets that women champion; she lies to herself as well as to others, and it keeps her in check.

We can only envision what wishful thinking existed in the lives of historical female figures such as Marie Antoinette and Anne Boleyn—women who were maligned, judged, and scrutinized while fighting for their survival. In reading Lady Antonia Fraser's account of the life of Marie Antoinette, *Marie Antoinette: The Journey*, I imagined how some wishful thinking might have eased her pain. Marie Antoinette, at the age of fourteen, in 1770, was sent by her mother, the Empress Maria Theresa of Austria, to marry Louis Auguste, the dauphin, who became Louis XVI of France in 1774, in order to secure relations between Austria and France.

From the time she arrived at court until she bore her first child eight years later, this young woman was unsure that her marriage would be consummated, a necessary act in the alliance between Austria and France. Although she was fortunate that her marriage eventually sufficed, at that point, it's likely that her wishful thinking shifted with the rumblings of a revolution that eventually became a reality.

Although Anne Boleyn, in sixteenth-century England, convinced King Henry VIII, her suitor and future husband, that she would give him a son, an heir to the throne if he married her, it was a tricky lie. Had she been more fortunate, it would have been successful, but once they were married, the only healthy child she bore was a girl (the future Queen Elizabeth I) and Henry did not forgive her. Anne paid the price with her life when Henry was ready to move on and had her executed in 1536 for trumped-up charges of adultery and treason.

These historical figures lived in an inverse reality, where women know the truth but lie to themselves in order to prevail. Famous modern-day women have faced their own set of challenges. For the late Princess Diana, it was that she was the last to know that her husband was in love with Camilla Parker Bowles. Diana's initial instinct appeared to be wishful thinking, followed by the facts. It's possible that neither the fact nor the lie enabled Diana to be heard or understood. Following this route provides a managing device, as we witnessed during the Hillary Clinton/Monica Lewinsky debacle. As the country tried to learn the truth, Hillary Clinton stood by her husband. She appeared on *The Today Show* in January 1998 stating that she believed the allegations against her husband were an effort "to undo the results of two elections," a "political campaign against [her] husband."

As with the lie we tell others, the lie to ourselves has limits.

Whether in the public or private sphere, many women today have described how wishful thinking and a lie to oneself has gotten them through tough times, but eventually they've had to face reality. Consider Darlene, forty-eight, a government employee, who suspected that her husband was gay for many years before confronting him.

I didn't want my marriage to end and we were so compatible. Plus, we had two babies. That was when I first suspected that something wasn't right. We lived in a small town and that made it worse, because I was supposed to be married and raising this family—nice husband, beautiful little boys. We both had decent jobs. So even though I had this hunch, this feeling that I couldn't explain, I told myself he was just overcome by how expensive life had become with kids, and how tired we both were. I made excuses for years—until one day he decided he wanted a divorce. That was when I had to ask why. It was weird how painful and freeing the truth was. But I also think that my way of handling it worked, up to a point. It kept the marriage together longer and it made me feel like we were a family, even if he was gay, and didn't want a wife, didn't want me, really.

Violet, thirty-seven, describes her experience with self-delusion and the aftermath:

I've tried everything to get my sister to know the truth about her husband, that he is a very bad guy. This was after years of my pretending he was okay, because that's what she wanted to hear. But whatever I do, it makes no difference—my sister is in some fantasy world and can't hear me, either way.

A woman's wishful thinking raises serious questions: How can we trust others if we lie to ourselves? How can we trust ourselves when we use our wishful thinking for the payoff, at any cost? What makes film and fiction so alluring is the complexity of the lies women tell themselves, and in the examples below, it's striking that as disparate as each narrative is, every story involves a woman as a wife.

The 2005 Academy Award–winning film *Brokeback Mountain* shows us how the wives of two gay men are affected by their husbands' love affair. Michelle Williams plays Alma, the wife of Heath Ledger's Ennis Del Mar. Alma is startled into reality by the discovery of her husband's male lover. Repulsed and rejected, she hasn't the luxury of wishful thinking; she divorces him and moves on. For Anne Hathaway's character, Lureen Newsome, the wife of Jake Gyllenhaal's character, Jack Twist, there is a vehement self-deception that lingers. After she is told that her husband is dead, she is unable to face what his life was about and that he might have been murdered for his sexual proclivities.

Another long-suffering wife of the silver screen is Julianne Moore's character, Cathy Whitaker, a fifties wife, in *Far from Heaven*, released in 2002. Dennis Quaid plays Frank Whitaker, a successful husband who is caught by his wife in the arms of a man. Not only does Cathy apply wishful thinking when it comes to "fixing" her husband's homosexuality, she applies the same ideology to befriending their black gardener, Raymond Deagan, played by Dennis Haysbert. Although Cathy puts her best foot forward to preserve her marriage and seemingly idyllic life as a privileged housewife in Hartford, Connecticut, no self-deception can save the day.

The film *A History of Violence*, based on the graphic novel of the same name, stars Maria Bello as Edie Stall and Viggo Mortensen as Tom Stall. The premise is that a supposedly ordinary family—wife, husband, two children—live a quiet life in a small town in Indiana. One day Tom Stall is confronted by his former enemies who know his real identity. Although Edie knows nothing consciously, she is in collusion with Tom's deconstruction of his past and her lie is almost greater than his, in order to keep her family together.

The female version of a heroic lie concerns Dolores Claiborne, the narrator of Stephen King's novel of the same name. Dolores, when questioned by the police, insists she did not kill her boss, Vera Donovan, for whom she worked as a housekeeper for many years. But Dolores has her own dark secret: that she's both a victim of domestic abuse and a killer, having murdered her abusive husband many years earlier (wishful thinking come true). In Dolores's painful confession is the conviction that Joe's death was what he deserved for how he treated her. Her self-deception is that the world will honor her cause and view the murder as necessary.

What about Nicole Kidman's character in the 2001 film *The Others*? Kidman plays Grace Stewart, a young mother who takes her two small children to a beautiful, mysterious house in Jersey, England, at the end of World War II to wait for her husband to return from service. While Grace carries on about specific rituals, such as her children not being exposed to any daylight, and her rigid rules for her set of strange new servants, it's all wishful thinking. Grace's horrifying secret is that she is dead, having killed herself and her children when she learned that her husband hadn't survived the war.

These female characters have taken a stance that few men would, and while extreme, what is known to us is how they've lied to themselves. In these somber stories, people suffer—Edie Stall's children are drawn into the drama, as her son witnesses his father's violent nature in *A History of Violence*, while Dolores has committed a murder in *Dolores Claiborne*, and Nicole Kidman's character has done the unspeakable, killed her children before taking her own life. In each tale we recognize the woman's plight.

Lying to ourselves is an art form, honed by women as young girls.

An article in *Scientific American Mind*, "Natural-Born Liars," states that the reason we lie well to others is because we do well at lying to ourselves. "Although we are often ready to accuse others of deceiving us, we are astonishingly oblivious to our own treachery. Experiences of being a victim of deception are burned indelibly into our memories, but our own prevarications slip off our tongues so easily that we often do not notice them or what they are," the article states. Self-deceptions, aka lying to ourselves, takes many forms. It suffices as both a dangerous trick, without boundaries, and as a necessary tool to get us through. Telling yourself you'll lose weight in six week's time or that a dissipating love relationship will rally or that your daughter will get off drugs is wishful thinking, but this specific form of lying to ourselves makes the day more bearable.

Sometimes it's just too difficult for women to *not* lie to themselves. I remember thinking this when I saw the 2000 film *Almost Famous*, when Penny Lane (Kate Hudson), a groupy to a band led by Russell Hammond (Billy Crudup), doesn't know Hammond is married. Or does she? Her rationale exemplifies the layers of wishful thinking. "Isn't it funny?" she says. "The truth just sounds different." Arianna, twenty-seven, involved with a married man for the past year, seconds the sentiments of Hudson's character.

Sure, I knew he was married, but I wanted to be with him, I keep thinking the circumstances will change, I keep believing they can be different. I act like he isn't married, like somehow I'll be with him.

GASLIGHTING

Blaming women for the truth and/or the lie is as old as the beginning of time. According to Greek mythology, Cassandra, the daughter of Priam, the king of Troy, was given the gift of seeing the future by Apollo. However, once she rejected Apollo, he made the gift a curse; she was able to predict the future but no one believed her, instead she appeared to be lying. When Cassandra foresaw the Trojan War and tried to warn people, she was dubbed a hysteric, a woman prone to drama and untruths. The moniker of being a female hysteric is traced today to Cassandra. In a modern-day film, Madeleine Stowe's role in *Twelve Monkeys*, that of Dr. Kathryn Railly, a physician who sees the future and is impotent to save anyone, echoes what Cassandra endured. The tragedy is not only that the women have an ability that is dismissed, but that their truth turned inward can be toxic.

Today, "gaslighting," a form of brainwashing, is something women undergo in unhealthy encounters. In this case, the abuser tries to convince his subject that she has the problem, something is wrong with her and her way of thinking. For example, Jeannette, fifty-one, a saleswoman, explains how she lied to herself about her husband's severe business problems, compounded by his drug use. Whenever she asked a question, she was made to feel she was an interloper.

I stay in this marriage because where would I go? But there are days that are so difficult for me, where my husband is such a disappointment. He has lost all of his capital and he definitely indulges in drugs—and I learned all this the hard way, after he kept fooling me, acting like I was crazy for asking him what he was up to, for being suspicious. When I met him, I thought he was successful, I thought we were going to have this great life. This is my second marriage and his third, and it's not something I can walk away from. I can't imagine starting again with someone else, and who knows what the next guy's problem would be? What bothers me about my husband is how everyone pulled the wool over my eyes. His sisters knew he was tanking and they could have warned me, or his mother even. We lived together before we got married and I just think they wanted me to be his wife and that was better to them than telling the truth. They got what they wanted by fooling me, making me seem like a gold digger or someone who didn't trust people, when I made any noise. Maybe I saw bits and pieces of it, but I always believed it was okay with him, that he was solid.

The term "gaslight" comes from the 1944 film *Gaslight*, starring Ingrid Bergman and Charles Boyer. In this story, Boyer tortures his vulnerable wife by dimming the gaslights in the house so that she thinks she is insane. Definitely this applies to the 1980 film *Private Benjamin*, starring Goldie Hawn. This tale of self-discovery features Hawn as a spoiled young woman whose husband dies on their wedding night. In shock and despair, she joins the army, succeeds at it, and meets a new man, played by Armand Assante. Assante's character, Henri, tries to "gaslight" Hawn's character, Judy Benjamin, when she accuses him of being unfaithful. Although at first she doubts herself and buys into his sketchy explanation, her suspicions are too strong for her to lie to herself for long, and she leaves him.

This treatment of women has existed for a long while—before "gaslighting" was a known phrase. In 1887, Charlotte Perkins Gilman chronicled such an experience. Two years after her daughter was born, Gilman's doctor prescribed a "rest cure" that kept her in a room where she felt imprisoned. She wasn't allowed to write, instead she studied the detailed pattern of the wallpaper and fought to remain sane under such conditions. The implication is that her husband was responsible for tampering with her reality, as documented in *The Yellow Wallpaper*, which she wrote upon her release and remains a feminist treatise.

Denise, forty-one, left her marriage of fifteen years because her husband chose to "gaslight" her.

We have four children together and my husband always made me feel like I was less, like I didn't matter as a mother. He had these inside jokes with the boys, and whenever I said something, they laughed at me. My one daughter never seemed caught up with my husband's meanness—that's really what it was. He was cruel to me and acted like I was the reason things didn't work out, everything from a delayed Little League game to dinner being cold because he got home later than planned. I felt sick inside and like maybe it was me, like if he and the boys acted like I was the one who couldn't get it right, maybe that was the case.

Then I went to visit an old friend and I told her the situation. She said he was playing with my mind and harming me. I thought about how it was so unbearable for me and I asked for a divorce. I had avoided it for years because I didn't want to break up the family. The weird thing is, he still does it to me, but now I'm not his wife, and not in his house. So if he says he'll pick up the kids on Thursday at four P.M. and he does a number on me about it, either canceling or showing up the wrong day and acting like I'm the mess, I know it's him— I'm far enough away to see that now. There's no lying to myself about it now, no thinking it's me when it's him, he's the mess.

In such situations, the truth speaks louder than any elaborate survival lie to oneself, and escape, as in *Private Benjamin,* or in Denise's case, is the solution. Yet women struggle with this issue and it could takes years before they face that it's not their fault, that they deserve better.

RESPONSIBILITY TO OTHERS VERSUS RESPONSIBILITY TO OURSELVES

We've now witnessed how the three dictates that I first described in Chapter 1 apply, depending upon what kind of secret is kept and which lie is told.

1. *The Shame Factor.* The Shame Factor is the first in the lineup of precepts women deal with in the web of secrets and lies. Women wrestle with what people will think and any shameful act puts them in jeopardy socially and harms their image. This doesn't mean that women forfeit the lie but that the lie is carefully constructed. This applies to addiction lies and family secrets in particular.

2. *The Guilt Game.* Just as with shame, women want no guilt attached to their secrets. While shame causes a woman to feel she didn't measure up, guilt evokes a sense of doing the wrong thing, but these emotions manifest differently. Those who have a sense of guilt want to be in the fold and those who feel shameful feel undeserving. Throughout the book, we've seen women who resist being bogged down by guilt and choose their lies with care.

3. *The Denial Quotient.* Without the denial quotient, women wouldn't be able to blow off the two previous emotions. Yet if women had less on their plates, they also wouldn't feel so disempowered and disenfranchised. Then their secrets and lies wouldn't come in so handy, or be as necessary. Jacintha's method of lying to others and lying to herself contains the denial quotient: she uses the lies as a way to protect herself, while she is denying her very reality.

Sissela Bok notes in her book *Lying: Moral Choice in Public and Private Life* that "any number of appearances and words can mislead us: but only a fraction of them are *intended* to do so. . . . We are beset by self-delusion and bias of every kind. Yet we often know when we mean to be honest or dishonest. Whatever the essence of truth and falsity and whatever the sources of error in our lives, *one* such source is surely the human agent, receiving and giving out information, intentionally deflecting, withholding, even distorting it at times." Bok's take on self-delusion is applicable to the women with whom I spoke for this section.

For example, Missie, forty-three, a teacher living in the South, had convinced herself that her life was satisfactory, when in truth she was in search of more.

> I have chosen the wrong men, the wrong jobs, even the wrong girlfriends by telling myself it's good for me, it works, when it doesn't. And I've gotten by with this way of doing things. I don't know how I eventually decided to do better for myself, but I really think it's that I had a job offer. They came to me and I decided to take the job and move to a new town. I met a nice guy and that was also new for me. It's not that I took charge but that I met better people, so it's better now.

This better life feels great, but the fooling myself was okay for years, too. In a strange way, it kept me from being depressed to tell myself things weren't so bad. I used to say to myself, at least you have a decent job and a nice house. Or a date on Saturday night. Now it's a full life, it's different. I've got children and a husband—if I'm going to fool myself it's not about missing out on this, now I have it.

Remember Becca from Chapter 5, who felt disenfranchised due to her mental illness? She explains how she "finally took matters into her own hands" to improve her life and lessen the wishful thinking.

In the last three years, I'd been getting worse. I bought stocks and lost all my money, and couldn't get my parents to advocate. Then I found a private doctor and realized I wasn't just depressed, I was lonely. So I signed up for match.com since it was the only way not to feel humiliated about dating and to be private. I haven't met anyone and then I worry if I do, I'd have to explain my story. I don't mind telling people I have a bipolar disorder, but I won't tell anyone I was hospitalized. I met one person who was too freaked out by the amount of medication I take. It freaked him out and this time I didn't just wish it away, act like his opinion doesn't matter. People so misunderstand why I use antipsychotic drugs. My only delusion is that I'll get married. I'm offering my secret so that other women can cope better; to say that at the drop-in center, it's easy to be who I really am. I'm taking the steps to be on the right track and I'm not hiding behind my disorder, I know my loneliness is very real.

If lying to ourselves is a defense mechanism, as evidenced in Missie's and Becca's interviews, women need the confidence to break a pattern. Missie says she wouldn't have left her "okay" boyfriend or "okay" job if the opportunity hadn't presented itself. Jessica, who we met in Chapter 2, tells us how being in a clinic after having been a prostitute as a teenager, forced her to face the truth. Yet out of fear of destroying her happiness by revealing her past, she chooses not to tell her husband any details, and to diminish the effect her experience had on her.

> I was so young and lonely and lost. I had run away from home and I prostituted myself to get through. I wanted a better life . . . it was horrible what I was doing. I tell myself today that my husband doesn't need to know all that happened to me. He's never learned about my prostituting and I don't want him to know. I did it out of desperation. I had no choice and I doubt he'd get what it was like. I can't lose him, who knows what he'd do if he knew. I want us to be together—we have children, we have this life. . . .

Similarly, Tina, twenty-five, from Utah, a volunteer in a local library, views her omission as a way to protect herself, a survival lie, as well as a way to rewrite the past.

> I wonder if lots of women have as strange a life as I do, or if it's just me. I haven't told my husband in detail what happened to me with my family. I doubt I'll ever say much. I tell myself it never happened and then I can face myself and my child. By keeping it a secret and telling myself a story, it makes it better.

Enough women describe themselves as triumphant, having somehow aced the system, convinced themselves of their own untruths. If a betterment lie told to oneself is cogent, women who are self-deceptive actually believe their own stories. Again, this comes back to how women are positioned in society and it's been going on for centuries.

In a roundabout way, women become honest by investing in the lies they've told themselves, laundering these tales into truths which come out clean.

The tragic heroine Tess, in Thomas Hardy's nineteenth-century novel *Tess of the d'Urbervilles,* questions the value of a woman telling the truth. Tess, a young beauty, is undone early in life when her wealthy cousin, Alec d'Urberville, forces her to have sex and she gives birth to a stillborn child. Once she escapes Alec, she meets Angel Clare, and falls in love. Tess attempts to tell Angel of her past, deluding herself that Angel will understand and she'll be exonerated. Instead, Angel doesn't forgive her, and tells her on their unconsummated wedding night, "You were one person; now you are another." He sends Tess out of his home, and in despair, after poverty and hunger, she becomes Alec d'Urberville's mistress. Soon after, she runs into Angel and in order to escape Alec and be with Angel once again, she slits Alec's throat. The authorities seek her out and she is hung at dawn. This cautionary tale encourages women to lie, to realize the truth is overrated, to weave a story for a chance at happiness.

For modern-day women in America, Margie Goldsmith tells us in her article "Turning Point," in *More* magazine (June 2006), how facing herself and dispelling the insincerity of her life enabled her to leave her marriage and begin anew. A rafting trip on the Colorado River caused Goldsmith to be self-reflective and to face that she and her husband had grown apart. She conjures up the courage to trade in her "Manolo Blahniks for hiking boots, running shoes, scuba fins and flip-flops," replacing wishful thinking with the right reality. Although Rosie, forty, is content with her marriage, it was her career that she had to reevaluate, by first facing the lies she told herself all these years.

> I went to law school thinking I'd love being a lawyer. My mother was a stay-at-home mom and I wanted to have this career and the prestige it brought. But after having children and commuting, I knew I couldn't do it anymore. And I hated the hours. What I didn't want to give up was my salary, so I kept acting like it was better than it was, acting like I still liked it. Then a friend became terminally ill and I woke up and saw that I had to change my life. I had to have another career, or even no career. But taking that step was hard and I don't think anyone can help you face yourself with an issue like this. I left after a year of deliberating and I'm ready to work from home, in a much less pressured environment, on something more creative.

EYES WIDE SHUT

I've always been fascinated by Blanche DuBois, the tragic heroine in Tennessee Williams's play *A Streetcar Named Desire,* and her ability to lie about her past. Blanche became a prostitute, something she would never admit to her sister, Stella Kowalski, and could hardly admit to herself. When Stanley, Stella's redneck husband, learns about it, Blanche is demoralized. As if it isn't treacherous enough for Blanche to have her secret be discovered, Stanley then rapes Blanche the night that Stella gives birth.

It's Stanley's word against Blanche's, and Blanche's story is too raw for Stella, who, with Stanley, arranges for her to be taken to an institution. Is the world today so different from this period piece of the fifties, for women in terms of male supremacy? It's as if Blanche's lies worked better than any truth she could tell when it came to her credibility. In rereading this play, I realized how many women are in jeopardy of being caught, *not* in having the secret and telling the lie.

Yet again, the "good girl" theory, women as pleasers, carries tremendous weight when it comes to lying to ourselves, one of the diciest ways in which women lie. This artifice is partly intrapsychic, partly cultural, and partly a survival technique. However, the blend is tricky, to what degree it works in a woman's favor versus to what degree it can backfire needs to be considered. Claire Owen, psychologist, remarks, "There is a defense mechanism that kicks in when women lie to themselves. This keeps women from being constantly unhappy in a relationship or with a life situation." Seth Shulman, a social worker, points out that a woman's denial and avoidance is a primitive response that can change over time. "As women get older, and more mature, there are some who are able to face their demons and no longer need to deny."

There is a delicate balance in lying to oneself.

Joanna, forty-eight, a journalist in Vermont, says:

Yes, I've consumed sweets, alcohol, shopped too much, and didn't tell my kids about their dad and why we're divorced. I told myself there wasn't any reason they had to know. I think my secrets served me well, especially with my children. And today, no one has 100 percent ownership over me. I'm entitled to this, I earned it, and what I do stays close to the vest. That's what my secrets have done for me.

Carly, thirty-eight, a physical therapist from a town in New England, says:

> What happened at that card table has been retold so many times. I doubt my mother even remembers what she made up. How could she live with herself otherwise? How could any of us know the truth? They never spoke again, my mother and her sister. Both lied, told stories, and got on with their day. My mom bought into her own story, and she used to say to me, give me a good lie or the basic truth.

While some women lie to *contain* their lives, other women rewrite their secrets for themselves, and this reconstructed truth is a reinvention. It's almost as if they've been sleepwalking through life, wake up and start again with a new canvas. If the female lies are about keeping the status quo, lying to oneself for the chrysalis-to-butterfly effect can be inspirational, if laborious.

The downside of lying to ourselves. If women don't recognize how and why they lie to themselves, the lies can affect all areas of their lives. Irene, whom we met in the introduction to this book, a thirty-seven-year-old mother who steals clothing and makeup, does it to create a secret place where no one can infiltrate. Although Irene is aware of the moral implications of stealing, she lies to herself by justifying her behavior.

Seeing is believing. When we compromise by lying to ourselves, it can be poisonous. This is the case with Joyce Carol Oates's novel *We Were the Mulvaneys*, which takes place in the mid-sixties in upstate New York. When a daughter is raped the night of her prom, evoking shame and blame by her family, her mother follows her father's lead, banishing their daughter from their home. The mother concedes her very essence by the lie she tells herself in order to satisfy her husband.

The upside of lying to ourselves. Whether it's realistic or not, there is a hopeful aspect of beguiling oneself that many women experience. This can be a Pollyanna response to stress and sadness, where women would prefer to soften the blow. "I'd rather fool myself than face another terrible truth," remarks Veronica, forty. "I'd rather lie about work, my kids, my husband, money, anything . . ." The lie to ourselves is often an enticing shortcut.

It's a relief to deceive ourselves if it means avoiding the shame that occurs when we are consciously spinning a yarn. When it has to do with sex, body image, mothering, aging, family matters, and addiction, the shame factor looms large, as Dr. Brené Brown points out in her book *Women & Shame*. Notwithstanding the benefits to believing our own lie, it has a component of risk. Yet Marguerite, forty-seven, defended her lie to herself voraciously, and feels triumphant.

> Years ago I convinced myself I made the right choice. When my kids were small, I would leave them with a sitter to visit my boyfriend who lived three thousand miles away. I told myself it would all work out, I would insist upon it! I denied to my mother that I was uncomfortable getting on a plane. I lied to myself because I had no choice. I had to travel to this man in order to get it right. I wanted him to marry me and he did, or I'd still be living in that hick town without any chances for any of us. The boyfriend became my husband and my kids love him.

Despite the downside of lying to oneself, women do it in record numbers. I found that 80 percent of my interviewees admitted to lying to themselves in some form. Whether it be a designated lie, such as Marguerite's situation, or Denise's betterment lie, to hold the family together, or the acceptable lies that Jacintha employs as a means to get through her day, these lies are frequently the basis for much of the secret keeping we do.

Or facing oneself is the answer and the self-deception evaporates. This transpired for Claudia, forty-eight, a stay-at-home mom who converted to her husband's religion when they were first married and returned to her own religion once they were divorced.

I thought that if I became their religion, my mother-in-law and my husband would take me in forever, no matter what. I thought it sort of cemented the deal, but it wasn't that way. Once the marriage didn't work, it was like I'd lied all along, they didn't think I was their religion and I knew I'd never been. We were all pretending, wishing we were the same when it mattered and then knowing it was a farce. I wanted to please my mother-in-law but I look back and what did I gain? I'm bitter about the marriage, more now because I'd done that whole conversion and had given up myself for them. We raised our daughter in this religion, too, with me always observing the holidays, more than anyone else in the family.

One thing about getting divorced is that I know the religion part wasn't worth it and I am so over it. I'm over wanting their acceptance. I feel like the family tried to trick me into the conversion, but it was my fault for buying into their plan for me, for telling myself it was okay, for selling my soul.

NINE

Bold Secrets: Lies That Make or Break Us

As I've come to see in the many interviews, women frequently use lies to create a world as they wished it existed. Or to better the world they live in. Whether it's a lie about sex or money or how motherhood actually depresses some mothers, the lie aids these women in their struggle to get through. In previous chapters we observed Sarah, who carries the burden of her paternity lie; Jollie, whose mother is a drug addict, a fact she's dealt with since she was a young girl; and Letia, thirty-four, who hides the tips she earns waiting on tables. Each of these women see a justification for her lie.

When I began this book, I anticipated that there would be a group of disbelievers when it came to the capacity that women have for lies and secrets. What we have seen in these pages, nevertheless, is how a lie can work for women. Many times, a woman feels an alternative wouldn't be adequate, and without the lie, she lacks a method. Then the lie keeps her on track, having evaluated the positive and negative features, for both short-term lies and long-standing secrets.

On the other hand, there are women who shuck the lie and go straight. This group has expressed an appreciation and a keen understanding of what gives credence to their former lies. Few of these women seemed remorseful over their secrets once they were behind them. Rather, they spoke of the trajectory of the discarded lie, and the merit it once had. Yet for these women, the formula that if you lie enough about it, it can become your reality, is no longer required.

At what price are these lies courageous or dangerous?

TRUTH OR LIE?

When Is It Okay to Lie?

A lie that protects those closest to us is a lie worth telling, a secret worth protecting, providing it doesn't endanger anyone in the process. A lie prevails for a woman who has much to lose by revealing her secret, and little to lose in keeping her cover.

Carol Ann views her omission of her son's father's pedophilia as falling into "the greater good" theory—her family's reputation and her son's emotional state.

My son had to have a chance and I wanted a normal life myself. So I hid who my ex really is. I divorced him over it and I kept it quiet. I thought it would be a bad thing for anyone to know. I told people his father was on a ship, he was traveling for months at a time. After a while no one asked when he came into port. Maybe they thought I'd never been married and I was making it up. I didn't care, as long as I lied about who he really was.

Earlier in the book we saw women who employed secrets when it came to their finances. For Elle, a thirty-eight-year-old freelancer, an accident in a parking lot became a source of found money. She absolves herself of any guilt when it comes to her actions.

> I might not have filed a claim when I slipped if it hadn't been such a tough year for me work-wise. So when I fell on my leg, I sued. I never thought it would pay off. One of my closest friends asked me if I didn't already have that problem, and I just looked at her. I don't know what she meant. I carefully watch myself in the decisions I make, this is one I can justify.

In listening to Nan, fifty-eight, living in New Mexico, with two grown children, there is her fear that had her husband learned of her brief affair, he would have left her. Her point of view is that not disclosing the affair saves her marriage and harms no one.

> I don't see the benefit of telling my husband what happened—he wouldn't understand and he'd hold it against me. It has nothing to do with him and he'd see it as a total betrayal. Besides, it's over, and I've decided I want my husband, not this other man. So whenever a conversation about infidelity comes up, with a girlfriend, or at a dinner party with couples, I say very little. I don't share my outlook and no one knows what I've done. No one. I worry too much about the consequences. I know he'd leave me if I tried to explain. If he asks me if I ever had an affair, I'll say no, to save us, as a couple.

Interestingly, Charlie, twenty-four, working at a not-for-profit, describes herself as having "cheated" on her boyfriend. Her guilt is definitely a heavy load, yet she has no intention of confessing.

> I wish I didn't feel so awful about what I did, but I do. I met a guy at work and we were friends at first. My boyfriend was out

of town and when he came back, I told him part of what happened. Not all of it. It was a mistake to get involved with this guy, it was a moment, that's all, and my boyfriend is my life. I think about telling him the rest, to get it out of my head. I don't do it though, 'cause I know it will make things worse, ruin things for me. I'm afraid to lose my boyfriend, so he can't know.

When we compare these two interviews, Nan's approach and Charlie's are not the same; age and life experience are a part of each woman's response. The commonality is how adamantly they hide their infidelity and their determination to sustain themselves. Charlie experiences deep regret and her characterization of "cheating" is a harsh judgment of herself. Meanwhile, Nan cuts herself some slack and is more forgiving. Both women express fear of being caught and of losing what they have, no wonder a lie is their best bet.

The fear factor might also be a part of the decision to lie for some women, as Louann Brizendine, M.D., explains in her book *The Female Brain.* According to Brizendine, women and men respond to fear and to safeness in different ways, based on what has happened to them in their lives. She writes, "The feeling of safety is built into the brain's wiring, and scans show that girls' and women's brains activate more than men's in anticipation of fear or pain. . . . Females find it harder than do males to suppress their fear in response to anticipation of danger or pain." We can conjecture that the female lie is a means to avoid feeling fearful and out of control.

What do you do if you've been the victim of a woman's lying? Not only do women lie to one another, but a woman can be the victim of another woman's lie. Women understand instinctively when they've been lied to by another woman, almost as a reflection of themselves. If the other woman's lie has been detrimental to you in some way, she should be confronted.

Keila, thirty-four, single mother of five, has made the decision to protect her secrets carefully, especially after her best friend spread the word.

I had to be closemouthed about my first marriage. I met a man at a restaurant, and we became good friends and then I fell in love with him. I would wonder if he knew more about me, would I win? I mentioned this to my best friend, who introduced us. But I didn't say much to this guy about my past and when it ended, I was pleased about that. Then he heard things anyway, things that weren't even true. Now I have a new boyfriend who would also like to know about my marriage, but I know he wouldn't be happy with the story. So I don't say anything. I told my best friend how secretive I'm being, almost lying by not saying a word. I explained how there are things I don't want to talk about with him about my ex-husband. It's not what he needs to know. On my last date with this guy, I realized he knew things, and it finally occurred to me that my best friend said something to him—she knows this man, too. I think I have to say something, to clear the air.

Also Renee, thirty-four, living in a small town in Wisconsin with three small daughters, working as an administrator for a corporation, has been watchful of her secret. Two years ago she stopped being an exotic dancer, but for the eight years that she did it to make ends meet, she was cautious about who knew her source of income.

I was trying to take care of my girls on my own and needed extra money. People close to me knew after a while, but it was years before anyone in my family knew. I didn't want them to know because I'd been raised in such a religious home. My father was a pastor and we all went to Bible school. It wasn't what I was suppose to do. I have never been married and there was no one to fall back on. This was how I could have enough money for us and I didn't get disowned, even though I thought I might, once they knew. I didn't feel guilty about it but I felt sick about it. It's no way to live. And my mother twisted what I did, she didn't understand, she had no idea what I was doing and saw it as evil.

For Betsey, fifty-seven, there have been a series of lies told about her since she moved back to her hometown after her divorce.

I suppose I should just hold a press conference so that women around here can stop talking about me. Especially the ones I know from years ago, from the store where we all worked. One of them told the others that my new boyfriend and I are breaking up. It isn't true; we're planning to live together. I think she is malicious but everyone believes her. Her lies about me make me wonder why I even came back here. What good could it possibly do?

Although Renee and Keila have each chosen a way to make their secrets work for them, they have been undermined by other women. Keila uses a survival lie to guard her past, and Renee to support her family. In Keila's case, her friend's actions were purposeful while Renee recognizes her mother's inability to grasp her predicament. In a different manner, Betsey finds herself maligned by old acquaintances. As Seth Shulman comments on a woman being verbally attacked by other women, "Women have been in a powerless place for a long while, and whenever they feel they can assume a higher status, even if it's a false higher status, they're going to do it."

What do you do if you're the chronic liar? There are women who are constant and compulsive liars and women who keep the lie going and won't stop, because the lie helps them in some way. "Women can find the lie an ongoing part of their lives," remarks Dr. Ronnie Burak. "Honesty is not always the best policy for women. There is a conspiracy theory for women, causing them to lie about their happiness, when they may not be happy at all. Or they lie and it makes them happier. Either way, they're lying for themselves." In either case, a woman would benefit from counseling to understand the underlying reason for her duplicity.

Michelle, thirty-five, a store manager in Springfield, Illinois, with a son and daughter, felt that lying about her father was preferable to finding people to believe the truth.

> My family was respected in our town and I knew from the time I was little that whatever was wrong, I couldn't say anything. There was this contradiction of our lifestyle and being religious, good citizens, and then who my father really was—an alcoholic who hit us. It wasn't safe to find help and tell the truth and our mom didn't want to do that. My sisters and I once told our friends' parents, but no one did anything, nothing at all. No one believed us. So after that I just acted like our mom taught us, to memorize the verses in the Bible and to do nothing at all. And strangely enough, it was a load off my shoulders, the lie was a relief.

Lee, fifty-six, has been embellishing every aspect of her life since high school. She doubts she's harmed anyone, but also admits she'd be hard-pressed to tell the "plain old truth."

> Maybe I'm just a natural-born storyteller, but I always exaggerate and my friends say I'm off base. I will tell you it rained for ten days straight when it was only five, I'll say we biked eight miles when we biked four, I'll say someone is brilliant when

they're maybe smart, at best. I'll say I heard gossip and when I spread it, it's very dramatic—and I will spread the word. Is this so awful, should I be punished? Can I quit the way I speak and think? I doubt it. This is who I am.

While Michelle found the lie a weapon and the truth an albatross, Lee is determined not to stop lying and defends her position as part of her essence. In both cases, we realize how secrets and lies have been threaded into their lives.

How can you tell when it's time to stop? In many instances, there is a statute of limitations on a secret and the accompanying lie. Once the lie is crippling a relationship, or stymieing the woman who lies, it's time to reevaluate why this secret exists at all and what is the advantage of lying. If a woman reveals the truth, and moves her life in a new direction, she has options and can reinvent herself.

It always comes back to the strength of the lie against the hovering possibility of being caught. In Jeffrey Eugenides's novel *Middlesex,* a secret is so dark and daring that it spooks the grandchild of the perpetrators. The narrator, Cal Stephanides, tells how his grandparents, Desdemona and Lefty, immigrated from Turkey to the United States as brother and sister, but embarked as an engaged couple on the ship and were married during the passage. Desdemona's bold secret, of marrying her own brother, surfaces in Cal's mind when his gender is in question. He then wrestles with his fate and the connection to his grandmother's dangerous lie. What is phenomenal about Desdemona's secret is how effortlessly she becomes Lefty's wife, considering the implications of incest.

Incest plays out in a tragic way for Faye Dunaway's character in the film *Chinatown.* In an unforgettable scene, Jack Nicholson's character, Jake Gittes, a private eye, confronts Dunaway's character, Evelyn Cross Mulwray, the daughter of a corrupt real estate developer, and learns that her daughter is also her sister. When Jake presses Evelyn about the young woman she is shielding, Evelyn says "My sister, my daughter, my sister, my daughter," while Jake and the audience alike are dumbfounded by the implications.

Other secrets have a beginning, middle, and end, as Royce, fifty-four, tells us. Living in Washington state where she is presently unemployed, divorced with two sons, she confesses to having lied for years to keep her life in balance.

> I wouldn't tell my husband's family how he treated me, that he was cheating on me for years. I decided it was better for me if they didn't know, as long as I decided to stay in the marriage, there was a reason to act like it was okay. We had these boys and I knew I had to protect his family from what he was like. They liked me better than they liked him and I wanted an extended family. I saw my in-laws as my family, and I wanted to be close to them, more than say a bunch of women friends.
>
> But it was getting harder and harder for me to hide this problem. We'd go on family vacations when the kids were little and he was so awful to me. He had a temper and was emotionally abusive. Finally, it was out in the open after some time since it stopped being worth it for me to lie about him and his ways.

At this juncture, Royce knew her lies to her husband about wanting intimacy had to stop; they were no longer effective.

> I was tired of hanging on, in fear of being stuck without a husband with a family to raise. Then I got strong again, and saw how the lies didn't work. I'd used the lies and it had been fine, but that time was over. It was a new phase, where I didn't want to share a room or a bed with him. That's when I stopped acting like it was okay to have sex, and stopped going through the motions.

Isla, forty-seven, has come to the same conclusion as Royce.

I was happy to lie about my husband's gambling until it was ruining our finances and he was missing work. I lied as long as it was a small problem and I was in on his secret. When it got to be a bigger deal, it was harder. I got so tired of lying, of hiding things, of the life. . . . I really suffered and then I blew it wide open. The time to lie was over.

In all three cases, the honesty arrives after the women have milked their lies dry. Some women say if only there was an ongoing defense of their lie, they'd hesitate before giving it up. It's often an arduous journey to the turning point, when it's clear that the truth is more important than the lie.

How can you tell if it's affecting your life in a negative way? If you are involved with a lie, be it your lie, your sibling's lie, a spouse's lie, or a child's lie, and it's oppressive, it's time to refuse to be in this partnership and move away from the drama. As we have seen with women who become prisoners to their lies, such as addicts and women who have been abused, the lie creates an obstacle to a healthy life. Or if the cover-up is so extreme that it demands more lies, then the original lie is of little use. Some interviewees who were able to fix their lives decided not to reveal their past, yet felt absolved.

This happened to Cari, forty-four, who knew since childhood that her older sister was a drug addict. Although torn between silence or helping her sister by blowing the whistle, she wanted to be loyal to her sister, and to this end kept the secret going.

Until my sister collapsed and needed to be rushed to the hospital a few years ago, I was willing to say she was okay when she wasn't. To my parents, her friends, her boyfriend, anyone who needed to be lied to. But it was too dangerous to be a part of her secret, and she was always lying, so I was always lying for her. Since I carefully lied about her, no one knows she's sober, no one knew she was an addict either. I leave it like this, I'm tired of lying but I don't want to explain the past either.

It's understandable that Cari doesn't want to talk about her sister now, but senses a stranger's curiosity. This applies in the news, too, where any sort of dark stories about women hold a perverse public fascination. When the secret is found out, the woman is often considered a transgressor.

This happened in 2006 in the book world, when a young undergraduate at Harvard, Kaavya Viswanathan, published a first novel with Little, Brown, *How Opal Mehta Got Kissed, Got Wild, and Got a Life*. *The Harvard Crimson* alleged that Viswanathan had plagiarized parts from a novel by Megan McCafferty, and within a few weeks, the publisher stated that they would not publish a revised version of Viswanathan's book, nor her second book scheduled for future publication. Did Viswanathan lie about the book being original material, and if so, why? After all, such a lie is conspicuous, imperiling her entire career. This raises more questions: Was it sheer ambition that caused this error in judgment? Did she not trust her own ability to write a book? What of the shame factor as a result?

Another news story that caught the eye of the public was the Jennifer Wilbanks, "runaway bride," story. Wilbanks, a thirty-two-year-old medical assistant planning to be married in May 2005 in front of six hundred guests in Georgia, instead feigned her own kidnapping in New Mexico several days before the wedding, as reported by cnn.com on May 2, 2005. It's one thing to change one's mind about a wedding, but boarding a Greyhound bus for Las Vegas as if you are abducted is quite another. With both Viswanathan and Wilbanks, the short-lived secrets resonate with the crash and burn of being discovered and dissected by the media.

Clarice, thirty-two, has discarded her secret happily. Living in New England, divorced with two sons, working as a caregiver, Clarice views her life as having gone either way, truth or fiction.

> I was miserable in my marriage and thought I should keep it to myself—for years. I stayed married because there were no complaints, the money was good, I had everything I needed. I thought things would improve, I always thought, there's another tomorrow and it will be better. Now I see that the problem was my husband, not me. He always said I wasn't a good wife, but a good mother. It wasn't true, I was a good wife, good enough to act like it was all okay when he had so many problems. Today I'm without him and it's much better, but much harder, too. The lie is off my shoulders, and that's a relief. I'm just learning about how to meet people and get out in the world, without any story to tell, anything to cover up. On the other hand, I was good at the lie. I might have worked that out, too.

What are your options: lying or coming clean? We have witnessed that women who conform to society are often the ones who believe their own lies. Recognizing your personal guidelines for the truth and the price paid for the lie is a measuring device; one that defines your options in lying to yourself and in lying to others.

Living the Lie

Here we see how deception can fortify a woman with what she wants. Lindy, thirty, working in retail and living in the South, used a man to become a citizen and lied about her feelings for him.

> I married a man for a green card and pretended to love him. We seem like a couple that belong together so it's better to act like I love my husband and have this life and be a citizen than

to chase love. I'd make the same decision again and it's a secret worth having—I don't see the harm. I look at this like a business transaction and it's fine. When I think of what I've given up, the chance to have a romance, I wish there'd been another way to get that green card. But why expose myself, why not just lie and stay put?

It's amusing that Catherine Zeta-Jones's character, Marylin Rexroth, in the film *Intolerable Cruelty,* fools men into marrying her so she can inherit their wealth, but we also identify with her goals. Women may disparage the term "gold digger," yet the realities of life for women, how things shake out in materialistic society, sustain why a betterment lie proves helpful. In the words of Rafie, a thirty-year-old wife and mother with whom I spoke:

> I want a certain kind of lifestyle and I did what I needed to do to get it, including marrying up and falsifying my credentials. This is a lie I support and a way for me to have a better life.

If Zeta-Jones plays the part of a conniving femme fatale on screen, Lindy, in real life, gladly plays a similar game for her green card, which she considers a noble cause.

> I can't make myself love him. So I don't, but I make it work, I live with my secret. I like that I had this choice.

In another arena, Brandy, thirty-nine, has opted for a lie rather than the truth. She tells us that she wouldn't have her twin daughters if she had been honest with her husband about having children.

> When I was first married, I wasn't sure I wanted kids and that was what my husband wanted to hear. Then I did and my husband didn't and I knew to keep my feelings a secret, to avoid a

big problem in our marriage. I knew that he'd say we had made a deal and he wasn't changing his mind. One time I was pregnant and I was secretly ecstatic and he was furious. He wanted me to have an abortion but I miscarried. Then I really knew where he stood and what I had to do. I went to a specialist on my own, I told my husband nothing. I took drugs and I got pregnant with twins. I manipulated things so that his family knew and was thrilled before he knew. I made it happen and to this day, he's in shock. After my miscarriage we were told it would be tricky, so he's scratching his head about how I got pregnant. I won't even say what I did. It was worth everything.

At thirty-five, Tanya has worked in the corporate world for the past ten years, and depends upon her lies for her success on the job.

I lied with purpose at work—first to get a foot in the door and then to climb the ladder. I saw no way to not lie, I had to embellish my résumé, my background, my experience, my private life. I did it all, told them everything they wanted to hear and it worked. If I'd come in as this inexperienced young woman off the street, it wouldn't have gotten me even my first job. I have used my lie wisely, in the workplace and with friends who are in high places. Will I ever get caught? I think about that, I think about how my past has to be a secret. Then I think how unfair the world is, or I wouldn't have had to do it this way to begin with.

Maylise, twenty-four, describes how her secrets have sustained her socially and emotionally. She lives in northern California and works in advertising.

If I wanted to be honest, I'd be left behind. I think it's a confidence issue for me. My mom was very young when she married and she was okay with it, with being stuck with kids and without any other plan. I didn't want it that way and I did whatever I needed to do so I wouldn't end up like her. I wanted to reinvent myself and I did. I see the results of rewriting my past with guys and with work. I have moved my life forward by not telling the truth about myself, about my family. It's all made-up and it works. I wouldn't give this lie up—it's better than any real-life story.

Coming Clean

In contrast to women who engage in their lies so comfortably, the women whose stories follow felt it was the right time to quit their double-dealing. Erica, thirty, who travels frequently for business, has made this decision.

I was always unfaithful in my supposedly monogamous relationships. Then I decided I didn't want to do it anymore, I didn't want to act one way when I was really doing something else. I didn't exactly have a confessional but I stopped the flirtations and one-night stands when I was out of town for work. This way, I can be free of the secret going forward. I don't owe anyone an explanation but I'm ready for this way of doing things—I'm trying honesty as a policy. It feels different, as if I've chosen another kind of life. It's lighter, and easier for me, I never have to think before I speak—I'm not hiding anything anymore.

Marissa, fifty-one, believes that the lies she told for her brother's sake worked, up to a point. Today she recognizes the fine line between protection and vulnerability.

I don't think there was much choice when I first started covering up for my brother. There was my mother, a single mother, to think of, plus his wife and kids and my children and all that would go wrong if people knew. Or if he got caught. So I stuck by this lie for years and it was the right decision for a while. Then he got so out of hand that I would ask myself what I was doing. Whatever could go wrong with my brother did, and he destroyed himself and took our money and squandered it. In the beginning my helping him was in good faith, I thought he'd clean up, be grateful. He can't help himself and I can't lie for him anymore.

Julia, sixty, working in human resources, claims the advantage to having a secret is knowing when to give it up.

For years I kept all sorts of secrets and told stories to cover my tracks. I would lie about my whereabouts, my kids, my plans. Mostly to my boyfriend, but also to my colleagues. Eventually it catches up with you, that's the thing. Now I'm honest to a fault—I didn't announce to the world, okay now I'm no longer a liar, I just made a decision to say what I really do, what I really feel, and that works better for me. I think I hid behind the secrets and I got tired of the game. Not that either way has gotten me where I'd like to be. It's just time to say the truth.

Sometimes it takes an uncovered secret, as well as a solidly held secret, for a woman to feel she's in control. An example of how unraveled secrets end up setting women free is evidenced in *sex, lies, and videotape* (1989). In the movie, Andie MacDowell is Ann Bishop Mullany, married to John Mullany, Peter Gallagher's character. John is having an affair with Ann's sister, Cynthia Patrice Bishop, played by Laura San Giacomo. This is Cynthia's secret and Ann hasn't a clue, she is too caught up in her own unhappiness in her marriage, which is her secret. When Graham Dalton, played by James Spader, arrives and spills his secret, that he's impotent, both sisters warm to him and allow him to film them on videotape. As the sisters' choices and lies are reevaluated by their interactions with Graham, they come to terms with their desires.

In real-life experiences, as in this film, there is the pragmatic quality of a woman's secrets, and the self-actualizing characteristics of being sincere. Whatever category of lie is told to achieve a goal, there is always the option to reverse this decision and reveal the truth.

Conclusion: The Female Talent for the Moral Lie

According to the *American Heritage Dictionary*, morality is defined as "a set of customs of a given society, class or social group which regulate relationships and prescribed modes of behavior to enhance the group's survival. A set of ideas of right and wrong." What I learned in writing this book is that while a woman's secret may not be moral by a community standard, it has a creed of its own. Women's experiences are not like men's, not culturally, emotionally, sexually, nor are women gratified in many of their endeavors and intentions. For this reason, as long as the male criterion prevails, women will cut corners, devise their own totality, and navigate a singular path.

Mora, a forty-two-year-old woman with whom I spoke, palliates her decision to have kept a secret from her son and daughters for many years.

> Had I told my son earlier to find his real father, before he was ready, he would have been bitter, and unforgiving. I led him to believe that my husband, who has been in his life since he was a small boy, is his biological father. My son asked me why I'd never told him and I said I wanted to keep the family together—I wanted him to feel equal. He has half-sisters who

he believed were his full sisters. I kept this secret and I insisted my husband go along with me. So now that he knows, at the age of seventeen, it's a shock for the girls, too, but the kids have had the benefit of a nuclear family, and my son's had a father figure. Maybe this secret was selfish, but I stand by my decision.

Was Mora's choice, a betterment lie, to mislead her son and daughters, the right decision? Did she preempt her son's ability to find his biological father or did she build a solid home life for her son? What remains to be seen is the fallout—how her son feels about the facts. It is significant that Mora purposely lied to protect her son, and her satisfaction is the close, undisrupted family life that her children experienced as a result.

"Socially, women generally feel misunderstood by men," Brenda Szulman, a therapist, tells us. "If they convey their inner thoughts, they could be thwarted and damned." Based on my study, the return on the investment of the secret and the lie can exceed any negative emotions, depending on the nature of the lie.

The shame factor influences women to be cautious, but not to forfeit the lies. Katie, thirty, explains her decision not to tell her husband that she'd been raped when she was fourteen. Still, carrying the weight of her secret, a survival lie, all these years has taken its toll.

It's always there but so is my reason not to bring it into my marriage. I've struggled with everything that happened, but I want to keep it to myself, I don't want to share it. It's better this way for me. I know my secret presses down on me but it's worth it, worth it as a secret.

THE OVERRATED TRUTH?

The harsh light of reality is often too much to bear. Consider Isabelle's beneficial lie about her son who has joined the armed forces. At forty-two, she is a single mother of three and works as a nurse in Pennsylvania.

> It isn't that my son hasn't done well, but that he's joined the army. I wouldn't have ever imagined this from him and now I have to worry about his safety. It wasn't what I taught him, it wasn't what I want for him and he knows that. I raised my children on my own and I wanted the boys to be in business. It's kind of a slap in the face, then I always think he can get a degree, like the ads on TV, through the army. I try to never look at the dangers or read the news about what happens to boys in Iraq. I act like he's not there, like he's in some reserve unit, that's how I get through, I have told very few people what he did because I'm not really proud of this. I wasn't born here and I'm not in favor of the war. I told no one in our family at home. I say he's working abroad, that's all.

Ironically, it appears that for some women in the news, it's the truth that could complicate their lives. On November 4, 2006, the New York *Daily News* featured the story "English Lather: Miss U.K. Stripped of Her Crown." Apparently, Danielle Lloyd, Miss Great Britain, lost her title after she revealed that she'd had an affair with a judge for the very contest she won. Corky Siemaszko, a staff writer at the *Daily News*, writes: "Memo to beauty pageant winners: If you want to keep your crown, don't blab about sleeping with a judge." Had Ms. Lloyd not boasted of a Christmas gift bestowed upon her by a soccer star judge, her boyfriend, Teddy Sheringham, no one would have figured out that the couple had been involved before the pageant, which is against the rules. Undeniably there is wisdom in such information remaining a secret in order to keep one's crown.

Similarly, Jeanine Pirro, the thrice-elected district attorney of Westchester County, New York, has been exposed for her secrets. Pirro made headlines in the summer of 2006 when the Republicans considered running her against Hillary Clinton for the Senate. All would have gone according to plan had Pirro not distrusted her husband. As reported by Steve Fishman in his article in *New York* magazine, "The Exclusive Marriage-Counseling Sessions," Pirro consulted Bernard Kerik, the former police commissioner of New York City, and allegedly "urged Kerik to bug her husband's boat." Because Kerik had problems of his own, the conversation with Jeanine Pirro was taped by federal investigators. Fishman writes, "Now the government is said to be investigating Jeanine. Portions of Jeanine's conversations with Kerik were leaked to WNBC, a leak targeted for maximum political damage."

If we consider how long Pirro had looked the other way (according to Fishman, Al Pirro had been unfaithful to his wife for many years, including having one tryst that produced a child), it's curious why she insisted on the truth. Would it not have served her better to lie about her marriage to her public or to have lied to herself about his latest affair and saved face?

Another female debacle regarding the truth occurred in October 1991. Anita Hill then testified at Clarence Thomas's Senate confirmation hearings that he had made sexual advances toward her when he was her supervisor at the Equal Employment Opportunity Commission (EEOC) during the early 1980s. Hill's objection to the confirmation of Thomas as a Supreme Court judge, based on her personal encounter, raised the issue of sexual harassment, which henceforth has defined the gold standard for propriety in the workplace. According to the Museum of Broadcast

Communications, "Thomas vehemently denied Hill's allegations and responded with outrage. Although the press described it as her word against his, the 'vastly differing recollections of events' kept the public from any revelation of the facts." Thomas was confirmed, but it was Hill's claims and her determination to speak out that have been beneficial for women ever since. Anita Hill created a new view of gender politics at work and the significance of a woman's word.

THE PERSISTENT SHADES OF GRAY

In his book *Why We Lie,* David Livingstone Smith notes that "the brain has no difficulty scrambling messages before they reach the conscious mind. The manipulation for information before it gets to the consciousness makes self-deception possible. There is nothing inherently incredible about the idea that our brains tendentiously manipulate information about our social interactions, just as they manipulate sensory and motor information." This applies to Deb, forty-four, divorced with three children, who decided not to marry her long-standing boyfriend after her compassionate lie kept her with him for three years.

> I promised my boyfriend that before I turned forty-five, I'd marry him. But now that the time is near, I doubt I can. There are too many complications and I wonder if I always knew this, if I was just plain lying to him. I was flattered that he wanted to be with me, with my kids, and after my bad divorce and all that still goes on with my ex. I wanted to be with him, too, but deep down, I knew it wasn't right for me. It's better to be honest now and see if he'll stay on my terms, without getting married. When forty-five was far off, in the beginning, it was better to lie, to say, sure, let's do it. It sounded right, it's

what you're supposed to do, marry again. I kept saying this to myself.

Leandre's experience also entails marriage as a goal. At forty-five, she is remarried, having "seduced" her husband six years ago, using a designated lie, in order to seal the deal.

We were dating for years and both of us were divorced. I knew that nothing further would happen unless we were connected more than we were. That meant getting pregnant. But he said he didn't want any more children and I knew that had to change. I had to get pregnant, so there was nothing to stop us from being together. I did it, and we have these darling twins and then both of us have children from our first marriages, who are older. What I did is a trick and I'd never tell him how deliberate it was. I remember acting like it was a happy accident when it was all planned, to get what I wanted. It's almost as if I didn't understand quite what he was saying when he said no more children. I had selective hearing and selective memory and I got it right.

Maybe Leandre is on to something when it comes to pregnancy and confessions. Justin Rocket Silverman reported at Newsday.com on November 21, 2005, that an unmarried pregnant teacher was fired from a Catholic school in Queens, New York, after announcing her pregnancy. Apparently, Michelle Mc-Cusker, twenty-six, had informed the principal at St. Rose of Lima School in Rockaway Beach, where she taught pre-k, of her condition. She subsequently filed a federal complaint of gender discrimination. When we review the fallout of her pregnancy and loss of revenue, one can't help wonder if McCusker might have done better to have created a ficticious husband or fiancé.

These shades of gray are prevalent among family secrets and

survival lies. For Marissa, who we met in the previous chapter, her lie for her brother's illicit habits drained her for years. But as he tanked, she knew the right thing was not to lie, but to speak up.

> This is some kind of personal journey for me. First I did a good job at the lie and now I'm getting good at the truth. It's about time and place.

In other circumstances, women use secrets as leverage. For example, Meryll, thirty-nine, is the mother of two small children and works in the computer industry. She has an $8,000 debt and a shopping addiction.

> I do it because I grew up in a large family and there was never enough. I go through money and into debt because I can't feel alive otherwise. It looks like I'm a model wife and mother, but really I have a controlling husband and I had a controlling father and I'm not okay from these men. Debt is a problem, but I don't see how shopping to act out is a problem. I need more money for it, that's all. I won't be telling anyone about this debt—I'll figure out a way to pay it. I know that material things can't make me happy, still it's the only time in my life when it's not about the children or work or my husband, so I like it for that, for me. I sort of make this work for me.

If Joann, forty-five, a journalist, hasn't left her live-in boyfriend of fifteen years but travels alone extensively in search of a more suitable mate, she feels she can't be faulted.

> I won't leave until a new person has proven his level of commitment and I don't think I need to tell my boyfriend that. I have broken up with him, stayed away, but I always go back. It's always the same, I think I should find someone else, but I

don't say a word. I take what works from this flawed relationship and keep on the lookout. If honesty is the best policy, that
doesn't apply here. My telling him that I'm looking for someone else, especially on business trips, would be a disaster. If
I'm asked on a date, I go, even though I live with someone. It
sounds insane, but it works for me.

*A woman's lie is predicated on societal prescriptions and lim-
ited choices.*

In general, there is a continuum of expectations that women
aren't capable of deceit of any sort, including overspending, having an affair, stealing merchandise, padding their children's college applications, taking drugs, or mismanaging money. Yet these
women are telling us they feel they have little recourse, as Seth
Shulman, a social worker, notes, "How stereotypically arrogant
men can be about a woman's behavior or the reasons behind it."
Shulman remarks, "Women are underestimated all the time. In
some ways, this provides extra room for a woman to have a secret
and a lie."

Although no one believed Bertha, Rochester's wife in Charlotte Brontë's classic novel *Jane Eyre,* her insistence that she
wasn't mad and was Rochester's proper wife only worsened the
situation. Meanwhile, Jane Eyre's wishful thinking granted
her Rochester's hand in marriage and, by going along with
Rochester's theory that his wife was crazy, Jane was rewarded.
Rochester's sight was miraculously restored, while Bertha, the
interloper in Jane's estimation, died in a fire. Jane prevailed by
believing Rochester's fable and won a husband in the process,
but the price is steep.

In contrast to Jane Eyre's decision to sell out for the husband,
we have a modern-day novel of remarriage and self-reflection. In

Joanna Trollope's novel *Other People's Children*, Elizabeth falls in love with Tom, who has been married twice with offspring from both marriages. Since Elizabeth has never been married, the idea of entering this extended, blended family is intimidating, but she loves Tom enough to try. When Tom's adult daughter makes life miserable, Elizabeth is unable to lie to herself for the sake of her future husband and the life they would share. Instead she faces that the dysfunction runs very high among the children and a former wife, and she breaks off the engagement. If one's goal is to be married, Elizabeth's decision and stark honesty might not be the best hand to play. Surely Jane Eyre wasn't going to dig around and find the dirt on Rochester and his first wife. To the contrary, she signs up so wholeheartedly for his lie that it becomes her lie.

THE FEMALE ADVANTAGE

The ongoing dilemma for women persists: to lie or not to lie, and what facilitates a better result.

In his book *Moral Minds*, Marc D. Hauser tells us that there is a universal taboo against lying. I couldn't help but think of the myriad women with whom I've spoken for this book and how little about their lives is so clear-cut that deception doesn't become part of the landscape, at the very least.

Despite the cheerleading for women, there is no status quo, no guarantee that any of the stages of their lives will be smooth and successful. What drives women to the numerous ways in which we guard secrets and tell tales is the degree to which we feign happiness and confidence, with all the complexities that our culture places upon us.

Based on my research, the majority of women have crafted ways to work the lie, even when the lie has an expiration date.

Secrets set the stage. My interviewees were quite clear about *why* they have their secrets and *how* they use their lies. Repeatedly women remarked, "I lie because it makes things work." "How else could I get by?" "I know what I'm doing and I'd do it again."

Operate from strength, not weakness. Is your friend's rivalry lie merely amusing or it is getting to you? Is your secret worth having or is it baggage you are prepared to toss? Consider the risk/reward ratio in choosing to perpetuate a secret and lie.

Weigh the white lies. Are women afraid to appear as we actually are in our overextended lives? These aren't survival lies, nor are they compassionate or betterment lies.The white lie is so close to us that we scarcely give it a thought. Yet this can be a less frequent tool if we demand that our families and friends become tolerant of our needs.

Juggling the lie. Women with multifaceted lying profiles and secrets at every turn claim that each secret has a place in the daily struggle. Still, a woman might do well to be discerning, carefully choosing when to keep a secret. If not, the lie can subsume her. The timing of both the lie and the truth is critical.

Consider the consequences of your lies. Ask yourself: Are you lying to keep an important secret? Are you lying to protect the innocent or the guilty? The lie might become so comfortable and familiar that the.truth feels threatening. It's wise to pay attention to the repercussions for our lies.

THE EXPIRED LIE

As I was about to wrap up the interviews for this book, I came upon two illuminating interviews. Valerie, fifty-four, who works in the music world, looks back fondly on the years she spent hiding her reality from her friends and coworkers.

In the mid- to late nineties I had a secret life. I was doing diet pills, drugs, and shopping like crazy. I had a boyfriend on the side and no one ever knew. To this day, my live-in boyfriend hasn't a clue. I was never where I was supposed to be, where I said I'd be. I would take my daughter to her friends' so I could do these things. I'd tell my office I had a meeting downtown when it wasn't the truth. I know this sounds odd, but it was a good period in my life and I always knew I was able to handle it. But things changed. My daughter was getting older and needed more of me, and I became more accountable. Then we moved away and I saw no reason to begin again, doing all that I'd done in secret for five years straight. I think I got over whatever made the secrets so important.

So no one knows what I did and that's fine, but it's different now. Now I'm who I'm supposed to be, who I was pretending to be. But those secrets sure got me through a tough time, when I wasn't certain about my career or my love life and I didn't feel like I looked good enough. I'm grateful I had this other life—it makes me appreciate my daughter and my boyfriend more than ever.

Gizelle, forty-two, didn't marry until she was forty. She describes her initial dislike of her stepdaughters as a secret worth keeping.

When I met my husband he was bruised from a bitter divorce. He had three teenage daughters and I knew it would be an issue. I never let on that I had trepidation or that I thought they were spoiled. These girls were always describing their mother to me as some perfect person. I kept pretending that I liked these wicked daughters, even though they were awful. I married their father, and part of why that happened, I think, is that I never said anything negative about his girls. It was an act, but I stuck with it, and after a while I got to know them and I like them. Today it isn't a lie that I care about my stepdaughters, it's the truth.

This is the kind of thinking shown to us in the lives of women who enlist their secrets. In learning how women ascertain their lies we learn how they perceive themselves—a reminder that a woman's deceit is not merely a negative response to a difficulty, but comprised of self-knowledge, self-awareness, and self-protection.

We understand Valerie's motivation at a point in time. She would describe her lies as both bold and beneficial, an attempt to expand her options. In defense of her lie, Valerie clings to the eternal good girl.

I didn't hurt anyone or make a problem. I thought it through and I lied when I needed to, end of story.

Gizelle's lie seems not only appropriate but easy enough, because, as we've witnessed in this study, women lie to position themselves, to alter their world, avoid obstacles, and attain power. It is Gizelle's success through her lie, as a means to a happy marriage and eventually a real relationship with her stepdaughters, that gives us hope. Her experience reminds us that the life span of the lie is as important as the lie itself.

Whatever the magnitude, the secrets and accompanying lies exist in the lives and hearts of women. The voices of the women themselves give us clear examples of the styles of female lies, each of which is partly acquired and partly innate behavior. In my research for *Little White Lies, Deep Dark Secrets*, I've come to recognize lying as an inestimable weapon in the female arsenal as women search for personal retribution and satisfaction.

ACKNOWLEDGMENTS

To the anonymous women who came forward to offer their experiences, I offer a heartfelt thank-you. Their voices are the soul of this book.

Meredith Bernstein, my agent, and Jennifer Enderlin, my editor, were at the fateful lunch where we discussed how women keep secrets and why women lie. Their endless support has propelled this book to life.

At St. Martin's Press (in alphabetical order), Sara Goodman, John Murphy, Sally Richardson, Frances Sayers, Colleen Schwartz, Matthew Shear, Dori Weintraub. For listening: Lori Ames, Gail Clott, Ashley Deiser, Susie Finesman, Brit Geiger, Meryl Moss, Judy Shapiro, Cynthia Vartan. Jennie Ripps, my muse, Robert Marcus, my lawyer, Emilie Domer, Ben Peryer, and Amanda Soule, my assistants. In academia: Elizabeth Irmiter, Suzanne Murphy, and Micheal Rengers at Sarah Lawrence College, Carol Camper, Lewis Burke Frumkes at Marymount Manhattan College. In Hollywood: Jon Avnet, Sally Robinson, Bruce Vinokour, Meredith Wagner, Allison Wallach, Ellyn Williams. The professionals who have contributed their thoughts to this book: Dr. Ronnie Burak, Dr. Donald Cohen, Claire Owen, Seth Shulman, Brenda Szulman. My parents, Selma and Herbert L. Shapiro, my in-laws Helene and Ted Barash, and dearest friends.

Jennie, Michael, and Elizabeth Ripps, my precious children. Lastly, Gary A. Barash, my husband, steadfast, knowing.

REFERENCES

Ahern, Vanessa Geneva. "Save Yourself from Holiday Debt." *Shape*, November 2004.

Ally McBeal. Created by David E. Kelley. Fox, 1997–2002.

Almost Famous. Directed by Cameron Crowe. Columbia Pictures, 2000.

American Demographics. "For Richer & for Poorer." July 2000.

American Society for Aesthetic Plastic Surgery (ASAPS). www.surgery.org.

Archives of General Psychiatry. http://archpsyc.ama-assn.org.

Armstrong, Mark. "Anna Nicole Smith's Plus-Sized Payday." *E! News Online*, September 28, 2000.

Associated Press. "DNA Confirms What Hurley Knew." CBS News, June 19, 2002.

Atwood, Margaret. *Cat's Eye.* Toronto: McClelland and Stewart, 1988.

Bachelorette, The. Created by Mike Fleiss. ABC, 2003–2005.

Banger Sisters, The. Directed by Bob Dolman. Fox Searchlight Pictures, 2002.

Barash, Susan Shapiro. *A Passion for More: Wives Reveal the Affairs That Make or Break Their Marriages.* Berkeley, Calif.: Berkeley Hills Books, 2001.

———. *Tripping the Prom Queen: The Truth About Women and Rivalry.* New York: St. Martin's Press, 2006.

Barrett, Jennifer. "Something Good Out of Something Bad." *Newsweek,* July 21, 2005.

Basic Instinct. Directed by Paul Verhoeven. TriStar Pictures, 1992.

Because I Said So. Directed by Michael Lehmann. Universal Pictures, 2007.

Belle de Jour. Directed by Luis Buñuel. 1967; Miramax Films, 1995.

Bennetts, Leslie. "Teri Hatcher's Desperate Hour." *Vanity Fair,* April 2006.

Benson, April Lane. *I Shop Therefore I Am: Compulsive Buying & the Search for Self.* Lanham, Md.: Jason Aronson, 2000.

Bergin, Michael. *The Other Man: John F. Kennedy Jr., Carolyn Bessette, and Me.* New York: Harper Collins, 2004.

Best, Ben. "Some Philosophizing About Lying." *Essays on Philosophy.* www.benbest.com/philo/lying.html (accessed June 12, 2007).

Bewitched. Created by Sol Saks. ABC, 1964–72.

Bhattacharya, Shaoni. "Fake Lie-Detector Reveals Women's Sex Lies." *Journal of Sex Research,* 40, p. 27.

Big Love. Created by Mark V. Olsen and Will Scheffer. HBO, 2006–.

Black, Edward. "96 Percent of Women Are Liars, Honest." *The Scotsman,* December 9, 2004.

Body Heat. Directed by Lawrence Kasdan. Warner Bros. Pictures, 1981.

Bok, Sissela. *Lying: Moral Choice in Public and Private Life.* New York: Vintage, 1999.

Breakfast at Tiffany's. Directed by Blake Edwards. Paramount Pictures, 1961.

Bridgforth, Glinda. "When Shopping Is a Sickness." *Essence,* August 2004.

Brizendine, Louann, M. D., *The Female Brain.* New York: Morgan Road Books, 2005.

Brokeback Mountain. Directed by Ang Lee. Paramount Pictures, 2005.

Broken Flowers. Directed by Jim Jarmusch. Focus Features, 2005.

Brontë, Charlotte. *Jane Eyre.* 1847; New York: Dover Publications, 2003.

Brown, Brené. *Women & Shame: Reaching Out, Speaking Truths and Building Connection.* London: 3C Press, 2004.

Burning Bed, The. Directed by Robert Greenwald. NBC, 1984.

Bushnell, Candace. *Lipstick Jungle.* New York: Hyperion, 2005.

Capote, Truman. *Breakfast at Tiffany's.* 1950; New York: Penguin, 1998.

Carey, Benedict. "The Secret Lives of Just About Everybody." *The New York Times,* January 11, 2005.

Catalyst, 2005. www.catalystwomen.org.

Cat on a Hot Tin Roof. Directed by Richard Brooks. M-G-M, 1958.

CBSNewsonline. June 2002, Elizabeth Hurley's paternity case.

Celebrity Couples Online. www.celebritycouples.net.

Centre for Addiction & Mental Health (CAMH). http://www.camh.net.

Center for Postpartum Adjustment. www.postpartumsupport.com.

Chicago. Directed by Rob Marshall. Miramax Films, 2002.

Chinatown. Directed by Roman Polanski. Paramount Pictures, 1974.

Chopin, Kate. *The Awakening.* 1899; New York: Avon, 1982.

Closer. Directed by Mike Nichols. Columbia Pictures, 2004.

CNN.com. "Charges Not Ruled Out for Runaway Bride," May 2, 2005. www.cnn.com/2005/US/05/01/wilbanks.found/index.html (accessed June 12, 2007).

CNN.com. "Hillary Clinton: 'This Is a Battle,'" January 27, 1998. www.cnn.com/ALLPOLITICS/1998/01/27/hillary.today/ (accessed June 12, 2007).

Coles, Joanna. "The Mommy Diaries." *New York,* July 24, 2006.

Conroy, Pat. *The Prince of Tides.* Boston: Houghton-Mifflin, 1986.

Crawford, Christina. *Mommie Dearest,* New York: William Morrow, 1976.

Crittenden, Ann. *The Price of Motherhood: Why the Most Important Job in the World Is Still the Least Valued.* New York: Henry Holt and Company, 2002.

Dangerous Beauty. Directed by Marshall Herskovitz. Warner Bros. Pictures, 1998.

Daniluk, Judith. *Women's Sexuality Across the Life Span: Challenging Myths, Creating Meanings.* New York: The Guilford Press, 1988.

Desperate Housewives. Created by Marc Cherry. ABC, 2004–.

Devil Wears Prada, The. Directed by David Frankel. 20th Century–Fox, 2006.

Dunaway, Faye. *Looking for Gatsby: My Life.* New York: Simon & Schuster, 1995.

Etcoff, Nancy. *Survival of the Prettiest: The Science of Beauty.* New York: Anchor Books, 2000.

Eugenides, Jeffrey. *Middlesex.* New York: Picador, 2002.

Eyes Wide Shut. Directed by Stanley Kubrick. Warner Bros. Pictures, 1999.

Far from Heaven. Directed by Todd Haynes. Focus Features, 2002.

Fatal Attraction. Directed by Adrian Lyne. Paramount Pictures, 1987.

Fessler, Ann. *The Girls Who Went Away: The Hidden History of Women Who Surrendered Children for Adoption in the Decades Before Roe v. Wade.* New York: Penguin Press, 2006.

Fingerman, Karen L. *Aging Mothers and Their Adult Daughters: A Study in Mixed Emotions.* New York: Springer Publishing Company, Inc., 2001.

First Wives Club, The. Directed by Hugh Wilson. Paramount Pictures, 1996.

Fischer, Agneta H. *Gender and Emotion: Social Psychological Perspectives (Studies in Emotion and Social Interaction).* New York: Cambridge University Press, 2000.

Fisher, Carrie. *Postcards from the Edge.* New York: Pocket Books, 2002.

Fishman, Steve, "The Exclusive Marriage-Counseling Sessions." *New York,* October 23, 2006.

Fitch, Janet. *White Oleander.* New York: Little, Brown, 1999.

Fitzgerald, F. Scott, *The Great Gatsby.* 1925; New York: Scribners, 1999.

Forward, Susan, and Craig Buck. *Obsessive Love: When It Hurts Too Much to Let Go.* New York: Bantam, 2002.

Fox, Kate. "Evolution, Alienation and Gossip: The Role of Mobile Tele-communications in the Twenty-first Century." Social Issues Research Centre. www.sirc.org/publik/gossip.shtml (accessed June 12, 2007).

Fraser, Lady Antonia. *Marie Antoinette: The Journey.* New York: Anchor Books, 2002.

Freydkin, Donna. "Reality-Show Contestants Raise Glasses, Concerns." *USA Today,* February 17, 2003.

Friends with Money. Directed by Nicole Holofcener. Sony Pictures, 2006.

Gabe Kapler Foundation. Tarzana, California. www.kaplerfoundation.org.

Gamblers Anonymous. www.gamblersanonymous.com.

Gamerman, Ellen. "Mismatched.com." *The Wall Street Journal,* April 1, 2006.

Gaslight. Directed by George Cukor. M-G-M, 1944.

Gift, The. Directed by Sam Raimi. Lakeshore Entertainment, 2001.

Gilligan, Carol. *In a Different Voice: Psychological Theory and Women's Development.* Cambridge, Mass.: Harvard University Press, 1993.

Gilman, Charlotte Perkins. *The Yellow Wallpaper.* 1892; New York: Dover, 1991.

Goldsmith, Margie. "Turning Point." *More,* June 2006.

Good Morning America. Mommy Wars segment, host Diane Sawyer. February 22 and 23, 2006.

Gordon, Meryl. "Duel at Sunrise." *New York,* June 6, 2005. http://nymag.com/nymetro/news/media/features/11909/ (accessed June 12, 2007).

———. "What Susan Sarandon Knows." *More,* April 2005.

Graduate, The. Directed by Mike Nichols. Embassy Pictures, 1967.

Grayson, Pamela Weiler. "Will Your Mother Soon Look Younger Than You?" *Harper's Bazaar,* October 2003.

Grifters, The. Directed by Stephen Frears. Miramax Films, 1991.

Guernsey, Diane. "The Dark Side of Weight Control." *Town & Country,* April 2006.

Hancock, Noelle, ed. "Denise Tells *US*: 'My Side of the Story.'" *US Weekly,* May 3, 2006.

Hanover, Donna. *My Boyfriend's Back.* New York: Penguin, 2005.

Hardy, Thomas. *Tess of the D'Urbervilles.* 1891; New York: Dover Publications, 2001.

HarperCollins German-English Dictionary. New York: HarperCollins, 1991

Hauser, Marc D. *Moral Minds: How Nature Designed Our Universal Sense of Right and Wrong.* New York: Ecco, 2006.

Hawthorne, Nathaniel. *The Scarlet Letter.* 1850; New York: Bantam Classics, 1981.

Heading South. Directed by Laurent Cantet. Shadow Distribution, 2006.

Hendrick, Susan S. *Understanding Close Relationships.* New York: Allyn & Bacon, 2003.

Herbert, Wray. "Psst. Want to Know a Secret?" *Newsweek,* August 21, 2006.

Hewitt, James. *Moving On.* London: Blake Publishing, Ltd., 2005.

Heymann, C. David. *Poor Little Rich Girl: The Life and Legend of Barbara Hutton.* New York: Random House, 1983.

History of Violence, A. Directed by David Cronenberg. New Line Productions, 2005.

Hite, Shere. *Women and Love: A Cultural Revolution in Progress.* New York: St. Martin's Press, 1989.

Hoffman, Ellen. "Stay Happy, Together." *Business Week,* July 24, 2006. www.businessweek.com/magazine/content/06_30/b3994409.htm ?campaign_id=aol_retire (accessed June 12, 2007).

Hollander, Dory. *101 Lies Men Tell—And Why Women Believe Them.* New York: HarperPerennial, 1997.

Holy Bible, The. "The Book of Luke." Standard English Version, Compact Ed. Wheaton, Ill.: Crossway Bibles, 2005.

Homeless to Harvard: The Liz Murray Story. Directed by Peter Levin. Lifetime, 2003.

Ice Princess. Directed by Tim Fywell. Buena Vista Pictures, 2005.

I Dream of Jeannie. Created by Sidney Sheldon. NBC, 1965–70.

I Love Lucy. Desi Arnaz, Executive Producer. CBS, 1951–57.

Imber-Black, Evan. *The Secret Life of Families: Making Decisions About Secrets: When Keeping Secrets Can Harm You, When Keeping Secrets Can Heal You—And How to Know the Difference.* New York: Bantam, 1999.

Indecent Proposal. Directed by Adrian Lyne. Paramount Pictures, 1993.

Intolerable Cruelty. Directed by Joel Coen. Universal Pictures, 2003.

Joe Millionaire. Fox, 2003.

Jones, Charisse. "Abuse Cases Face Double Standard." *USA Today,* February 11, 2005.

Josephson Institute of Ethics, The. http://josephsoninstitute.org.

Kaiser Permanente Medical Care Program. www.kaiserpermanente.org.

Kantrowitz, Barbara. "Sex & Love: The New World." *Newsweek,* February 20, 2006.

Kennard, Jerry. "When Does Gambling Become a Problem? Men and Compulsive Gambling." http://menshealth.about.com/od/psychological issues/a/Men_Gambling.htm (accessed June 12, 2007).

Kidd, Sue Monk. *The Mermaid Chair.* New York: Viking Penguin, 2005.

Kindlon, Dan. *Alpha Girls: Understanding the New American Girl and How She Is Changing the World.* Emmaus, Pa.: Rodale Books, 2006.

King, Stephen. *Dolores Claiborne.* New York: Viking, 1993.

Kovaleski, Serge and William Rashbaum. "Astor Son Claims Vindication Over Words in Judge's Ruling." *The New York Times,* December 6, 2006.

Kuczynski, Alex. "A Woman's Work Is Never Done." *Vanity Fair,* September 2006.

Kuffel, Frances. *Passing for Thin: Losing Half My Weight and Finding My Self.* New York: Broadway, 2004.

Larry King Live. "Inside Madonna's Adoption Controversy." CNN, October 18, 2006.

League of Their Own, A. Directed by Penny Marshall. Columbia Pictures, 1992.

Legends of the Fall. Directed by Edward Zwick. TriStar Pictures, 1994.

Little Children. Directed by Todd Field. New Line Cinema, 2006.

Madigan, Nick. "Actress Sentenced to Probation for Shoplifting." *The New York Times,* December 7, 2002.

Madonna. "Material Girl." *Like a Virgin.* Warner Bros., 1985

Match Point. Directed by Woody Allen. DreamWorks, 2005.

McCullough, Colleen. *The Thorn Birds.* New York: Harper & Row, 1977.

McKay, Jeff. "Judge Says Government Misled Public on 9/11 Air Quality." CNSNews.com, February 6, 2006. www.cnsnews.com/ViewNation .asp?Page=%5CNation%5Carchive%5C200602%5CNAT20060206a .html (accessed June 12, 2007).

Mean Girls. Directed by Mark Waters. Paramount Pictures, 2004.

Media Matters for America. "Defending Coulter, O'Reilly and Limbaugh Claimed She 'Doesn't Lie.'" June 9, 2006. http://mediamatters.org/ items/200606090014 (accessed June 12, 2007).

Melanie Griffith Official Web Site. www.melaniegriffith.com.

Mellan, Olivia. *Overcoming Overspending: A Winning Plan for Spenders and Their Partners.* New York: Walker and Company, 1997.

Mellody, Pia, and Andrea Wells Miller. *Facing Love Addiction: Giving Yourself the Power to Change the Way You Love.* San Francisco: HarperSanFrancisco, 1992.

Me Without You. Directed by Sandra Goldbacher. Fireworks Pictures, 2001.

Miller, Rebecca. "The Art of Spontaneous Shopping." *Harper's Bazaar,* April 2005.

———. *Personal Velocity: Three Portraits.* New York: Grove Press, 2002.

Mills, Patricia Jagentowicz. *Woman, Nature, and Psyche.* New Haven: Yale University Press, 1987.

Minnesota Prevention Resource Center, Minnesota Institute of Public Health for the Chemical Dependency Program Division, Minnesota Department of Human Services. "Minnesota State-Funded Gambling Treatment Program's Final Report." July 21, 1997.

Mr. & Mrs. Smith. Directed by Doug Liman. 20th Century–Fox, 2005.

Museum of Broadcast Communications. "Anita Hill Hearings Report." Chicago, 2006.

National Adoption Foundation. www.adopt.org.

National Center of Addictions and Substance Abuse at Columbia University. www.casacolumbia.org.

National Center on Elder Abuse (NCEA). www.elderabusecenter.org.

National Institutes of Health (NIH). www.nih.gov.

National Institute of Mental Health (NIMH). www.nimh.nih.gov.

National Mental Health Association. Alexandria, Virginia. www.mental health.samhsa.gov.

Nip/Tuck. Created by Ryan Murphy. FX Network, 2003–.

Notes on a Scandal. Directed by Richard Eyre. Fox Searchlight Pictures, 2006.

Nussbaum, Emily. "Mothers Anonymous." *New York,* July 24, 2006.

Oates, Joyce Carol. *We Were the Mulvaneys.* New York: Plume, 1996.

O'Connor, Karen. *Addicted to Shopping . . . and Other Issues Women Have with Money.* Parker, Colo.: Harvest House, 2005.

Ogunnaike, Lola. "Sex, Lawsuits and Celebrities Caught on Tape." *The New York Times,* March 19, 2006.

O'Leary, Kevin. "Denise Speaks." *US Weekly,* May 15, 2006.

Once and Again. Created by Marshall Herskovitz and Edward Zwick. ABC, 1999–2002.

O'Neal, Tatum. *A Paper Life.* New York: HarperEntertainment, 2004.

Ontario Substance Abuse Bureau. Ontario Ministry of Health and Long-term Care. Toronto, Ontario. www.health gov.on.ca.

Opdyke, Jeff D. "Intimate Betrayal: When the Elderly Are Robbed by Their Family Members." *The Wall Street Journal,* August 30, 2006.

Oprah Winfrey Show, The. WABC-TV. April 18, 2006.

Others, The. Directed by Alejandro Amenabar. Miramax Films, 2001.

Pauley, Jane. *Skywriting: A Life Out of the Blue.* New York: Random House, 2004.

Peabody, Susan. *Addiction to Love: Overcoming Obsession and Dependency in Relationships.* New York: Celestial Arts, 2005.

Pollack, Daphne, "Learning Curve." *More,* March 2006.

Pretty Woman. Directed by Garry Marshall. Touchstone Pictures, 1990.

Private Benjamin. Directed by Howard Zieff. Warner Bros. Pictures, 1980.

Proof of Life. Directed by Taylor Hackford. Warner Bros. Pictures, 2000.

Renfrew Center Foundation for Eating Disorders. www.renfrew.org.

Reuters. "Lea Fastow Arrives Early for Prison." *USA Today,* July 12, 2004.

Roberts, Selena. "The Beauty and the Burden." *The New York Times,* September 10, 2006.

Rose, Isabel. *The J.A.P. Chronicles: A Novel.* New York: Doubleday, 2005.

Rosenbloom, Stephanie. "Honk If You Adore My Child Too." *The New York Times,* January 5, 2006.

Runaway Bride. Directed by Garry Marshall. Paramount Pictures, 1999.

Scarlet Letter, The. Directed by Roland Joffé. Buena Vista Pictures, 1995.

Schaeffer, Branda. *Is It Love or Is It Addiction?* Ontario: Hazelden, 1997.

Scientific American Mind. www.sciammind.com.

Secret Lives of Dentists, The. Directed by Alan Rudolph. Manhattan Pictures International, 2002.

Sex and the City. Created by Darren Star. HBO, 1998–2004.

sex, lies, and videotape. Directed by Steven Soderbergh. Miramax Films, 1989.

Shields, Brooke. *Down Came the Rain: My Journey Through Postpartum Depression.* New York: Hyperion, 2005.

Siemaszko, Corky. "English Lather: Miss U.K. Stripped of Her Crown." New York *Daily News,* November 4, 2006.

Silber, Kathleen, and Phylis Speedlin. *Dear Birthmother: Thank You for Our Baby.* San Antonio, Tex.: Corona Publishing Co., 1991.

Silverman, Justin Rocket. "Unmarried Pregnant Teacher Sues Catholic School Over Firing." Newsday.com, November 21, 2005.

Silverman, Sue William. *Love Sick: One Woman's Journey Through Sexual Addiction.* New York: W. W. Norton, 2001.

Sleeping with the Enemy. Directed by Joseph Ruben. 20th Century–Fox, 1991.

Smith, Aidan. "Jane Birkin Ditches Hermès Bag for Sporran." *The Scotsman,* March 19, 2006. http://heritage.scotsman.com/news.cfm?id=432982006 (accessed June 12, 2007).

Smith, David Livingstone. *Why We Lie: The Evolutionary Roots of Deception and the Unconscious Mind.* New York: St. Martin's Press, 2004.

Steinem, Gloria. *Outrageous Acts and Everyday Rebellions.* New York: Henry Holt and Company, 1995.

———. "Ruth's Song (Because She Could Not Sing It)." In *Making Sense of Women's Lives: An Introduction to Women's Studies.* Lanham, Md.: Rowman Littlefield Publishers, 2000.

Stepmom. Directed by Chris Columbus. TriStar Pictures, 1998.

Sunshine for Women. www.pinn.net.

Supreme Court of the United States. *Roe v. Wade.* Texas, 1973.

Sweet Home Alabama. Directed by Andy Tennant. Touchstone Pictures, 2002.

Talk Surgery. www.talksurgery.com.

Taraborrelli, J. Randy. *Jackie Ethel Joan: Women of Camelot.* New York: Warner Books, 2000.

Taylor, Gabrielle. *Pride, Shame, and Guilt: Emotions of Self-Assessment.* London: Oxford University Press, 1985.

Tkach, Chris, and Sonja Lyubomirsky. "How Do People Pursue Happiness? Relating Personality, Happiness-Increasing Strategies, and Well-being." *Journal of Happiness Studies.* Netherlands: Springer, June 2006, 7 (2).

TopTenREVIEWS. www.toptenreviews.com.

Trollope, Joanna. *Other People's Children*. New York: Berkley, 2000.

Truth About Cats and Dogs, The. Directed by Michael Lehmann. 20th Century–Fox, 1996.

Tucker, Judith Stadtman. "Motherhood, Shame and Society: An Interview with Brené Brown," August 2004. The Mothers Movement Online, www.mothersmovement.org/features/bbrown_int_1.htm (accessed June 12, 2007).

Twelve Monkeys. Directed by Terry Gilliam. Universal Pictures, 1995.

28 Days. Directed by Betty Thomas. Columbia Pictures, 2000.

Tyre, Peg. "Poker Buddies for Life." *Newsweek*, February 20, 2006.

Unfaithful. Directed by Adrian Lyne. 20th Century–Fox, 2002.

United States Census Bureau. www.census.gov.

United States Department of Labor in the Twenty-first Century. www.dol.gov.

UrbanBaby. www.urbanbaby.com.

Viswanathan, Kaavya. *How Opal Mehta Got Kissed, Got Wild, and Got a Life: A Novel*. New York: Little, Brown, 2006.

Volver. Directed by Pedro Almodóvar. Sony Pictures, 2006.

Waldman, Ayelet. *Love and Other Impossible Pursuits*. New York: Doubleday, 2006.

Wallace, Amy. "Jamie Lee Curtis: On Growing Older & Wiser." *More*, September 2002.

Waller, Robert James. *The Bridges of Madison County*. New York: Warner Books, 1992.

Warner, Judith. *Perfect Madness: Motherhood in the Age of Anxiety*. New York: Riverhead, 2005.

Webster's Collegiate Dictionary. Tenth Edition, Springfield, Mass.: Merriam-Webster, 1993.

Wharton, Edith. *House of Mirth*. 1905; New York: Virago Press, 2006.

When a Man Loves a Woman. Directed by Luis Mandoki. Touchstone Pictures, 1994.

When Harry Met Sally. Directed by Rob Reiner. Columbia Pictures, 1989.

Wilcox, W. Bradford, and Steven L. Nock. "What's Love Got to Do with It? Equality, Equity, Commitment and Women's Marital Quality." *Social Forces*, 84 (3), March 2006.

Williams, Bernard. *Shame and Necessity*. Berkeley, Calif.: University of California Press, 1994.

Williams, Juanita H. *Psychology of Women: Behavior in a Biosocial Context*. New York: W. W. Norton and Company, 1987.

Williams, Tennessee. *A Streetcar Named Desire*. New York: Dramatists Play Service, 1947.

Woods, Judith. "An Appetite for a Bit on the Side." *The Daily Telegraph*, January 8, 2005.

INDEX